THE BATTLE
OF
SOUTH MOUNTAIN

JOHN DAVID HOPTAK

Maps by Mannie Gentile

Charleston — London

THE
History
PRESS

Published by The History Press
Charleston, SC 29403
www.historypress.net

Cover image: The Battle of South Mountain, Maryland. Lithograph by E.B. & E.C. Kellog.
Courtesy of the Maryland Historical Society

First published 2011

Manufactured in the United States

ISBN 978.1.59629.401.1

Library of Congress Cataloging-in-Publication Data

Hoptak, John David, 1978-
The Battle of South Mountain / John David Hoptak ; maps by Mannie Gentile.
p. cm.
Includes bibliographical references and index.
ISBN 978-1-59629-401-1
1. South Mountain, Battle of, Md., 1862. 2. South Mountain, Battle of, Md.,
1862--Pictorial works. I. Title.
E474.61.H67 2011
973.7'336--dc22
2010052258

Notice: The information in this book is true and complete to the best of our knowledge. It is
offered without guarantee on the part of the author or The History Press. The author and
The History Press disclaim all liability in connection with the use of this book.

Dedicated to

my Baba, Anna Mitsock,
who departed this world on April 12, 2010

and my beautiful niece, Mary Anna,
who entered it eight weeks later, on June 8

Contents

Preface   7

1. "The Enemy…Means to Make Trouble in Maryland":
   Lee Drives North   13
2. "Hell Itself Turned Loose": The Struggle for Fox's Gap   37
3. "My Men Were Fighting Like Tigers. Every Man Was a Hero":
   The Fight for Frosttown and Turner's Gaps   87
4. "The Victory Was Decisive and Complete":
   The Battle of Crampton's Gap   131
5. "God Bless You and All with You. Destroy the Rebel
   Army If Possible": The Road to Antietam   167

Order of Battle   183
Notes   195
Bibliography   209
Index   217
About the Author   223

Preface

On Sunday, September 28, 1862, Lieutenant M. Edgar Richards, adjutant of the 96th Pennsylvania Volunteer Infantry, wrote a letter to his sister in Pottsville. Two weeks earlier, Richards's regiment lost nineteen men killed and seventy-one wounded while storming the Confederate defenses at Crampton's Gap during the Battle of South Mountain. So heavy were the 96th's casualties and such was the intensity and savagery of the combat that its commander, Colonel Henry Cake, declared that the regiment had covered itself with "horrid glory." Three days later, on Wednesday, September 17, near the banks of the Antietam Creek, the 96th was again brought to the front. There, however, it would be kept out of action and remained in reserve, losing just two men killed by an errant Confederate shell. The 96th was fortunate to have escaped Antietam with such little loss, for around these men raged what became the bloodiest single-day battle in all of American history.

In a little more than twelve hours of combat on an otherwise pleasant late summer day, some 23,100 Americans were killed, wounded, captured or listed among the missing in action at Antietam. The following night, General Robert E. Lee marched his defeated Army of Northern Virginia across the Potomac River and then turned south in retreat. His invasion of the North had failed; his primary objective of gaining a decisive victory on Union soil had not been realized. Five days later, on Monday, September 22, President Abraham Lincoln built on the Federal victory at Antietam by issuing a preliminary proclamation of emancipation, thereby transforming the Union war effort. No longer was this civil war being waged solely to reunite a divided nation; from this point forward, it also became a crusade to abolish slavery.

With such unimaginable loss and because of its significant consequences, Antietam almost entirely eclipsed the fierce battle that had occurred three days earlier at South Mountain, just as Lieutenant Richards of the 96th Pennsylvania feared it would. To his sister, Richards wrote, "I am afraid the large battle of Wednesday will entirely overshadow our division's fight at Crampton's Pass," where his regiment had suffered so much loss. And so it has.[1]

South Mountain was the first major battle fought north of the Potomac River, and it was there, not at Antietam, where Lee's first northern invasion was initially met and turned back. It had been just ten days since Lee's confident gray- and butternut-clad columns first waded across the Potomac in the wake of a remarkably successful spring and summer, during which they had soundly defeated two powerful Union armies, driving the dispirited Federals into the safety of Washington's extensive fortifications. Lee, having assumed command of the Army of Northern Virginia just three months earlier, was hoping to maintain his hard-won initiative by sweeping north. Having already taken the conflict from the gates of Richmond to the doorsteps of Washington, Lee now headed north across the Potomac and, for the first time since the commencement of the war nearly a year and a half earlier, led a Confederate army onto Union soil. He came north seeking another battlefield victory, for such a victory, he thought, might go a long way toward ending the fratricidal conflict in the Confederacy's favor.

But things went poorly for Lee once in Maryland, and just ten days into the campaign he lost the initiative and was forced on the defensive. Having first marched north to Frederick and then west across South Mountain, Lee divided his army, with General James Longstreet's columns moving north to Hagerstown and Thomas J. "Stonewall" Jackson's men heading south in order to clear Harpers Ferry of a Federal garrison stationed there, a force Lee mistakenly assumed would retreat in response to his invasion. His army was thus widely separated when the Union Army of the Potomac, some seventy-five thousand men strong and under the command of Major General George Brinton McClellan, arrived at Frederick and began pushing west toward South Mountain. Lee, caught off guard, was forced to make a stand on South Mountain lest his army, as McClellan envisioned, be "cut in two and beaten in detail."

The Battle of South Mountain was a daylong affair, spread out across many miles of rugged, mountainous terrain, as McClellan's men attempted to force their way across several key mountain gaps and Lee's men, outnumbered but enjoying a strong defensive position, desperately tried to prevent the Federals from doing so. The fighting was deadly, at times vicious, and costly to both sides. By nightfall, the Army of the Potomac emerged triumphant, having driven the Confederate forces from their positions and having secured all the gaps, save for one, which Lee would soon abandon. That Sunday night, with McClellan's forces secure on the mountain and with more Union troops stacking up behind them, Lee realized he had been defeated, and with his army still divided, he knew his situation was critical. "The day has gone against us," Lee famously declared while ordering a retreat. Lee was prepared to abandon his campaign. He withdrew his forces from South Mountain and led them westward toward the Potomac River crossing near Shepherdstown while at the same time sending orders to his commanders at Harpers Ferry to forfeit their operations.

Yet as the hours ticked by early the next morning—Monday, September 15—the fruits of the Union's hard-won victory at South Mountain began to wither on the vine. The Federal pursuit of Lee's retreating forces was not as aggressive as McClellan had wished, and at 8:00 a.m., the hapless Union garrison at Harpers Ferry, after a three-day siege, surrendered to Jackson's forces. It was then that the results of the Confederates' stubborn defense on the mountain became clear. Although forced off the mountain, Lee's battered forces had succeeded in delaying the Union army long enough to give Jackson the time he needed to complete the siege. The Union's tactical victory at South Mountain was also a strategic one for the Confederacy. When Lee learned of the fall of Harpers Ferry, he was at once reenergized. Perhaps, he thought, all was not lost. He called off the retreat and instructed Jackson to march his men north to Sharpsburg, where Longstreet's and D.H. Hill's men—who had fought so valiantly on the mountaintop the day earlier—were then gathering. Lee knew he could either use Sharpsburg as a rallying point from where he could continue his campaign north or, if need be, form a defensive line of battle along the nearby Antietam Creek.

Despite the battle's heavy casualties, which exceeded five thousand, and despite its centrality to the September 1862 Maryland Campaign—arguably the most significant of the entire war—South Mountain has long remained understudied, languishing in the shadow of Antietam. It was not until 1992 that the first full-length study of the battle appeared with the publication of John Michael Priest's exhaustively researched *Before Antietam: The Battle of South Mountain.* The next was Timothy Reese's *Sealed with Their Lives: The Battle for Crampton's Gap*, an excellent, finely written account authored by the leading authority on this fierce struggle. Chapters on the Battle of South Mountain have appeared in all the leading studies of both the Maryland Campaign and Antietam, including James Murfin's *The Gleam of Bayonets* (1965), Stephen Sears's *Landscape Turned Red* (1982), Joseph Harsh's *Taken at the Flood* (1999) and, more recently, Ethan Rafuse's helpful *Antietam, South Mountain & Harpers Ferry: A Battlefield Guide* (2008) and Ezra Carman's *The Maryland Campaign of September 1862*, Volume 1 (2010), brilliantly edited by Thomas Clemens. A number of in-depth articles on various aspects of the battle have also appeared over the years, including some written by participants in the fight, such as Jacob Dolson Cox, Joseph Jackson Bartlett and Daniel Harvey Hill, as well as more recent studies, specifically "My God! Be Careful: Morning Battle at Fox's Gap" and "It Looked Like a Task to Storm: The Pennsylvania Reserves Assault on South Mountain," both penned by D. Scott Hartwig. Yet in terms of books that focus exclusively on South Mountain, Priest's and Reese's stand alone. Thus, when I was approached by Doug Bostick, managing editor of the History Press's Civil War Sesquicentennial Series, to write a book-length narrative history of the Battle of South Mountain, I jumped at the chance. With this book, if I can contribute in some small way to our further understanding of this important battle, then I will have succeeded in my efforts.

I would like to take this opportunity to thank all those who assisted me in this undertaking. My thanks go to friend and fellow Civil War historian Eric Wittenberg, who first put me in touch with Doug Bostick, for his continual assistance and support. To Doug Bostick, Laura All, Adam Ferrell and everyone at The History Press, I would also like to extend my appreciation for all their guidance along the way. No words can truly express the great honor and privilege it is to work at the Antietam National Battlefield and alongside some of the nation's finest park rangers. To all my colleagues and friends at Antietam, thank you for making the past five years some of the best of my life. Special thanks go to Ranger Brian Baracz for reading the manuscript, catching my errors and offering helpful suggestions and to Ranger Mannie Gentile, who once more brought his talents to bear in developing the maps for this book. I must also thank Christopher Gwinn, friend and former colleague at Antietam, for reading and reviewing the manuscript, as well as Isaac Forman, a great go-to guy for anything South Mountain related. For their help along the way, I thank Dave Maher and Dan Vermilya, as well as Jim Rosebrock, Kevin Booth and Maura James, each of whom helped me sound out the fighting at Fox's and Crampton's Gaps, discovering more about the battles there by some good old-fashioned battlefield tramping. Thanks also to Ronn Palm, for opening up his incredible collection of Civil War images to see the faces of those who fought and died at South Mountain and for providing copies of some of these images. For reading the manuscript, providing support along the way and responding to all my numerous inquiries, I must thank Dr. Thomas Clemens, a leading authority on the Maryland Campaign; Ted Alexander, Antietam's chief historian; and Scott Hartwig, chief of interpretation at Gettysburg National Military Park, all experts in the field of Civil War history who have each helped me tremendously. Finally, for everything they have done for me over the years, and for their unfailing support, I must thank my parents, David and Colleen Hoptak; my sister, Dr. Angie Hoptak-Solga; and, of course, my incredible wife, Laura, the source of continual encouragement and support.

1

"The Enemy...Means to Make Trouble in Maryland"

Lee Drives North

In early September 1862, the United States was in great peril. The fortunes of war, which had shone so brightly on the Union war effort just several months earlier, had taken a decided turn in favor of the Confederacy. Out West, Southern forces under Generals Braxton Bragg and Edmund Kirby Smith were sweeping north through Tennessee and into Kentucky, while in the East, where most of the eyes of the world were focused, the situation appeared even brighter for the nascent Confederate States of America. There, General Robert E. Lee, following up a summer's worth of battlefield victories, decided to maintain his army's hard-earned initiative and launch an invasion of Union soil. By early September 1862, America's fratricidal conflict—which at its outset many believed would last only a few months after one strong show of force—had already been raging for nearly a year and a half, and at this point, it appeared as though the Confederacy might prevail.

Such had certainly not been the case just several months earlier. Indeed, in the early spring of 1862, in both East and West, the Union was triumphant. In February, Forts Henry and Donelson fell into Union hands, as did the city of Nashville. More good news followed when reports arrived of the Union victory at Shiloh. By the end of March, General Ambrose Burnside was completing a successful expedition along the North Carolina coastline, during which his men captured all the state's important ports, excepting Wilmington. Port Royal, South Carolina, had also fallen to the Union, as had Norfolk, the Confederacy's most important naval yard. And, as if all this was not bad enough, near the end of April, Admiral David Farragut captured New Orleans, the Confederacy's largest city and principal port. Such success prompted the *New York Herald* and many others in the North to predict the war's end by the Fourth of July.[2]

While news from throughout the South during that spring of 1862 was unsettling for the Confederacy, most of the attention centered on General George McClellan's mammoth, 100,000-man-strong Army of the Potomac, creeping up the peninsula formed between the York and James Rivers and approaching dangerously close to the Confederate capital of Richmond. By the end of May, McClellan's forces were within just a few miles of the city. Panic reigned in Richmond, and the Confederate government began taking steps to prepare for the city's evacuation. These were certainly dark days for the Confederacy. Yet the pendulum of war would soon reverse its course.

On June 1, 1862, fifty-four-year-old Robert Edward Lee assumed command of the Army of Northern Virginia, taking the place of General Joseph Johnston, who had fallen wounded the previous day at the Battle of Seven Pines. In Lee, the Confederacy found an audacious commander, ever willing to assume bold risks, even in the face of seeming adversity. With McClellan's army stalled

General Robert E. Lee, commander, Army of Northern Virginia. *Library of Congress.*

on the doorstep of the capital, Lee launched a weeklong series of attacks, unprecedented in its bloodshed and known collectively as the Seven Days' Battles. Although he lost a higher percentage of men than did McClellan, Lee's offensive did the trick. Convinced that he faced overwhelming numbers, McClellan ordered his army to retreat, falling back to the safety of the Federal gunboats on the James River. The threat to Richmond was gone, and the Confederacy breathed easier. Confederate war clerk John B. Jones spoke for many when he succinctly noted that Robert E. Lee had "turned the tide" of the war.[3]

Yet Lee could not rest on his laurels. With the Army of the Potomac neutralized on the James, Lee turned his attention to another Union army just then organizing in northern Virginia. Patched together with Union forces that Stonewall Jackson had thumped in the Shenandoah, and augmented by Burnside's newly arrived Ninth Corps, the Federal Army of Virginia was headed by Major General John Pope. Lee hoped to defeat Pope's force before it could be reinforced by McClellan's army, which was already being withdrawn from the James for that very purpose. Leaving a force behind to defend Richmond, Lee swept north and, during the waning days of August, achieved a smashing victory over Pope at Second Manassas, forcing the shattered Army of Virginia back to the safety of the Federal capital.

Within just ninety days, Lee had succeeded in taking the war from the gates of Richmond to the outskirts of Washington, along the way defeating two Union armies and clearing most of Virginia of Federal troops. By early September, hope had replaced the despondency that had prevailed throughout the Confederacy just three months earlier. And while the Confederacy was at its zenith, the Union had fallen on its darkest days. The Fourth of July came and went, and no longer were there any newspaper predictions of the war's imminent end. Two armies—one shattered and one dispirited—limped back into Washington, while a growing dejection began to sound throughout the land, both on the homefront and in the ranks. Sergeant Henry Keiser of the 96th Pennsylvania summed up this sentiment nicely when he declared, "Things look blue."[4]

Nevertheless, Robert E. Lee now found himself faced with a difficult dilemma: what to do next? He did not have many viable options. Despite fears in Washington, Lee entertained no thoughts of following up the retreating Union columns and attacking the capital. The fortifications were simply too strong and his army too weak for such an extensive undertaking. The countryside around Manassas, made desolate by war, was unable to support his army. He could not simply wait there and prepare for the next Union offensive, and falling back toward a more defensible line was simply out of the question. Both of these options would effectively give the Federals time to regroup from their defeats and surrender to them the hard-won initiative, which Lee would not allow. There was really only one choice that made sense: a drive north, across the Potomac; an invasion of Union soil.

Such a movement had much to offer. It was nearly harvest time, which meant Lee's army would be able to gain some much-needed provisions from Maryland's lush agricultural countryside. Taking the war across the Potomac would also relieve Virginia of the burdens of war and give the people of

Lee's native state a well-earned reprieve. There was even a possibility, however remote, that a sweep into Maryland would encourage the people of this slave-owning border state, with pockets of strong Southern leanings, to rise up and cast its allegiance to the Confederacy. These factors alone were a strong inducement to Lee, but he realized there was much more to be gained by a drive north, much more than just a gathering of food and fodder and the possibility of adding another star to the Confederacy's banner. By sweeping north, Lee was hoping, above all else, to achieve yet another battlefield victory, this one on Union soil. Such a victory, thought Lee, might just go a long way toward ending the conflict in the Confederacy's favor. Lee neatly summarized his chief motivation for launching the invasion in a postwar interview, "I went into Maryland," declared the aging warrior, "to give battle."[5]

With the North's seemingly endless supply of manpower and its vastly superior industrial and manufacturing capabilities, Lee understood that the longer the war continued, the less chance at victory the Confederacy would have. To prevail in this conflict, thought Lee, the Confederacy would have to wear down the North's willingness to fight, and the surest way to do this was to defeat its armies on the field of battle, to convince the Union that this was a war it would be unable to win. Such a mindset helps to explain Lee's willingness throughout the war to assume many bold risks, and this was what motivated him in early September 1862 to lead his men across the Potomac and into Maryland. The timing of this campaign was also very important for Lee. The 1862 midterm elections were less than two months away, and Lee was hoping to capitalize on the growing antiwar movement in the North, further exacerbating the political and social divisions there, and bear an outcome on the elections, thus making it even more difficult for President Lincoln to continue to prosecute what was fast becoming an unpopular war.

Having thus decided on his plan of action, Lee began developing his strategy. He would cross the Potomac near Leesburg and drive straight north to Frederick, threatening both Washington and Baltimore. This action would also force the Union army to follow before it had time to catch its breath and heal its wounds from its summertime defeats and before the tens of thousands of new volunteers, arriving daily in Washington, could be properly trained and organized. From Frederick, Lee planned to turn west across both the Catoctin and South Mountain ranges and into the Cumberland Valley. This would allow him to establish safer lines of supply and communication south through the Shenandoah Valley and would also draw the Federals farther from their base at Washington. At this stage, Lee imagined, he could compel the Federals to attack him on good, defensible ground, and if all went well, he would achieve the victory he went north hoping to gain.

Late on September 3, General Lee summoned his military secretary Armistead Long to his headquarters near Dranesville, Virginia. Several days earlier, Lee had been thrown from his horse, spraining both wrists and fracturing a bone in one of his hands. With his hands wrapped in splints, Lee was unable to write what would become one of the more famous dispatches in the annals of the Army of Northern Virginia; instead, he dictated to Long. To President Jefferson Davis, Lee famously announced, "The present seems the most propitious time since the commencement of the war for the Confederate Army to enter Maryland." The two main Federal armies that had been operating in Virginia under McClellan and Pope had been driven out of the state and were "much weakened and demoralized." Although he could not attack them in the extensively fortified U.S. capital, by sweeping north across the Potomac, he would compel his opponents to follow. Such a move would free Richmond of any immediate threat, and seeking to further convince Davis of the advantages of such a campaign, Lee noted, "If it is ever desired to give material aid to Maryland and afford her an opportunity of throwing off the oppression to which she is now subject, this would seem the most favorable."

Lee most likely did not have much faith in the people of Maryland rising up in great number to throw its support behind the Confederacy, but he did know this was a Confederate goal from the outset, and by including this in his justification of a northern campaign, he was making his case to Davis that much stronger. Lee admitted that a drive across the Potomac was attended with much risk and that his army was "not properly equipped for an invasion of an enemy's territory. It lacks much of the material of war, is feeble in transportation, the animals being much reduced, and the men are poorly provided with clothes, and in thousands of instances are destitute of shoes. Still," said Lee, "we cannot afford to be idle, and though weaker than our opponents in men and military equipments, must endeavor to harass if we cannot destroy them."[6]

Confident in the president's approval, Lee did not wait for a response from Davis; he instead ordered his columns to make their way toward the Potomac River crossings near Leesburg.

At the outset of the campaign, Lee's Army of Northern Virginia was only loosely organized. Instead of neatly organized corps, Lee went into Maryland with an army composed of various wings, divisions and independent commands, an arrangement that would prove unwieldy and would come to haunt him in the days ahead. General James Longstreet's command consisted of two divisions, under Generals David R. Jones and John Bell Hood, and one independent brigade, under Brigadier General Nathan Evans. Stonewall Jackson commanded Lee's other large command, or wing. He had three divisions, including his old Stonewall Division, which began the campaign under General William Starke; Ewell's Division, under Alexander Lawton; and A.P. Hill's famed Light Division. Augmenting Longstreet's and Jackson's wings was a general reserve division under Major General Richard Anderson. On September 2, Longstreet and Jackson each had roughly twenty thousand men in their commands while Anderson had an additional fifty-seven hundred. Lee's army was strengthened further by the arrival of three strong divisions from Richmond, which linked up with the army at the beginning of the Maryland Campaign. Lafayette McLaws brought seventy-six hundred men in his division; Daniel Harvey Hill added another eight thousand, while Brigadier General John Walker's division contributed five thousand more. Each of these divisions would operate independently during the majority of the campaign, excepting brief periods when they were temporarily attached to either Longstreet or Jackson. Commanding the Confederate cavalry was Major General Jeb Stuart; he had roughly fifty-five hundred troopers, a number that included the recent arrival of Wade Hampton's Brigade.

On paper, then, Lee had more than seventy thousand troops of all branches when he launched his campaign into Maryland, and although he would lose thousands of these men to straggling, he went north with a much larger army than has been traditionally described. Most accounts place Lee's numbers at anywhere between forty to fifty thousand men, but this is simply too low a number. Even a commander as audacious as Lee would not have embarked on such an important operation with so few troops, and he certainly would not have separated his army five ways and spread it across more than twenty miles of unfriendly territory—as Lee would do within a week of coming north—if he had but forty or fifty thousand men. Bold, yes, but Lee was certainly not foolish.[7]

The Confederate invasion of Maryland commenced on September 4 when the first of Lee's columns waded across the cool waters of the Potomac at White's Ford, near Leesburg. It was a stirring scene, one that portended great things and one long remembered by those present. Heros Von Borcke, a Prussian-born officer serving on Jeb Stuart's staff, left perhaps the most vivid portrait of Lee's veterans splashing through the waters while being serenaded by regimental bands:

Confederate soldiers
crossing the Potomac.
*Battles & Leaders of the
Civil War.*

It was, indeed, a magnificent sight as the long column of many thousand horsemen stretched across this beautiful Potomac. The evening sun slanted upon its clear placid waters, and burnished them with gold, while the arms of the soldiers glittered and blazed in its radiance. There were few moments, perhaps, from the beginning to the close of the war, of excitement more intense, of exhilaration more delightful, than when we ascended the opposite bank to the familiar but now strangely thrilling music of "Maryland, my Maryland."[8]

By September 7, all of Lee's columns had crossed the river and were either already encamped near or converging on Frederick, Maryland's second-largest city, roughly forty-five miles northwest of Washington and fifty miles west of Baltimore.

The campaign began with much hope. Lee was confident and had great faith in his men and in the soundness of the campaign, believing a victory on Union soil would bring the Confederacy another step closer to victory.

Yet almost from the start, things began unraveling for the Confederate army commander.

The condition of Lee's army was cause for concern. Despite their confidence, Lee's men were worn-out, hungry and in such poor shape that one young Marylander famously described them as "the dirtiest men I ever saw, a most ragged, lean, and hungry set of wolves."[9] Of more immediate concern was the amount of straggling from the ranks. This was such a persistent and severe problem for Lee that he wrote of it frequently in his communications and reports on the Maryland Campaign. "One of the greatest evils…is the habit of straggling from the ranks," Lee wrote to Davis on September 7. "It has become a habit difficult to correct. With some, the sick and feeble, it results from necessity," said the army commander, "but with the greater number from design. These latter do not wish to be with their regiments, nor to share in their hardships and glories. They are the cowards of the army [who] desert their comrades in times of danger." Lee mentioned straggling again in a letter to Davis dated September 13, in which he declared that his ranks have been "very much diminished—I fear from a third to one-half the original numbers."

Lee was certainly not alone in bemoaning the problem of straggling. General D.H. Hill credited the "enormous straggling" as one of the reasons why the Army of Northern Virginia met with defeat in Maryland. "Doubtless the want of shoes, the want of food, and physical exhaustion had kept many brave men from being with the army," said the gruff division commander, "but thousands of thieving poltroons had kept away from sheer cowardice. The straggler is generally a thief and always a coward," described Hill, "lost to all sense of shame; he can only be kept in ranks by a strict and sanguinary discipline." It is impossible to determine with certainty, but the number of stragglers from Lee's army easily stretched into the thousands. Lee's columns simply melted away as they made their way through Maryland.[10]

Another problem, one not nearly as severe as the straggling but no doubt very disappointing to Jefferson Davis, was the lukewarm reception provided to Lee's men as they made their way north. Lee may have anticipated this sort of reaction, particularly in the agricultural regions of central and western Maryland, where Unionist sympathy was strong, but in a letter dated September 7, Lee advised Davis not to get his hopes up; Marylanders would not come flocking to the Confederacy. "Notwithstanding individual expressions of kindness that have been given," said Lee, "I do not anticipate any general rising of the people in our behalf."[11]

Disappointing, yes, but Lee was far more focused on achieving his military goals than on securing another state for the Confederacy. Despite the problems already encountered with the straggling and the unreceptive citizenry, Lee was determined to continue with his campaign. But things would only continue to worsen for Lee.

Lee planned to cross the Potomac and move north to Frederick, thereby threatening both Washington and Baltimore and forcing the Union army to pull its troops from south of the river and follow. He then called for his army to move west from Frederick, over the Catoctin and South Mountain ranges and into the lush Cumberland Valley, with Hagerstown his desired destination. This movement would threaten Pennsylvania and would naturally compel the Union army to move even farther from Washington, tenuously extending its supply and communication lines and placing several mountains between it and its capital. By moving west across the mountains, Lee was also planning to reestablish his own supply and communication lines south through the friendly Shenandoah Valley. The farther he moved north while east of the mountains, the more exposed his lines became; by moving west, he would not only solve this problem but would also have a secure way of receiving supplies forwarded from Richmond. It was a sound strategy and one Lee had decided on early in the campaign. Yet in the execution of this plan, Lee encountered another problem, one that would entirely derail his campaign.

In order to establish his supply lines through the Shenandoah Valley, it would necessarily need to be free of Federal forces. However, this was not the case. Even as the Army of Northern Virginia was preparing to move west from Frederick, two small Federal garrisons remained in the lower valley, one stationed at Martinsburg, numbering three thousand men under General Julius White, and a larger one—ten thousand men strong—at Harpers Ferry under Colonel Dixon Miles. The presence of these Union soldiers came as no surprise to Lee; he was well aware of their positions. He had assumed, however, that these troops would evacuate their posts once he crossed the Potomac and placed his army between them and Washington. In measured understatement, Lee later noted that in this assumption, "I was disappointed." Not only were these Union soldiers in a position to threaten Lee's proposed new lines of supply and communication, but they would also be directly to the rear of his army once it crossed South Mountain and moved north toward Hagerstown. These Union troops were the proverbial thorn in Lee's side, but he was not initially overly concerned. He would be forced to change his plans to clear Martinsburg and Harpers Ferry of these Federal troops, but this, Lee believed, would only be a temporary deviation from his overall strategy—a quick, clean operation of no more than a few days' duration. Yet, as events would prove, in this, too, Lee would be greatly disappointed.[12]

On the afternoon of September 9, Lee met with Jackson and Longstreet to explain how he intended to deal with the stubborn Union forces still in the valley. Jackson would lead the army's advance early the following morning and, with his three divisions, march west along the National Pike across the mountains toward Sharpsburg. He was to then cross the Potomac "at the most convenient point" and, by Friday, September 12, capture the Federal garrison at Martinsburg and "intercept such as may attempt to escape from Harpers

Ferry." Longstreet's command, along with the army's supply and baggage trains, was to follow behind Jackson until reaching Boonsboro. Lafayette McLaws, with his own division, plus that of R.H. Anderson, was directed to follow behind Longstreet as far as Middletown, where he was to then turn south toward Harpers Ferry. McLaws's joint command, totaling roughly fifteen thousand, was by Friday morning to take possession of Maryland Heights, which overlooked Harpers Ferry from the north, and "endeavor to capture" the Federal garrison there. And while McLaws approached Harpers Ferry from the north, General John Walker's division was to recross the Potomac and take possession of Loudoun Heights, which loomed high over Harpers Ferry from the south, working "as far as practicable" to cooperate with McLaws and Jackson in "intercepting" the enemy.

After clearing the valley, the commands of Jackson, McLaws and Walker were to move north and reunite with the army's "main body" at either Boonsboro or Hagerstown, depending on circumstances. Meanwhile, General D.H. Hill's hard-fighting division was to form the army's rear guard, following behind Longstreet and preceded by the army's reserve artillery, ordnance and supply trains. The final assignment fell to Jeb Stuart. His cavalry was to "cover the route of the army, bringing up all stragglers that may have been left behind" and keeping a careful eye on any Federal advance from Washington.[13]

It was a bold plan. Lee was dividing his footsore army, already plagued by straggling, into five parts and spreading it thin across largely unfriendly territory. Jackson initially opposed the idea, wishing to give battle east of the mountains, near Frederick, but Lee quickly dismissed this suggestion. It was imperative, he said, to move west, open the Shenandoah Valley and lure the Union army over the mountains. Longstreet also opposed the wide separation of the Confederate army and was able to convince Lee, for the moment at least, to allow him to halt his command at Boonsboro and not go to Hagerstown as Lee originally intended. Lee then dismissed his two highest-ranking subordinates and dictated this daring plan to his chief of staff, who recorded it as Special Orders No. 191. Copies of these orders were prepared and distributed to each of the commanders listed therein. Lee then retired for the night, confident that by Friday, just three days distant, the Federals would be cleared from the valley and his army would again be united to continue with the overriding objective of this campaign: defeat the main Federal army and gain a stunning victory on Northern soil.[14]

Part of the reason why Lee was willing to undertake such a risky venture as spelled out in Special Orders No. 191 was because of a false sense that time was on his side. What he did not realize was how quickly his time was running out. Another significant problem for Lee in Maryland was that he had seriously misjudged the advance of the Union army out of Washington, an error that can be largely attributed to his cavalry chief Stuart, who did a poor job of keeping Lee informed on the progress of the Federal advance. Indeed, Lee was so ignorant of the location of the main Union army that on September 8, while in Frederick and just one day before issuing No. 191, he wrote to Davis, "As far as I can learn the enemy are not moving in this direction, but continue to concentrate about Washington." Yet by this very day,

General Jeb Stuart, commander, Confederate cavalry. *The Photographic History of the Civil War.*

the Army of the Potomac had already advanced more than ten miles from the capital's fortifications, and there had been some sharp skirmish fights between the opposing cavalry forces at Pooleville and Hyattstown. The following day, September 9, the Army of the Potomac's advance carried it to the halfway point between Washington and Frederick, and by September 11, even as the final elements of Lee's army were evacuating Frederick to carry out their orders assigned in No. 191, the leading blue columns were already well within ten miles of the Maryland city. Making matters worse, not only was the Union army moving rapidly on Lee's divided forces, but the Confederate army commander had also established an unrealistic timetable for the successful execution of the orders set out in No. 191. The valley operation would quickly fall behind schedule.[15]

Jackson did get off to a good start, beginning the march west from Frederick at 4:00 a.m. on September 10. Before noon, his men had crossed both Catoctin and South Mountain, but after this strenuous march, Jackson called a halt outside Boonsboro. There his men remained for the duration of the day, having covered just thirteen miles from Frederick. The next day, instead of marching west to Sharpsburg, Jackson turned his columns northwest to Williamsport, where his men forded the Potomac. Instead of approaching the Union garrison at Martinsburg from the east, Jackson's columns would now be converging from the north and west. Meanwhile, farther back and just as Jackson's men were splashing across the Potomac, Longstreet's command arrived in Boonsboro. It did not stay there for long. Learning of large quantities of flour in Hagerstown and hearing reports of a large body of Pennsylvania militia supposedly moving south from Chambersburg, threatening the rear of Jackson's command, Lee directed Longstreet to continue north to Hagerstown. Already Lee was significantly deviating from the plan spelled out in No. 191 and was spreading his army even wider apart. Longstreet again protested this further separation of the Confederate army, allegedly declaring to Lee, "General, I wish we could stand still and let the damned Yankees come to us!"[16]

Longstreet's command arrived in Hagerstown the following day, September 12, the same day Lee had hoped would end his valley operation and the day he hoped to be able to rejoin his divided columns. But this would not prove to be the case. About noon, Lee, who had traveled with Longstreet to Hagerstown, learned from Jackson that the Federal garrison at Martinsburg had fled. However, although Martinsburg was now cleared, the Federal force there had simply fallen back to Harpers Ferry, augmenting Colonel Miles's command by another three thousand soldiers. Knowing the now-strengthened Harpers Ferry force to still be the thorn in Lee's side, Jackson led his men south. To both Jackson and Lee, it had now become apparent that Miles's force would not obligingly flee as had been hoped and that a siege operation would be necessary to finally dislodge it. Jackson's men marched through the day and arrived on Bolivar Heights, west of Harpers Ferry, the following afternoon, Saturday, September 13.

As Jackson's men moved south toward Harpers Ferry on September 12, Generals McLaws and Walker continued to follow their orders spelled out in No. 191, but both had already fallen behind schedule. It would not be until the late afternoon of September 13 that McLaws, after a tough, bloody fight, gained possession of Maryland Heights and Walker placed his men atop Loudoun Heights. With the arrival of these troops, and with Jackson's men by then occupying the high ground to the west, Harpers Ferry was at last surrounded. Still, Colonel Miles was under orders to hold out to the last. For the moment, and even as the Confederate artillery was being wheeled into position on the heights surrounding the town, he planned to do just that.[17]

General Robert E. Lee, a commander celebrated in Civil War historiography for his supposed ability to *read* his opponents, was wrong in thinking the Federals would voluntarily leave their post in Harpers Ferry, a

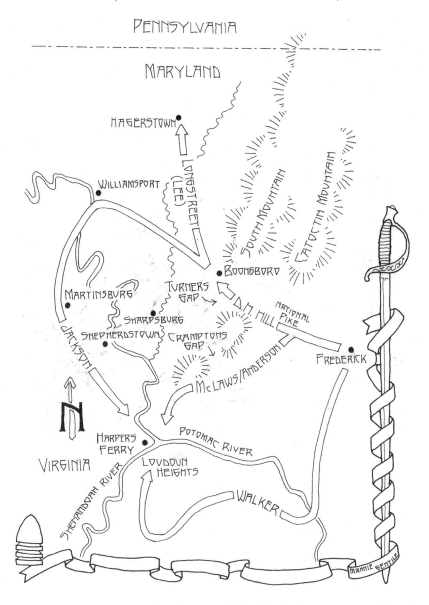

miscalculation that caused his plans to fall behind. But more significantly, Lee, based partly on the scarcity and inaccuracy of reports he had received Stuart, had entirely misjudged the advance of the main Federal army from Washington. On September 13, whether he fully appreciated the extent of it, Lee was in serious trouble. The afternoon before, the advance elements of the Union Army of the Potomac had entered Frederick; their commander, Major General George McClellan, arrived in the city the following morning,

25

and by the afternoon of September 13, Union troops were already pushing west, heading toward South Mountain and Lee's widely dispersed army. Lee had lost the initiative; it now lay directly in the hands of his opponent, and McClellan would not let it slip away.

It had been less than two weeks since McClellan reassumed Union army command. On the morning of September 2, the thirty-five-year-old general was enjoying his breakfast at his residence in Washington when he was visited by General in Chief Henry Halleck and President Abraham Lincoln. The two had come to give the young general command of all the forces then gathering in the capital. McClellan accepted, although he considered it a "terrible and thankless task." It was, at the very least, a daunting one. In the wake of the disaster at Second Manassas, with Lee's triumphant Confederate army on the doorstep of the capital, with panic and despair the prevailing mood, McClellan had to take command of two dispirited Federal armies—his old Army of the Potomac and Pope's Army of Virginia—and get them back in fighting shape. "You don't know what a task has been imposed upon me!" McClellan wrote to his wife, Mary Ellen, a few days later. "I have been obliged to do the best I could with the broken & discouraged fragments of two defeated armies defeated by no fault of mine—nothing but a desire to do my duty could have induced me to accept the command under such circumstance," the army commander explained. Still, McClellan was confident and placed his faith in God. "Again I have been called upon to save the country," he wrote on September 5. "The case is desperate but with God's help I will try unselfishly to do my best & if He wills it accomplish the salvation of the nation. My men are true & will stand by me to the last."[18]

The decision to reinstate McClellan to army command was by no means an easy one for Lincoln, nor a popular one among the president's cabinet. In view of McClellan's failings on

General George B. McClellan and his wife, Mary Ellen. *Library of Congress.*

the peninsula and during the Seven Days' Battles, and because he believed McClellan had deliberately failed to support Pope during the Second Bull Run Campaign, Secretary of War Edwin Stanton sought McClellan's court-martial. Salmon Chase, secretary of the treasury, stated that McClellan ought to have been shot. Although perhaps not as strong, Lincoln had his own reservations about the young commander, having lost much faith in him. Still, Lincoln had no other choice. He offered army command to Burnside, who refused, believing himself not cut out for it. So Lincoln turned again to McClellan, and with great energy, McClellan immediately went to work.[19]

On the afternoon of September 2, McClellan and his staff rode to Upton's Hill, where they encountered John Pope, just then returning from the front with his defeated army. McClellan notified Pope that his men were now under his command. Word of McClellan's return spread quickly among the troops, and the effect was electrical. For all of McClellan's character flaws, and despite his previous failings, he was simply beloved by his men, as highly venerated by his soldiers as any general during the Civil War. Lincoln realized this; to Secretary of the Navy Gideon Welles, the president stated simply that McClellan "has the army with him." And so he did. Almost in an instant, morale improved. Cheers rent the air, sweeping up and down the ranks, while caps were tossed high. Lieutenant Colonel Rutherford B. Hayes of the 23rd Ohio, serving for the first time under McClellan, spoke of this in a September 3 letter to his uncle: "General McClellan is undoubtedly a great favorite with [the] men under him. Last night it was announced that he was again in command…Everywhere the joy was great, and was spontaneously and uproariously expressed. It was a happy army again."[20]

McClellan at once prepared for the difficult task that lay ahead. That Lee would cross the Potomac and head into Maryland came as no great surprise to the Union's military men. General Pope, in one of his last dispatches to Halleck, written on the morning of September 2, declared that "the enemy…means to make trouble in Maryland." George McClellan, a master strategist, surely knew that Lee had no other feasible option. He was confident that Washington was safe from attack—that Lee dare not attack so fortified a city—and he knew Lee would not sit idly by and await the next Union offensive. There was no other choice for Lee but a strike north. On September 4, a message sent from the Union signal station on Sugar Loaf Mountain confirmed that Confederates were indeed crossing the Potomac. Prepared for this, McClellan began organizing the pursuit, placing his army on the roads leading north and west from Washington. In describing the march from Washington, Colonel Joseph J. Bartlett, commanding a brigade in the Sixth Corps, wrote, "Bands played, then men stepped out with that veteran swing which is only acquired by troops after long and continuous campaigning, and the Army of the Potomac seemed to be itself again."[21]

McClellan merged Pope's forces into the Army of the Potomac while at the same time organizing the dozens of new regiments arriving daily in the capital, formed in response to Lincoln's July call for 300,000 more men. Keeping two corps behind to man Washington's forts, McClellan set out in pursuit of Lee with five corps, a division of the Fourth Corps under General Darius Couch and George Sykes's division of U.S. Regulars from the Fifth Corps. To expedite the march, McClellan adopted a wing structure. The right wing, under Burnside, consisted of the First Corps, now under Joseph Hooker, and the Ninth Corps, under Jesse Reno, two corps that were unfamiliar to McClellan, never having served under his command. To command the army's center wing—the Second and Twelfth Corps—McClellan tapped Major General Edwin Sumner, while William Franklin took charge of the army's left wing, which consisted of his own Sixth Corps plus Couch's division. Screening the army's advance was the Union cavalry, under Alfred Pleasonton, while Sykes's division brought up the rear as a general reserve.

On a map, the advance of the Army of the Potomac resembled a large pitchfork; McClellan was forced to cast a wide net to defend against all contingencies. Burnside's right wing moved north and then turned west in order to defend against any Confederate advance toward Baltimore. Sumner brought up the middle, pushing northwest directly toward Frederick, while Franklin's wing moved along the Potomac to the south. The army commander set off for the front on September 7, still hopeful. "We are well & the entire army is now united, cheerful & confident," wrote McClellan to his wife. "You need not fear the result for I believe that God will give us the victory."[22]

At first the Union army moved off at a slow rate of advance, covering just a few miles a day, but its pace accelerated once McClellan became more aware of Lee's movements and intentions. And while McClellan may have initially sought a limited objective—to drive Lee from Maryland—he would come to adopt a more aggressive one, believing he had an opportunity to inflict a crippling blow on the Army of Northern Virginia even though he was well aware of the heavy stakes involved. Often overlooked was the tremendous pressure resting on McClellan's shoulders during the Maryland Campaign. Simply stated, following a summer's worth of defeats and with Confederate forces on the move across a thousand-mile front, McClellan could not afford to lose another battle, especially one fought on Union soil. As he rather plainly stated to Halleck on September 11, "If we should be defeated, the consequences to the country would be disastrous in the extreme." In another letter to Halleck, McClellan added that it was "upon the success of this Army the fate of nation depends."[23]

Although he set out with no clear idea of exactly where the Confederate army was headed, McClellan sensed that the purpose of Lee's drive north was to bring the Army of the Potomac to battle and not to capture cities or key geographic landmarks, as many believed. Halleck, for instance, was convinced that Lee's movement across the Potomac was merely a feint to draw McClellan out of Washington. Lee would then recross the river and attack the now lightly defended capital from the south. McClellan never seemed to have given more than a passing thought to this. Besides, even if Washington fell, as McClellan wrote to Pennsylvania's governor, Andrew Curtin, it would not "bear comparison with the ruin and disasters which would follow a signal defeat of this army." Instead of attacking Washington or Baltimore, or even heading north toward Harrisburg, said McClellan, "Everything seems to indicate that [the Confederates] intend to hazard all upon the issue of the coming battle." McClellan was not going to shrink from the challenge. "You may be sure," the army commander promised Curtin, "that I will follow them as closely as I can, and fight them whenever I can find them."[24]

Believing Washington and Baltimore were not in any danger, McClellan continued his pursuit toward Frederick. By September 11, the same day the last of Lee's columns left Frederick, the Army of the Potomac had already arrived to within a hard day's march of the city. Federal cavalry had recaptured the key Sugar Loaf Mountain, and McClellan received reports that day that Lee's men had

Colonel Dixon S. Miles, commander, Harpers Ferry Garrison. *Library of Congress.*

evacuated Frederick and were marching west. He issued orders for Burnside to move into Frederick the following day and sent repeated requests to Halleck to send up more men. McClellan also repeated his request that Colonel Miles's command be at once ordered to abandon Harpers Ferry and join up with his army, but Halleck refused to vacate the strategic town and, by this act, inadvertently forced Lee to alter his campaign and divide his forces.

On September 12, the Army of the Potomac continued its drive westward, and although certain that Lee had left Frederick and had crossed the mountains farther west, McClellan received conflicting reports that Confederate forces were moving both north toward Hagerstown and south toward Harpers Ferry. He did not have a clear idea of where Lee was heading, as is evidenced by a letter he penned to Mary Ellen at 3:00 p.m. that Friday. "From all I can gather secesh is skeddadelling...I begin to think that he is making off to get out of the scrape by recrossing the river at Williamsport...He evidently don't want to fight me—for some reason or other." Still, McClellan's men continued their march, and at 4:30 p.m., the first Union troops, General Jacob Cox's Kanawha Division, Ninth Corps, entered Frederick, but not without a little dust-up.

Colonel Augustus Moor, commanding a brigade in Cox's division, along with a small escort, galloped ahead of his men, apparently caught up in the moment, and noisily entered the city. Hearing the commotion, Confederate cavalrymen from Wade Hampton's Brigade, just then galloping out of Frederick, turned around and dashed directly toward Moor's party. The result was the capture of ten Union soldiers, including Colonel Moor. Satisfied with their catch, the Confederate cavalrymen sauntered out of town with their prisoners in tow, clearing the way for Cox's Federals. The Union men were greeted with a perfect ovation from the people of Frederick, who felt their liberators had at last arrived.[25]

McClellan entered the city at nine o'clock the following morning, welcomed as a hero. "I can't describe to you for want of time the enthusiastic reception we met with yesterday at Frederic," wrote the army commander the next day, "I was nearly overwhelmed and pulled to pieces." Still, touched as McClellan was with this display of affection, there was serious work to be done. Late the evening before, McClellan received a note from Lincoln, who had heard reports of Confederate forces crossing the Potomac near Williamsport. "Please do not let him get off without being hurt," urged the commander in chief, and McClellan did not intend to. He had already ordered Pleasonton to advance west from Frederick, with the Ninth Corps instructed to follow

McClellan entering Frederick, by Edwin Forbes. *Library of Congress.*

behind. Franklin was directed to advance that day to Buckeystown, south of Frederick, and at the foot of Catoctin Mountain, while Hooker's First Corps, the Second and Twelfth Corps under Sumner and Sykes's Fifth Corps division were all instructed to continue to Frederick.[26]

Colonel John Farnsworth's cavalry brigade led Pleasonton's advance west of Frederick on September 13, setting off along the National Pike. About 2:00 p.m., it came under fire from several cannons in position at Hagan's Gap in the Catoctin Range, supported by dismounted cavalrymen of the Jeff Davis Legion. Jeb Stuart, having fallen back from Frederick, had set up a defensive screen along Catoctin Mountain. Hampton's men trailed behind D.H. Hill's columns as they marched out of Frederick and were forced to contend with the main Union thrust, while Colonel Thomas Munford's two regiments—the 2nd and 12th Virginia Cavalry—moved several miles south, to Jefferson Pass. General Fitzhugh Lee's cavalry brigade had been ordered far to the north and was that day some twenty-five miles northeast of Frederick at Westminster. By this time, Stuart was well aware of the proximity of McClellan's troops but was still not too concerned. He did not know that the Confederate army remained divided on the other side of South Mountain; instead, he was under the impression that the valley operation had been completed and that Lee was already endeavoring to reunite his forces.

Farnsworth's blue-clad troopers of the 3rd Indiana and 8th Illinois Cavalry came under what Pleasonton described as a "severe cannonading and several warm volleys with carbines" in their attack against the small Confederate force defending Hagan's Gap. They were able to force their way through, driving the Confederate horsemen several miles back to Middletown, where Hampton set up another defensive line. After another brisk fight, Hampton's men were again driven back. Stuart then directed Hampton to take his brigade south to Burkittsville to reinforce Munford's small brigade. Galloping south, Hampton noticed a column of blue troopers advancing along a parallel road. He detached Cobb's Legion, which turned left and galloped into the Federal horsemen near the Quebec Schoolhouse. This clash of sabers left four Confederates dead and nine wounded, while the Union troopers, belonging to the 3rd Indiana, lost thirty men killed and wounded before withdrawing.

With their way now clear and free of any Federal pursuit, Hampton continued on to Burkittsville, where he linked up with Munford's command. Like Hampton's troopers, Munford's men had also been driven from their position on the Catoctin Mountain. Union troops converged on Munford's men at Jefferson Pass from three directions, with the main thrust coming

General Alfred Pleasonton, commander, Union cavalry. *Library of Congress.*

from Frederick. The Pennsylvanians of Richard Rush's cavalry brigade, reinforced by elements of Colonel Harrison Fairchild's Ninth Corps brigade, drove the Virginia cavalrymen from the pass, with Rush's Lancers following the retreating Confederates all the way to Burkittsville at the eastern foot of South Mountain. There, Munford set up a defensive line along Mountain Church Road and placed some guns halfway up the mountain slope, astride the road leading to Crampton's Gap.[27]

By nightfall, Union cavalrymen, supported by the soldiers of the Ninth Corps, drove Jeb Stuart's forces from Catoctin Mountain, through the Middletown Valley and all the way to South Mountain. By this time, Stuart had learned that the valley expedition had fallen behind schedule and that the Confederate army remained divided. The seriousness of the situation began to sink in. Stuart sent reports to both Lee and D.H. Hill, whose division—the rear guard of the Army of Northern Virginia—was nearest South Mountain at Boonsboro. Yet Stuart believed that the Army of the Potomac, surely on its way to rescue the beleaguered Harpers Ferry garrison, would move primarily on the roads to the south, through Burkittsville and Crampton's Gap or to Wevertown. He reported that only two Union brigades were advancing along the National Pike toward Turner's Gap and notified D.H. Hill that only one brigade would be sufficient to hold the gap. Hill sent the Georgians and Alabamians of Alfred Colquitt's Brigade to the critical mountain pass. Stuart conversed briefly with Colquitt, telling him there was only a small Union force in the valley ahead and that he was heading south to Burkittsville. The next morning, without notifying either Colquitt or D.H. Hill, Stuart detached Colonel Thomas Rosser's 5th Virginia Cavalry at Fox's Gap, one mile south of Turner's, and then continued south, galloping toward Crampton's Gap.[28]

With his horsemen pushing west of Frederick on the afternoon of September 13 and the rest of his army in motion, converging on the city, George McClellan set up his headquarters. About noon, while entertaining a group of Frederick businessmen, McClellan was unexpectedly handed a copy of Robert E. Lee's Special Orders No. 191.

When the Confederate army commander issued these orders four days earlier, he had ensured that a copy be made for each of the commanders mentioned in the orders, which of course included General Daniel Harvey Hill, whose division Lee regarded as an independent command. Stonewall Jackson, however, believing that Hill was under his command and was now being detached, prepared a copy of No. 191 for Hill. Because of the loose structure of Lee's army, two copies of the same orders were thus sent to Hill's headquarters; somehow, one of them ended up lost. When the Union

Twelfth Corps settled in for a rest on the morning of September 13 in a meadow south of Frederick, which just a few days earlier had served as the site of Hill's headquarters, Corporal Barton Mitchell of the 27th Indiana happened upon an envelope. Stuffed inside were three cigars, wrapped together by a piece of paper, which turned out to be Lee's lost orders. The envelope and its contents were rushed quickly up the chain of command until they landed in the hands of McClellan.

After a quick glance at No. 191, McClellan was elated with this surprising discovery, famously boasting to General John Gibbon, "Here is a paper with which if I cannot whip Bobbie Lee, I would be willing to go home" and promising Lincoln that he would soon send him trophies. "I think Lee has made a gross mistake and that he will be severely punished for it," wrote the army commander to the president. "I have all the plans of the Rebels and will catch them in their own trap." However, upon more careful examination, McClellan realized that Special Orders No. 191 raised more questions than it answered. First, it was dated September 9 and identified September 12 as the day Lee wished for the Harpers Ferry operation to be completed. McClellan, of course, had to determine whether his opponent was still following these orders. At 3:00 p.m., he sent a copy of No. 191 to Pleasonton, whose horsemen were just then advancing toward Middletown, having busted their way through Hagan's Gap an hour earlier. Pleasonton was instructed to "ascertain whether this order of march has thus far been followed by the enemy." McClellan believed that it had been, and from the artillery fire coming from the direction of Harpers Ferry, which must have sounded like distant thunder, he surmised that Lee had fallen behind schedule and that Miles's garrison force still held out.[29]

Aside from seeking to verify the information contained in No. 191, McClellan carefully scrutinized the wording of the orders, seeking to deduce the size of Lee's army. Throughout the Maryland Campaign, and as had been true on the peninsula and outside of Richmond, McClellan believed himself to be heavily outnumbered. The estimates McClellan received of the size of Confederate forces in Maryland ranged anywhere from 80,000 to 200,000 men. He took a lower-end figure, somewhere between 110,000 and 120,000—still far greater than Lee's actual strength. There was, of course, no specific mention of actual numbers in No. 191, only words such as "command" and "division," and Lee's willingness to so thoroughly divide his forces was just further evidence to McClellan that he did, indeed, face a superior foe.[30]

Still, Special Orders No. 191 made it clear that Lee had divided his forces, and McClellan knew that they remained divided on the other side of South Mountain. Numbers aside, McClellan realized he now had an opportunity not only to drive Lee out of Maryland but also to destroy the Army of Northern Virginia in detail. By the evening of September 13, McClellan had formed his plan of attack. The bulk of the Army of the Potomac, spearheaded by Reno's Ninth Corps, would advance along the National Pike, heading west from Frederick and toward the "main body" of the Confederate army—Longstreet's command and D.H. Hill's division—which McClellan assumed to still be at Boonsboro. Of course, McClellan did not know that Longstreet's command had already marched to Hagerstown, leaving only Hill's division at Boonsboro. Whether these Confederates, whom in McClellan's mind numbered around sixty thousand, would remain in Boonsboro or defend South Mountain at Turner's Gap did not matter. With the Ninth Corps, followed by Hooker's First Corps and backed up by Sumner's center wing, McClellan sought only to keep the main Confederate body at bay while his Sixth Corps, under Franklin, delivered the key blow to the south. Franklin, whose Sixth Corps soldiers had settled into bivouac at Buckeystown on the night of September 13, was to move at daybreak, cross over Catoctin Mountain and sweep through the valley to Burkittsville. He was to then ram through any Confederate force that might be defending Crampton's Gap and, once across, turn south and either capture or destroy McLaws's command on Maryland Heights, thereby lifting the siege of Harpers Ferry. With Miles's liberated command now augmenting his force, Franklin was to either turn back north and assist Burnside—with the Ninth and First Corps—in his battle or, if Burnside had by this time defeated Lee's "main body," head west toward the Potomac to cut off any of Longstreet's and D.H. Hill's men attempting to escape. "My general idea," McClellan wrote to Franklin, "is to cut the enemy in two and beat him in detail," while also relieving the Harpers Ferry garrison. It was an aggressive plan—perhaps too aggressive, especially as it pertained to Franklin. Still, McClellan was confident.[31]

While confidence prevailed at Union army headquarters, anxiety overtook Lee at his headquarters at Hagerstown. Stuart's reports of the Union advance from Frederick were strengthened by one sent by D.H. Hill. After dark, Alfred Colquitt, alone on South Mountain at Turner's Gap, saw the area around Middletown lit up with thousands of campfires. It was clear that there was a far greater threat to his front than Stuart had let on. Colquitt informed Hill of this and sought reinforcement. Hill ordered Samuel Garland's North Carolinians and the guns of Captain John Lane's battery to Colquitt's support on the mountain and then sent a report to Lee informing him of the large Federal force just on the other side of South Mountain. Lee now realized the danger he faced. He no longer held the initiative, and with his army split and with McClellan's men "advancing more rapidly than was convenient" from Frederick—as Lee later mildly put it—the Confederate army commander knew he was in serious trouble.

He was most concerned about McLaws, whose two divisions were positioned on Maryland Heights and along the banks of the Potomac. If the Union army punched through at Crampton's Gap to the rear of McLaws's positions, it could very well cut off a full 20 percent of Lee's army. Lee sent repeated messages that night to McLaws, urging him to hurry things along and keep a careful eye on the roads leading from Frederick toward his rear. Lee also decided to turn Longstreet's men around and get them moving back in the direction of Boonsboro at first light on September 14. Longstreet again objected, wishing instead for Lee to pull his entire army back toward Sharpsburg, but Lee would not consider this. He could not abandon McLaws, and he certainly could not order a retreat; he had come north to give battle, and to retreat now would be an admission of defeat. He would make his stand on the mountain, attempting to hold back McClellan's men as long as possible.

After sending his urgent notes to McLaws, Lee sent another to D.H. Hill, ordering him to oversee the defense of Turner's Gap. He could not know which of the gaps McClellan would use, but with Longstreet's command heading back toward Boonsboro, Lee knew they could be sent to either Turner's or Crampton's, depending on the circumstances.[32]

On the night of September 13, all attention focused on South Mountain, an extension of the Blue Ridge Mountains, rising precipitously to heights of nearly one thousand feet above the surrounding valley floors and running in a southwesterly direction from central Pennsylvania to the Potomac River near Harpers Ferry. The countryside surrounding the mountain was idyllic and peaceful, while the slopes of the mountain were rugged and wooded. There were only a few good roads leading across South Mountain from west of Frederick. The National Pike was the main thoroughfare, crossing the mountain at Turner's Gap, but there were others, such as the Old Sharpsburg Road, which ran through Fox's Gap, and the Burkittsville–Rohrersville Road, which passed over the mountain six miles farther south at Crampton's Gap. The soldiers of McClellan's Army of the Potomac would use these roads and these critical gaps the following day in their effort to force their way across the mountain. Before the night of September 13, Lee had no intention of defending South Mountain. Now, caught off guard, he was forced to, lest his army be cut in two and beaten in detail.

2

"Hell Itself Turned Loose"

The Struggle for Fox's Gap

Early on the morning of Sunday, September 14, in that quiet, gray calm between daybreak and sunrise, General D.H. Hill enjoyed a quick cup of coffee before riding from his headquarters near Boonsboro to Turner's Gap, at the summit of South Mountain. As he rode, Hill no doubt contemplated the heavy burden now resting on his shoulders. As per Lee's instructions in Special Orders No. 191, Hill's division—composed of five veteran brigades and numbering somewhere between seven and eight thousand men—had been assigned to Boonsboro to serve as the army's rear guard and to defend the roads leading north through Pleasant Valley in order to prevent Federal troops from escaping the noose tightening around Harpers Ferry. Such an assignment, said Hill, had already "required a considerable separation" of his command. Then, on the afternoon of September 13, Hill had received a note from Jeb Stuart, stating that two brigades of Federal infantry were pushing westward and driving his horsemen back toward South Mountain. He appealed to Hill for one brigade to halt this Federal advance. Hill responded by sending Colquitt's Brigade of Georgians and Alabamians. He later sent up Brigadier General Samuel Garland's hard-fighting North Carolinians, as well as Captain James W. Bondurant's Alabama artillery and Captain John Lane's Georgia battery. With these men redirected back to Turner's Gap, later that night Hill received yet another more urgent note, this one from the army commander. Not entirely confident in Stuart's ability alone to defend the gap, Lee directed Hill to go in person to help oversee its defense.[33]

Whatever anxieties Hill had as he made his way up the mountain were magnified when he arrived on the summit about 5:30 a.m. Although the

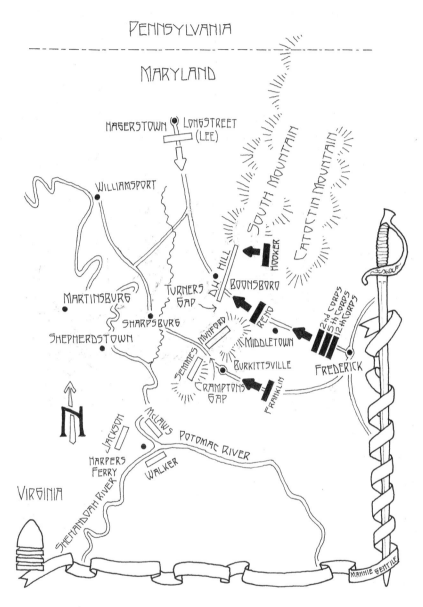

previous day Stuart had indicated that one brigade would be sufficient to
defend the pass, a quick examination of the terrain convinced Hill that
it "could be only held by a large force, and was wholly indefensible by a
small one." Making matters worse, Hill discovered that he had been entirely
abandoned by Stuart. The cavalryman left a note stating that he had galloped

south with his command toward Crampton's Gap, where he believed the Federals would concentrate their efforts. "He was too gallant a soldier to leave his post when a battle was imminent," Hill later wrote, with some underhanded criticism, "and doubtless he believed that there was but a small Federal force on the National road."[34]

What made Hill's task so daunting was that in order to defend Turner's Gap, he also had to guard three other passes, all along a five-mile front. Three miles north of Turner's Gap was

General Daniel Harvey Hill. *The Photographic History of the Civil War.*

the little-used Orr's Gap. More immediate and thus more threatening was Frosttown Gap, approximately one mile to the north. Completing the passes Hill would have to defend was Fox's Gap, roughly three-quarters of a mile to the south. It would be a trying ordeal, but Hill immediately went to work. At that early hour, Hill had just two batteries and two of his brigades on hand: Garland's, which was bivouacked near the Mountain House, and Colquitt's, which was deployed astride the National Pike on the mountain's eastern slope. For the time being, Hill kept Garland where he was until he gained a better understanding of the ground. He then sent several aides racing down the mountain with instructions for his three brigade commanders still at Boonsboro. Hill was reluctant to call up all of his men. The Federal garrison at Harpers Ferry continued to hold out, and it was thus still necessary to guard the roads running north through Pleasant Valley. Hence, only Brigadier General George Burgwyn Anderson's Brigade, some twelve hundred North Carolinians, was immediately sent for. Brigadier General Roswell Ripley was directed to detach the 4th Georgia and send it north to Orr's Gap, while the balance of his brigade, along with that of Brigadier General Robert Rodes, was to remain at Boonsboro. After sending out these orders, Hill quickly

39

surveyed Colquitt's line, finding himself satisfied with its placement. With his adjutant, Major J.W. Ratchford, Hill then rode south along the crest of the mountain to reconnoiter Fox's Gap.[35]

Hill and Ratchford wandered along the wood road, a narrow, rough trail running along the summit, connecting the two gaps. As they neared Fox's, however, the sound of muffled voices and rumbling wheels brought their reconnaissance to an abrupt halt. Assuming that Federal troops had already gained possession of Fox's Gap, Hill turned around and quietly made his way back to Turner's Gap. What Hill did not know was that the voices he heard were from soldiers of Colonel Thomas Rosser's 5th Virginia Cavalry. Stuart had earlier detached Rosser's small command of 250 men, along with two guns under Captain John Pelham, to guard the pass. Stuart neglected to inform Hill of this, and as the division commander later wrote, since Rosser "was not directed to report to me...I did not suspect his presence." Upon returning to the Mountain House, Hill found Garland's Brigade under arms and ready for deployment. Believing his right to be endangered, Hill explained the situation to Garland and directed him south with orders to hold Fox's Gap "at all hazards." The fate of Lee's entire army, said Hill, was at stake. Bondurant's Alabama artillerists followed behind Garland's men with their four guns. Hill watched as the column moved out, later recording that Garland "went off in high spirits."[36]

Born in Lynchburg, Virginia, in December 1830, Samuel Garland had already accomplished much in his thirty-one years. He graduated from Virginia Military Institute in 1849 and then, two years later, from the University of Virginia Law School. A successful young attorney in his native Lynchburg, Garland also maintained an active role in the Virginia state militia. With the outbreak of war, Garland entered service as a captain in the 11th Virginia Infantry. Rising quickly to regimental command, Garland was shot in the elbow while leading the 11th at Williamsburg in May 1862 and had made such a strong impression on his superiors that, less than three weeks later, he was again promoted, this time to brigadier general. D.H. Hill described Garland as "the most fearless man I ever knew, a Christian hero, a ripe scholar, and most accomplished gentleman." It was an estimation shared by most. In Lee's army, Garland ranked among the brightest young stars.[37]

Not entirely sure what to expect as he led his brigade south along the wood road, Garland was doubtlessly relieved when he encountered Rosser. As best he could, Rosser explained the terrain to Garland and helped the young Virginian deploy his brigade. The Old Sharpsburg Road, which branched off the National Pike several miles to the east of South Mountain, near

Catoctin Creek, crossed the mountain at Fox's Gap. A Union artillerist later described the roadway as being "rough with stones and ruts, and narrow as a farm lane." While the Old Sharpsburg Road was the most important, there were also several secondary roads that were to play vital roles in the combat. The wood road, running along the crest of the mountain from Turner's Gap, intersected the Old Sharpsburg Road at Fox's Gap. Running south from Fox's Gap, and also along the crest of the mountain, was the ridge road, bordered for nearly three hundred yards with stout stone fences. Approximately three-quarters of a mile south of Fox's Gap, the ridge road intersected the loop road, which then ran in a northeasterly fashion down the eastern side of South Mountain, where it ultimately connected with the Old Sharpsburg Road at the mountain's base. At the summit of South Mountain at Fox's Gap stood the modest cabin home of farmer Daniel Wise and a four-acre clearing known as Wise's Field. These roadways, in reality no more than narrow, crooked trails, and Wise's once peaceful mountaintop farm formed the stage of operations for the savage combat that would soon be waged for control of the gap.[38]

The terrain and all the various approaches forced Garland to stretch his brigade thin. Garland's command consisted of five veteran North Carolina regiments, but because of heavy casualties sustained throughout the spring and summer, it totaled just eleven hundred men fit for action. Many of these men were rookie conscripts who had joined up during the summer and had yet to witness battle. Garland placed Colonel Duncan McRae's 5th North Carolina on the far right of his line, near the intersection of the ridge and loop roads. With four hundred men, the 5th was Garland's largest

Looking south at Fox's Gap, Wise's Cabin can be seen on right. *Battles & Leaders of the Civil War.*

regiment. To the right front of the 5th, and on a commanding piece of high ground, went Rosser's cavalrymen and Pelham's two guns. The 12th North Carolina, whittled down to just ninety men and commanded by a captain, went into position to the left of McRae's troops. Continuing Garland's line to the north was Colonel Daniel Christie's 23rd North Carolina, which went into position behind the stone wall along the ridge road, to the left of the 12th. Captain Bondurant's "Jeff Davis Artillery" unlimbered next to the 23rd North Carolina, its two twelve-pound Napoleons and two three-inch rifles dropping trail in an open field, south of Wise's Field. Garland's remaining regiments, the 13th and 20th North Carolina, went into position north of the Wise Cabin, their right resting on the Old Sharpsburg Road. Between the right of these two regiments and the left of the 23rd North Carolina was a gap of some 250 yards, only somewhat covered by Bondurant's gunners. Thus deployed, Garland's line stretched 1,300 yards, across a wide front. It was a lot of ground to cover, but Garland had no other choice. His deployment was the best he could do under the circumstances. However, although spread thin, Garland's men did enjoy the defensive advantage, since any attack against their position would have to be made uphill. Having posted his brigade, Garland found Rosser, and the two further discussed the situation. Minutes later, gunfire erupted. It was 9:00 a.m.[39]

The musket fire, at first desultory but soon steady, was coming from the far right of Garland's line. After initially positioning the 5th North Carolina, Garland had instructed McRae to advance a body of skirmishers "into the woods to our right-oblique front, to go as far as possible and explore." McRae sent forward fifty men. As he later reported, "they had not passed 50 steps from where we then stood when they encountered the enemy's skirmishers and the fight commenced." Those enemy skirmishers belonged to the 23rd Ohio, leading the advance of Brigadier General Jacob Cox's Kanawha Division of the Ninth Army Corps.[40]

The Kanawha Division had led the Federal advance west of Frederick the previous day and had settled into camp near Middletown, five miles east of South Mountain. The Ninth Corps, which, along with the First, composed Burnside's Right Wing, was in position to lead the Army of the Potomac's main thrust across South Mountain at Turner's Gap, keeping Lee's "main body" at bay while Franklin's Sixth Corps punched through at Crampton's Gap, six miles to the south. Franklin's movement was the key to McClellan's entire operation, since it would drive a wedge in Lee's army while at the same time relieving Dixon Miles's hapless command at Harpers Ferry. McClellan trusted Franklin with this important assignment and accompanied Burnside in his movement west along the National Pike. Still relying on the information contained in Special Orders No. 191, and unaware that Longstreet's command had marched to Hagerstown, McClellan had no way of knowing that only D.H. Hill's small division remained at Boonsboro on the mountain's western base. He thus believed that both Hill *and* Longstreet were still to his front with upwards of sixty thousand men. The Union army commander predicted battle on the fourteenth. Early that morning, McClellan penned a few lines to his beloved Mary Ellen: "I have only time to say good morning this bright sunny Sunday," wrote McClellan, "& then start to the front to try to relieve Harper's Ferry, which is sorely pressed by secesh. It is probable that we shall have a serious engagement today & perhaps a general battle."[41]

Pleasonton's horsemen drove Confederate forces out of the Catoctin Valley on September 13, pushing Stuart's gray-clad troopers all the way back to South Mountain and prompting Stuart to appeal to D.H. Hill for support, which in turn resulted in Colquitt and Garland being sent to Turner's Gap. When the Union cavalrymen drew within sight of Colquitt's Brigade deployed astride the National Pike, it was already growing dark, and the advance was halted. Pleasonton sought infantry support for his continued reconnaissance the following day and sent back a request for reinforcement to Burnside. The Union cavalry chief then rode back toward Middletown and located Cox's division going into bivouac. Pleasonton found Cox, explained the situation and asked for support. A single brigade, said Pleasonton, would suffice. Even after his meeting with the cavalry commander, Cox apparently did not fully grasp the strategic circumstances since, as opposed to McClellan, he did not anticipate a serious battle.[42]

By 6:00 a.m. Sunday morning, while D.H. Hill was reconnoitering the mountain gaps and preparing for their defense, Colonel Eliakim Scammon's brigade was on the road, leading Cox's advance, the rising sun warming the soldiers' backs as they marched west from their camps at Middletown along the National Pike. Cox accompanied Scammon at the front of the column, curious about how Pleasonton planned to use the brigade. Scammon's brigade was a mixed unit of infantry, cavalry and even some artillery. It consisted of the 12th, 23rd and 30th Ohio Regiments, two small companies of independent western Virginia cavalry and Captain James McMullins's battery of six ten-pound Parrotts. In total, Scammon could count roughly fifteen hundred men present for action that day. Believing their mission to be only a reconnaissance, the Ohioans left their knapsacks behind and moved out in light marching order.[43]

Not long after their advance commenced, Scammon's Ohioans heard the faint, though distinct, rumble of artillery fire. Up ahead, Pleasonton's troopers were already busy scouting the various roadways and examining the mountainous terrain. Pleasonton directed the reconnaissance from near the small village of Bolivar. Near this small gathering of dwellings and on a high knoll to the left of the National Pike, the cavalry commander had placed Captain Horatio Gibson's Battery C&G, 3rd U.S. Artillery, and Lieutenant Samuel Benjamin's Battery E, 2nd U.S. Artillery, a total of ten long-range guns, which he ordered to fire into Turner's Gap, hoping to draw a return fire. The response soon came from Lane's six guns, positioned on a high, clear field north of the Mountain House. At times, this artillery exchange grew quite heated, but the Federals were having the best of it, silencing Lane on several occasions and forcing the Confederate artillerist to reposition his outnumbered guns. It was the combined salvos of these guns that Cox's Ohioans heard as they marched west, the rumbling growing louder with each step.[44]

Cox and Scammon sauntered along in front of the blue column. Soon after crossing Catoctin Creek, however, both officers reined to an unexpected stop, astonished to see Colonel Augustus Moor standing beside the road. Moor, who began the campaign in command of the Kanawha Division's Second Brigade, had been captured by Wade Hampton's cavalry in the streets of Frederick two days earlier when Cox's troops first entered the city. When asked what had happened, Moor told Cox he was taken as a prisoner beyond South Mountain but had been paroled the evening before. He was now making his way back to the Union lines. Moor then asked Cox where he was heading. The division commander explained that Scammon's men were advancing in support of Pleasonton in a reconnaissance of Turner's Gap. "My God! Be careful!" exclaimed Moor. Then, realizing he was still honor-bound to comply with the terms of his parole, the Ohio colonel simply turned away and continued on his hike. Moor's exclamation was enough to convince Cox that there might be some trouble ahead. He instructed Scammon to continue westward and locate Pleasonton while he headed back to Middletown to order up his Second Brigade, now under Colonel George Crook. As he rode back, Cox singled out each of Scammon's regimental commanders, "warning them to be prepared for anything, big or little—it might be a skirmish, it might be a battle."[45]

Arriving back at Middletown, Cox directed Crook to move his brigade out in support of Scammon. After firing off a brief note to Jesse Reno, apprising the Ninth Corps commander of the developing situation, Cox then wheeled and galloped his way back to the front. Trotting along the National Pike, Cox passed Crook's men just moving out. Like Scammon's Brigade, Crook's was a mixed unit. It contained three regiments of infantry—the 11th, 28th and 36th Ohio—as well as Captain Frederick Schambeck's company of Chicago Dragoons and the six rifled Parrotts of Captain Seth Simmonds's Kentucky Light Artillery. Like Scammon, Crook could also count fifteen hundred men present for action.[46]

Crook's men were just getting underway when Cox arrived back at the front. He found Pleasonton near the still booming cannons of Benjamin's and Gibson's batteries, continuing to hurl shells toward Lane's artillerists in Turner's Gap. From Pleasonton, Cox discovered that Scammon's brigade had already filed off the National Pike and was now approaching South Mountain along the Old Sharpsburg Road. Scammon had reported to the cavalry commander a short time earlier. During their conversation, Pleasonton told Scammon that Turner's Gap was too heavily defended for a direct attack up the National Pike. His troopers, however, had discovered two roads, "one on the right and the other to the left of the gap," that, if gained, would turn the Confederate position in Turner's Gap on either flank. Pleasonton instructed Scammon to advance along the road to the left—the Old Sharpsburg Road, which crossed South Mountain at Fox's Gap. After gaining the crest, Scammon was to then turn north and strike the Confederate rear at Turner's. Scammon nodded in approval and deployed his Ohioans accordingly. While Scammon executed this maneuver, Pleasonton's horsemen would divert the Confederates' attention by demonstrating toward Turner's Gap. Cox also discovered that four of Captain McMullins's six artillery pieces had unlimbered next to Gibson and Benjamin, adding to Pleasonton's firepower. A short time later, two of Captain Seth Simmonds's twenty-pound Parrotts deployed here. Cox approved of the plan, told Pleasonton to expect Crook's men in roughly half an hour and then rode off to catch up with Scammon.[47]

Scammon's men had roughly two miles to cover along the Old Sharpsburg Road before reaching South Mountain, and, as Cox later recorded, "as it was a pretty sharp ascent the men marched slowly with frequent rests." Confederates on the mountaintop detected their advance, and it was not long before Bondurant's gunners, recently arrived at Fox's Gap, began lobbing shells into the Ohioans' ranks. Under fire and believing Fox's Gap to be heavily defended, Scammon turned his men off the Old Sharpsburg Road and onto the loop road, which branched off the Old Sharpsburg Road near the mountain's base and which they would follow south before the road turned to the right. Scammon was hoping to utilize this road to sweep around the Confederates' right and rear. Meanwhile, a courier from Ninth Corps headquarters caught up with Cox and informed him that Reno had approved of his movements and had already ordered up the remaining three divisions of the corps, which would be advancing to his support.[48]

Local farmer John Miller guided Scammon's march along the loop road, riding forward with his leading regiment, the 23rd Ohio, commanded by Lieutenant Colonel Rutherford B. Hayes. The Ohioans now moved unseen by the Confederates, marching parallel with the crest of the mountain until they reached the point where the loop road turned to the right and climbed up the mountain's eastern slope. At this point, Scammon called a halt and deployed his brigade. Hayes's 23rd Ohio held the far left of the line; his instructions were to "move through the woods on the left of the road, crossing the mountain so as to attack the enemy on the right and rear of the right flank." Scammon also instructed Hayes to capture a two-gun battery believed to be there, no doubt referring to Pelham's pieces attached to Rosser's 5th Virginia Cavalry. Hayes inquired what to do if instead he found six guns and a strong infantry support. "Take them, anyhow," replied the brigade command before riding off to position the rest of his command.[49]

Colonel Carr B. White's 12th Ohio went into line to the right of the 23rd. Its mission promised to be a deadly one as it was to simply charge uphill across the open fields to its front and attack a Confederate force posted behind a stone wall on the crest. Completing Scammon's line to the north was the 30th Ohio, under Colonel Hugh Ewing, which formed to the right of the 12th. The 30th Ohio was to advance uphill and engage the Confederates posted in Fox's Gap, including Bondurant's guns, drawing the Confederates' full attention while Hayes and White moved around their right flank and rear. With his line thus formed and the orders delivered, it was time for the attack. It was just minutes before 9:00 a.m.[50]

Hayes's 23rd Ohio led the attack. The 12th and 30th moved out a short time later. Advancing up the mountainside and through difficult, wooded terrain, Hayes deployed

Brigadier General Eliakim Parker Scammon. *The Photographic History of the Civil War.*

Company A as skirmishers and led the rest of the 23rd forward. Hayes's skirmishers soon encountered those of the 5th North Carolina, and a sharp firefight broke out. It was this exchange of rifle fire that had alerted Garland, who then turned to McRae and instructed him to advance his entire regiment to support his skirmishers. As directed, McRae led the 5th North Carolina forward, through a wood so thick and dense with undergrowth that "it was impossible to advance in line of battle."[51]

McRae's advance caught the attention of Lieutenant Colonel Hayes. Having already advanced Company A as skirmishers and Companies I and F as flankers, and with these men now sparring actively with the Confederate skirmishers, Hayes ordered the balance of the regiment forward. Hayes later recorded that the 23rd "formed hastily in the woods" and then "pushed through bushes and rocks and over broken ground towards the enemy; soon received a heavy volley, wounding and killing some. I feared confusion; [I] exhorted, swore, and threatened." Better positioned, McRae's North Carolinians enjoyed the advantage. As McRae noted, "The enemy's skirmishers had advanced almost to the very edge of the woods nearest us, and, as we appeared at the edge, a sharp skirmish fire ensued, with much more effect on our side than on that of the enemy, as we lost no men and several of the enemy were seen to fall." Under this heavy fire, and with his men falling rapidly, Hayes feared his line would break. To prevent this, the one-time lawyer turned warrior ordered a charge. Preparing his men, Hayes, at the top of his voice, shouted, "Now boys, remember you are the Twenty-Third and give them hell! In these woods, the Rebels don't know but we are ten thousand; and…we are as good as ten thousand, by God!"

"Men of the Twenty-Third," exhorted Hayes, "when I tell you to charge, you must charge." With that, he gave the order, and the Ohioans swept forward, charging directly toward McRae's line.[52]

The North Carolinians unleashed a deadly volley, which felled many of Hayes's men. Yet the soldiers in blue advanced. Unnerved by the sight of hundreds of Federals heading right for them, their glistening bayonets pointed forward, some of the rookie soldiers on the right of McRae's line who had never before been under fire gave way. McRae attempted to rally them but found his safest course of action was to withdraw his entire command back up the slope to the nearest tree line. After doing so, McRae was able to briefly re-form his line, and his men delivered a more destructive fire into Hayes's charging Ohioans, halting the Federal advance. "I soon began to fear we could not stand it," said Hayes, "and again ordered a charge." With this second surge, McRae's line fell back once more, this time up the mountainside to its original position. Hayes's men pursued through the trees and then emerged on an open field, where they came under a severe fire that once again brought the charge to a halt.[53]

Minutes earlier, General Garland had ordered the 12th and 23rd North Carolina to advance in support of McRae. Daniel Christie's 23rd North Carolina moved forward about forty yards from the ridge road, where it found some shelter behind a hedgerow and piles of stones and delivered a crushing fire into Hayes's surging Federals. Colonel McRae, thankful for the support, remembered that "with great coolness" that the 23rd poured a "constant and destructive fire into the enemy as they attempted to pass from the woods… and to advance upon our position." The 23rd North Carolina, concluded McRae, behaved "most gallantly." The same was not the case with the 12th North Carolina. At just ninety-two men, the 12th was not even the size of a full company, and at South Mountain, the regiment was under the command of a rather inexperienced officer, Captain Shugan Snow. Snow led his men to the front but then quickly gave the order to "fire, then fall back." The 12th delivered just one volley before fleeing back up the slope, Snow leading the way. The 12th ran itself away from the fight, although some thirty to forty members later fell in with the 13th North Carolina on the far left of Garland's line.[54]

Even with the departure of the 12th, the Confederates were still able to halt Hayes's attack. The 23rd Ohio went into line behind a stone wall at the edge of the woods, keeping up a heavy fire on McRae's men to their front and Christie's troops on their right front. Soon, fire erupted to their left. Colonel Rosser's 5th Virginia Cavalry, some 250 strong, advanced dismounted from the high ground to the right of McRae's original line. The cavalry's fire, combined with canister delivered from Pelham's two guns, was taking a fearful toll, and it was here, struck on three sides, that the 23rd Ohio suffered its greatest loss. Rutherford Hayes believed the only way out was another charge, but before he could give the order, he felt a "stunning blow" to his left arm and fell to the ground. A bullet struck

Lieutenant Colonel Rutherford B. Hayes, 23rd Ohio. *The Photographic History of the Civil War.*

him just below the elbow. Fearing a severed artery, he had one of his men tie a handkerchief above the wound. "I soon felt weak, faint, and sick at the stomach," recounted Hayes. However, while lying on the ground some twenty feet behind his line, Hayes said he was comfortable and from there "could form a pretty accurate notion of the way the fighting was going...I could see wounded men staggering or carried to the rear; but I felt sure our men were holding their own."[55]

Even while lying wounded and in terrible pain, Hayes continued to direct the 23rd. Hearing reports of heavy fire on the left, Hayes called out to Captain James Drake, commander of Company H on the far left of the regiment's line, ordering him to wheel his company to the left in order to face this attack. Drake did as ordered, calling his company back about twenty yards. However, upon seeing this retrograde movement, the rest of the regiment followed suit, falling back to link up with Drake's new line. This left Hayes in a no-man's-land between the two lines of battle. For the next twenty minutes, the fighting continued until it eventually sputtered out, the two sides seemingly agreeing to take a brief rest. As the gunfire quieted down, the wounded Hayes yelled out, "Hallo Twenty-Third men! Are you going to leave your colonel for the enemy?" At least six of Hayes's men leaped forward in an effort to retrieve their commander, prompting an immediate response from the North Carolinians. The combat renewed, and Hayes directed his men back, "telling them they would get me shot and themselves, too." Minutes later, and under a covering fire, Lieutenant Benjamin Jackson crawled forward and brought Hayes back to the safety of the Union line. Dr. Joseph Webb, the regimental surgeon and brother of Hayes's wife, Lucy, released the tourniquet and treated the wound while providing the colonel with some brandy and opium. Hayes was later taken by ambulance to Middletown, where in the weeks ahead he recuperated in the home of Jacob Rudy, cared for by Lucy, who had traveled from their Ohio home. With Hayes's departure, Major James Comly assumed command of the 23rd Ohio.[56]

While the 23rd Ohio battled on the far left, action was also picking up along the rest of Scammon's line. After Hayes advanced with the 23rd on its right, two companies of Colonel Carr White's 12th Ohio went forward as skirmishers followed by the rest of the regiment. Finally, on the far right of Scammon's line, Colonel Hugh Ewing sent forward a large skirmish force under his second in command, Lieutenant Colonel Theodore Jones, and then led the remaining companies up the slope behind the skirmishers. As soon as the 30th began its attack, it came under a sharp fire from Bondurant's

Print depicting the attack of the Kanawha Division at South Mountain. *Library of Congress.*

guns on the summit. Fire soon erupted from Lane's guns, far to the north, near Turner's Gap, and combined with that from Bondurant's pieces, it caught Ewing's men in a crossfire. Cox later wrote that the 30th Ohio swept uphill "in the face of showers of canister and spherical case." Yet, Ewing's Ohioans continued their advance, and soon began to pepper Bondurant's gunners with musket fire.[57]

On the summit, General Samuel Garland was busy directing his troops. The fiery brigadier was everywhere along his now beleaguered line, galloping back and forth, shouting out commands and ordering changes of position. With Bondurant's battery under fire from Ewing's men, the gunners and horses being struck down one after the other, Garland ordered the artillerists to withdraw, but not before they delivered several well-directed blasts of canister in the ranks of the 30th. Moments later, Colonel McRae, whose 5th North Carolina had been heavily engaged all morning on the right of the line, reported to Garland, expressing his concern about an enemy force gathering in large numbers in a woodlot farther to his right, thus threatening his flank. He wanted Bondurant to shell the woods to dislodge this force, but the Alabamians had already limbered up and galloped northward along the ridge road. Bondurant eventually halted near Wise's garden and there deployed his guns. With his right endangered and his line showing signs of cracking, Garland sent a staff officer galloping off with orders for Colonels

Thomas Ruffin and Alfred Iverson to advance their regiments—the 13th and 20th North Carolina, respectively—from their positions in the open fields north of the Old Sharpsburg Road south toward the fighting. Looking over his shoulder and growing anxious, Garland galloped away from McRae to place the 13th and 20th as they entered the fray.[58]

While Garland rode north along the summit, the 30th Ohio continued to push its way up the slope south of the Old Sharpsburg Road, while the fighting still raged, intermittently, on the opposite end of the line. Before long, Garland located Iverson and directed him to place his 20th North Carolina to the left of Colonel Christie's 23rd, still engaged in desultory fire with Hayes's 23rd Ohio. Because of the nature of the terrain, however, Iverson was unable to form a direct link with the 23rd. Instead, he formed his men along the ridge road, to the left and behind Christie's men. Iverson later recalled that while his men were concealed within the tree line, there were open fields directly to their front that sloped down the steep mountain slope. Unable to see what lay at the bottom of this slope, Iverson sent forward his skirmishers. As Iverson's men settled into their new position, the 13th North Carolina formed to their left front. The deployment of these two newly arrived regiments had come none too soon, for just minutes later the Federals renewed their efforts, and the action picked up in intensity.[59]

Colonel Eliakim Scammon, a West Point graduate whom some soldiers derisively dubbed "Old Granny," believed that with the 23rd and 30th Ohio drawing Confederate attention on their right and left flanks, respectively, it was now time to spring the 12th Ohio in a determined attack against their center. Some three hundred yards to their front, Iverson's skirmishers were seen advancing. Knowing the time had arrived, Colonel White had his men fire a volley and then gave the order to charge. With bayonets fixed and with loud hurrahs, the 12th surged forward, sweeping uphill across open pasture fields, immediately coming under what Cox described as a "most galling" and "murderous" fire. As the cheering Federals neared the summit, Iverson's skirmishers fled back to the regiment's main line along the ridge road, but not before losing between fifteen and twenty men dead or wounded. White's men succeeded in gaining the summit; however, they were now exposed to a heavier fire from the 20th North Carolina, sheltered behind stone walls in the tree line to their front, and from some of Christie's men of the 23rd North Carolina to their left. Having already advanced beyond the 23rd Ohio to his left and the 30th Ohio to his right, and with his men under this intense fire, White ordered his panting soldiers to lie down, hoping that the regiments on either flank would soon link up with his own. It was an unenviable situation to be in—White and his men, lying prone in an advanced and exposed position, bullets whistling over their heads as they looked back, waiting for their sister regiments to advance.[60]

White's anxious soldiers did not have to wait too long, for pushing up the hill to their right rear was the 30th Ohio. But as had happened to the 12th minutes earlier, the 30th immediately came under heavy fire as it reached the mountaintop. Artillery fire from Bondurant's pieces erupted to its front while reports arrived that a Confederate force—Ruffin's 13th North Carolina—was advancing to its right. Ewing changed front to face this threat. He had his skirmishers advance to the shelter of a rail fence while the rest of the regiment formed in the tree line to the rear. It was not long before Ewing's Ohioans and Ruffin's North Carolinians were trading volleys.[61]

Samuel Garland was with Ruffin when this gunfire erupted. Fearless in battle and never afraid to lead from the front, Garland sat stoically on his horse coolly watching the action unfolding and no doubt inspiring the men of the 13th by his example. Yet Ruffin was concerned, believing the brigade commander was needlessly exposing himself.

"General, why do you stay here?" inquired Ruffin. "You are in great danger."

"I may as well be here as yourself," replied Garland.

"No, no," said Ruffin, "it is my duty to be here with my regiment, but you could better superintend your brigade from a safer position."

Seconds later, Ruffin fell, shot through the hip and seriously wounded. Garland glanced down at his stricken subordinate and then turned in his saddle to give orders to a staff officer. As he was doing so, a bullet tore through Garland's chest. He fell to the ground, writhing in pain, his life quickly slipping away. Carried from the field, Garland was soon dead. The Army of Northern Virginia had lost a shining star and D.H. Hill a trusted subordinate and friend. In reporting his death, Hill referred to Garland as "that pure, gallant, and accomplished Christian soldier…who had no superiors and few equals in the service." With Garland's mortal wounding, Colonel Duncan McRae assumed brigade command.[62]

McRae inherited a difficult assignment. The Confederate line was beginning to crack. Captain Snow's 12th North Carolina, with the exception of those men who joined up with Ruffin, had already fled the field, while grim mutterings of Garland's demise spread along the wavering line dispirited the men. With his line in trouble, McRae sent an aide racing north to beg D.H. Hill for help.

Although in terrible pain, Ruffin remained in command of his regiment. After Garland's fall, he ordered his men to fall back to the ridge road, where they linked up with Iverson's regiment. Bondurant's artillerists were still blazing away at Ewing's men to their right front. Under what Ewing described as "a hail of grape," the winded soldiers of the 30th Ohio were also ordered to fall back to just beneath the crest of the summit, an order they quickly obeyed.[63]

If McRae was feeling uneasy about the integrity of his line and the continued determination of his men, his adversary, Colonel Scammon, was growing increasingly frustrated at his brigade's inability to break through. On his left, the 23rd Ohio

Brigadier General Samuel Garland. *Battles & Leaders of the Civil War.*

continued to spar with Rosser's troopers to its left front and with the 5th and 23rd North Carolina to its immediate front. Colonel White's 12th Ohio and Ewing's 30th had reached the top, but both regiments now lay prone, trading shots with Iverson's and Ruffin's men along the ridge road and still exposed to Bondurant's annoying fire. If infantry alone was unable to break the Confederate position, thought Scammon, then perhaps the artillery could. He sent back to Cox for some guns. Cox obliged by sending forward a section from Captain James McMullin's battery, two guns under the command of Lieutenant George Crome. It was now nearly 11:00 a.m., and the struggle for control of Fox's Gap had been raging for roughly two hours.

The battery's horses labored up the steep slope. Realizing that they alone would not be able to bring the guns into position, Crome's gunners and a handful of volunteers from the 12th Ohio sprang to their feet to help shoulder the burden, sweat dripping from their brows as they wheeled the two ten-pound Parrotts forward. Arriving at the summit, the guns were quickly unlimbered in the open field directly in front of the prone men of the 12th Ohio, the men and horses perfect targets for Iverson's North Carolinians protected behind a stone wall just forty yards to their front. Thinking quickly, Iverson sent Captain James Atwell's company forward to the right of Crome's guns in order to pour an enfilading fire directly into the Federal cannoneers. Crome's men fell fast. Some of White's infantrymen ran forward to help man the pieces, but there was little they could do. Still, despite the heavy losses, Crome's two guns managed to blast four rounds of double-canister fire into the Confederate line. Lieutenant Crome was conspicuous on this deadly occasion, serving as gunner of one of his pieces. While loading the gun, Crome was struck through the heart. He fell backward, mortally wounded. Captain McMullin reflected that Crome's "loss is deeply regretted, for he was a brave and noble man, who at the first call of his country left the endearments of home for its defense." The survivors of Crome's shattered section fled the field, leaving the Parrotts behind. Atwell's skirmishers returned to the 20th's position, the North Carolinians realizing the futility of trying to capture the guns.[64]

While Iverson's men may have been relieved at having driven back Crome's gunners, they no doubt watched in growing apprehension as new waves of Federal blue rolled up the mountainside. George Crook's brigade, fifteen

hundred men strong, had arrived and was now being sent forward to bolster Scammon's line. The 11th Ohio, under command of Lieutenant Colonel Augustus Coleman, swung south to link up with the 23rd Ohio on the far left of the Kanawha Division. By this time, Major Comly had ordered the 23rd to advance, and the men crawled forward until they at last connected with the left of the 12th Ohio on the crest. Lieutenant Colonel Melvin Clark, in command of Crook's largest regiment, the 36th Ohio, was sent forward to fill a gap that had formed between the 12th and 30th Ohio. Crook's final regiment, the 28th Ohio, was directed to fall in behind the 30th Ohio, south of the Old Sharpsburg Road, in

Colonel George Crook. *The Photographic History of the Civil War.*

order to protect the division's right flank. McRae watched nervously as these Federals stacked up to his front. Yet reaching the field at this same time were some badly needed Confederate reinforcements, in the form of the 2nd and 4th North Carolina of Brigadier General George B. Anderson's Brigade.[65]

Earlier that morning, D.H. Hill had summoned G.B. Anderson's men from their camps at Boonsboro. When the four regiments reached the Mountain House, Hill initially deployed them north of the National Pike. However, when McRae's plea for support reached Hill, he detached the 2nd and 4th North Carolina, placed both regiments under command of Colonel Charles Tew and sent them racing south toward Fox's Gap. Tew galloped in advance of his men, his pace quickening as he heard the salvos from Crome's guns. He reported to McRae, informing him that his two regiments, some 450 men total, would soon be arriving. Knowing that Tew's commission predated his own, McRae offered to turn command of the field over to the aristocratic officer, but Tew, having just arrived, rightly declined and offered to send his men wherever McRae directed. McRae had them fall in next to Ruffin's 13th North Carolina, extending the Confederate line north along the ridge road. Tew's men arrived in position and for several minutes, a brisk fire opened between them and Ewing's 30th Ohio. Colonel Bryan Grimes of the 4th North Carolina recorded that as soon as they arrived in this position, his "best marksmen" shot down Ewing's men "whenever they appeared," killing several. As the musket fire escalated, Tew realized the vulnerability of the Confederates' Fox's Gap line, particularly its left flank, and sent an aide racing back to General Anderson with a request that he send down his remaining two regiments, the 14th and 30th North Carolina.[66]

The veteran North Carolinians on the mountaintop doubtlessly knew what was coming, their anxieties building as they readied for the inevitable Federal charge. Colonels McRae and Tew watched the action from the left of the line when orders reached Tew from G.B. Anderson. Concerned about the left, Anderson, although nearly a mile away, directed Tew to sidestep back to the north, filing back in the direction from which they had just arrived. Obeying Anderson's order, Tew obligingly flanked to his left, taking his men back toward the Wise cabin and the intersection of the ridge road and Old Sharpsburg Road and thus breaking the connection between his right and Ruffin's left. McRae responded by ordering Ruffin to follow in Tew's footsteps in order to maintain their connection. Ruffin did as directed, but this movement created a three-hundred-yard gap in the middle of the Confederate line, between Ruffin's right and the left flank of Iverson's 20th North Carolina. McRae thought perhaps he could fill this gap with the 5th

North Carolina, but realizing the 5th was itself preoccupied with the 23rd Ohio to its front, he quickly thought better of it and instead sent another courier racing north to D.H. Hill, again pleading for reinforcements. Moments later, and with the gap in his line haunting him, McRae heard a "long-extended yell" and soon, noted the harried brigade commander, the Federal troops "burst upon our line."[67]

Shortly after 11:30 a.m., the four regiments of Cox's Kanawha Division then in position on the crest of the mountain surged forward, their bayonets glistening in the light of a brilliant sun. General Cox, on horseback, watched as his men swept forward. "The enemy opened with musketry and shrapnel," the division commander later wrote. "Our men fell fast, but they kept up their pace, and in a few moments they were on and over the wall." On the left of Cox's line, Major Comly of the 23rd Ohio shouted to his men, "Up and at them!" No sooner had Comly's men risen than Colonel Christie's 23rd North Carolina let loose a deadly volley that staggered the Ohioans. The Buckeye State men closed ranks and charged forward across thirty yards of open ground, losing men at every step before crashing over the stone wall and into the North Carolinians. A short, though fierce, hand-to-hand mêlée erupted. Overwhelmed, Christie ordered a retreat. To his right, Captain Thomas Garrett, who assumed command of the 5th North Carolina following McRae's elevation to brigade command, tried in vain to stem the tide. With his sword drawn, he stopped the regiment's flag bearer in the ridge road, hoping his men would rally on the colors. Within moments, the 5th's color sergeant fell in a heap, and his men, too, joined in the retreat.[68]

With the 23rd and 5th North Carolina gone, Colonel Thomas Rosser, on the extreme southern end of the Confederate line, ordered his 5th Virginia Cavalry to withdraw. Pelham's gunners delivered a few final volleys before they limbered up their hot pieces and galloped away. Their retreat came none too soon, for advancing directly toward their position was the 11th Ohio. A soldier of the 11th later remembered that the "laurel being in places almost impenetrable, the Regiment became somewhat disorganized, but Col. Coleman rapidly reformed the broken ranks, and moved forward to the fray." The 11th soon occupied the high ground held all morning by Rosser's dismounted men.[69]

As the 23rd Ohio swept forward on the left of Cox's line, to its right Carr White led his 12th Ohio forward, while to its right rear the 36th Ohio also advanced. Anticipating a deadly volley, such as the one that tore into Comly's ranks to his left, White, after first ordering his men to charge, quickly thereafter yelled at them to lie down. The 12th Ohio dropped as one,

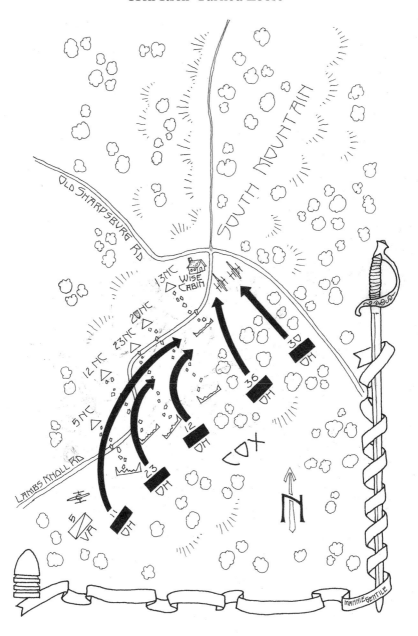

a round of Confederate bullets fired by Iverson's 20th North Carolina sailing harmlessly overhead. In an instant, the soldiers of the 12th were again on their feet, screaming as they charged headlong into Iverson's men along the ridge road. Colonel White proudly wrote, "My regiment dashed over the crest and into a thicket of laurel under a severe fire. In this charge we drove the enemy in great confusion and inflicted serious loss upon him, killing several with the bayonet." Solomon Smith, a soldier in White's 12th Ohio, perhaps summed up this murderous, confused fighting the best when he labeled it a "carnival of death; hell itself turned loose."[70]

There was little Iverson could do. With the 12th Ohio crashing into his center, with some of the 23rd Ohio now swarming around his right and with the 36th Ohio advancing into the trees to his left, the Confederate colonel ordered a retreat. His men "fled like deer" while he, too, made "terrific leaps down that mountain." Scurrying down the western slope of South Mountain, Iverson's survivors collided with those of the 5th and 23rd North Carolina. It was a mad dash, but at the mountain's western base Colonel McRae, together with Thomas Garrett, Daniel Christie and a now panting Alfred Iverson, took a moment to gather themselves before attempting to rally their broken commands. For the men of 5th, 20th and 23rd North Carolina, after a tenacious stand of nearly three hours on the mountaintop, their day of battle was over. As D.H. Hill later noted, these men, "demoralized by [Garland's] death and by the furious [Federal] assault," had been "too roughly handled to be of any further use that day." As the survivors of these shattered Confederate regiments regrouped west of the mountain, on the summit more than two hundred of their comrades, many of them wounded, fell into Union hands.[71]

Colonel Alfred Iverson, 20th North Carolina. *Gary Kross Collection.*

Among the captured were five men of the 20th North Carolina who had surrendered to Corporal Leonidas Inscho, of Company E, 12th Ohio Volunteers. As he charged toward the wall, Inscho was stunned when a bullet struck his left hand. He fell behind the stone wall, examining his wound, when he noticed a North Carolina captain just on the other side of the wall. Inscho grabbed the captain and told him to surrender. The captain refused and pulled his revolver on Inscho. Acting fast, the Ohio corporal grabbed the barrel and turned it skyward as the Confederate pulled the trigger. He managed to disarm the captain, but a fistfight broke out. "He struggled vigorously and struck me in the face several times," said Inscho, "but I got him over the wall and knocked him down compelling him to surrender." Inscho then noticed a group of Confederates huddled behind a tree. Using the captured revolver, he demanded their surrender, and soon Inscho had four more prisoners. He marched them to the rear and ultimately delivered them to Colonel White. For his actions, Corporal Inscho later received the Medal of Honor.[72]

Colonel Ruffin's 13th North Carolina and Bondurant's Alabama gunners were now alone on the mountain. Ruffin's men were busily engaged with the 30th Ohio to their front, as that regiment swept up the mountainside to the right of the 36th Ohio. In his regiment's sidestep to the left, Ruffin believed Iverson's 20th North Carolina had also moved northward and was initially unaware of the large gap that had developed in the line. When a hail of bullets came tearing into his men from the right, however, the wounded colonel sent his adjutant to see what was going on. The staff officer returned a short time later, out of breath, and reported that the Confederate line was gone and that Federal troops were swarming on the mountain. These were the victory-flushed soldiers of the 36th and 12th Ohio. The 12th Ohio actually pushed farther west than the rest of the Union line, pursuing Iverson's retreating Carolinians. Yet they soon came under fire from Bondurant's guns, still delivering deadly blasts. The gunners manned their pieces in the Wise garden, behind Ruffin's men, and had turned the barrels southward after the 12th Ohio had punctured the center of the Confederate line, roughly six hundred yards away. A red-faced Colonel Scammon ordered Carr White to turn his 12th Ohio north to capture Bondurant's guns, which all morning had taken a fearful toll on his brigade. White remembered moving his cheering men "through a dense laurel under a heavy fire" until they emerged behind Bondurant's gunners, delivering a few well-directed shots. The Alabama gunners realized their position was lost and quickly limbered up and galloped away, racing across the open fields north of the Old Sharpsburg Road.[73]

Bondurant's withdrawal left only Ruffin's stout warriors of the 13th North Carolina. Federal troops began closing in on the 13th from all sides. With the 30th Ohio pressing his front, Ruffin ordered a retreat. However, his men soon encountered the 12th Ohio, which had just chased Bondurant, while the 36th Ohio was still peppering the 13th from the south. Ruffin sought to turn left and link up with the 2nd and 4th North Carolina under Tew, but unknown to Ruffin, these regiments had also evacuated the field and were now in position farther north along the wood road. Instead of finding Tew's men, Ruffin encountered some of the 30th Ohio now closing in on his left. His men were now surrounded on all sides. Yet he did not panic. Instead of ordering a cease-fire and a raising of arms in surrender, Ruffin resolved to fight his way out. He first ordered a charge forward, directly into the unsuspecting 30th Ohio. With that regiment momentarily reeling, Ruffin now turned his regiment to face south, quickly engaging the 36th and 12th Ohio, which had been on his right. The fighting grew savage, with bullets flying thick and the smoke of battle obscuring farmer Wise's cabin and once peaceful fields. The color-bearer of the 13th North Carolina climbed the stone wall enclosing Wise's garden, waving the banner in proud defiance. Admiring this display of courage, the Federals ceased fire and called on him and his comrades to surrender. When they refused, the Ohioans loosed a hail of bullets. The 13th's flag bearer fell dead, pierced by a dozen shots; the colors were later secured by Private Hoagland of the 12th Ohio as a trophy of war.

Ruffin was losing men with each passing second, yet his heroics did stall the 12th Ohio's advance. Thinking fast, Ruffin turned his regiment around and ordered them now to the north. The fragments of the 13th clawed their way through Ewing's Ohioans, who had seeped into Ruffin's rear, and at last emerged from the closing vise. It was a narrow escape. Their colonel leading the way, the exhausted survivors of the 13th North Carolina fell in with their fellow Tar Heels of George B. Anderson's Brigade, in columns along the wood road. General Anderson had advanced along the wood road from Turner's Gap with his remaining regiments—the 14th and 30th North Carolina—having been directed south by D.H. Hill in order to reestablish contact with Colonel Tew's men of the 2nd and 4th. D.H. Hill appeared a short time later in the van of more troops, personally leading them toward the gap. In a postwar letter to Hill, Colonel Ruffin wrote, "I shall never forget the feelings of relief I experienced when I first caught sight of you. You rode to me, and, shaking my hand, said that you had given us up for lost and did not see how it was possible for us to have escaped."[74]

It was now minutes after noon. After three hours of intense fighting and after wrecking Garland's Brigade, Cox's Kanawha Division held Fox's Gap. The smoke of battle began to drift away, and a tense lull settled over the field as the cries of the wounded now took the place of the rattle of musketry and booming of cannons. Both sides caught their breaths and took stock of the situation. With Federal forces now in possession of Fox's Gap, D.H. Hill realized his position at Turner's Gap was in jeopardy. The grizzled division commander wrote long after the war that he did not remember "ever to have experienced a feeling of greater loneliness. It seemed we were deserted 'by all the world and the rest of mankind.'"

"There was nothing to oppose him," said Hill, contending that Cox could have (and should have) immediately continued moving north in order to turn Colquitt's right flank and thus gain possession of Turner's Gap. But such an advance would have been impossible for Cox.[75]

Hill was in error when he said there was nothing to oppose a continued Federal advance since G.B. Anderson's fresh brigade stood along the wood road ready to contest any further movement. In addition, Cox's men were by this point thoroughly exhausted, having begun the day in Middletown and having already wrestled control of a difficult position from a determined and tenacious enemy in a good defensive line. And while losses in Garland's Brigade were heavy—his North Carolina brigade lost 44 men killed, 168 wounded and nearly 200 captured, for an almost 40 percent casualty rate—Cox's losses were high as well. Scammon lost 262 men killed and wounded, with the heaviest losses taking place in the 23rd Ohio. Casualties in Crook's brigade, which arrived just in time to participate in the final charge, numbered 62 men killed or wounded. Moreover, Cox learned from prisoners that D.H. Hill's remaining brigades, plus Longstreet's entire command, were within supporting distance. With that, Cox made the right decision in halting and pulling his men back to a more sheltered position along the mountain's crest, awaiting the promised reinforcements. "It was time to rest," declared Cox. "Three hours of up-hill marching and climbing had been followed by as long a period of bloody battle, and it was almost noon. The troops began to feel the exhaustion of such labor and struggle...The two Kanawha brigades had certainly won a glorious

General Jacob Cox. *The Photographic History of the Civil War.*

victory, and had made so assured a success of the day's work," concluded the division commander, "that it would have been folly to imperil it."[76]

As Cox's tired men began to settle in, Confederate artillery fire broke the silence. Bondurant's gunners were at it again, firing from the open field north of the Old Sharpsburg Road. Fire also came from Lane's guns near the National Pike and from Pelham's two pieces, which had gone into position on a piece of high ground northwest of Fox's Gap. "The enemy's artillery kept up a pretty steady fire," Cox later reminisced,

> *but the infantry rested on their arms, the front covered by a watchful line of skirmishers, every man at his tree. The Confederate guns had so perfectly the range of the sloping fields about us and behind us, that their canister shot made long furrows in the sod with a noise like the cutting of a melon rind, and the shells which skimmed the crest and burst in the tree tops…made a sound like the crashing and falling of some brittle substance, instead of the tough fiber of oak and pine. We had time to notice these things as we paced the lines waiting for the renewal of battle.*

They would have a long wait. The battle would not be renewed for another three hours.[77]

While affairs at Fox's Gap settled down during the early afternoon hours of September 14, more Union and Confederate soldiers were making their way to the front, approaching South Mountain from opposite sides. The first to reach the summit were the Confederates of Roswell Ripley's and Robert Rodes's Brigades, which Hill had summoned earlier from their camps near Boonsboro. While Hill sent Rodes's men to the left, or north of the National Pike, he dispatched Ripley's Georgians and North Carolinians south to Fox's Gap. Hill must have felt somewhat relieved with the arrival of these men. Still, he could not quell a sense of foreboding as he gazed off to the east and saw "the vast army of McClellan spread out before me. The marching columns extended far back as eye could see in the distance…It was," declared Hill, "a grand and glorious spectacle, and it was impossible to look at it without admiration. I had never seen so tremendous an army before, and I did not see one like it afterward." Yet Hill did realize the larger, strategic picture. Despite the massive blue columns advancing and stacking up in front of him the hard-fighting native South Carolinian wrote that the "sight inspired more satisfaction than discomfort; for though I knew that my little force could be brushed away as readily as the strong man can brush to one side the wasp or the hornet, I felt that General McClellan had made a

Alfred Waud sketch of Union soldiers marching through Middletown on their way to South Mountain. *Library of Congress.*

mistake." As Stuart had earlier that morning, Hill believed McClellan would have surely sent the bulk of his army south to Crampton's Gap in order to have a greater chance at lifting the siege of Harpers Ferry. But with the waves of Federals advancing toward him, he knew the longer he could delay McClellan, the more time Jackson would have to complete the capture of Miles's Harpers Ferry garrison and for Lee's divided army to once again be reunited. Hill was perfectly willing to sacrifice his own division for the good of the army.[78]

Roswell Ripley moved south with his brigade along the wood road, having been directed to report to General G.B. Anderson. When Ripley, a native Ohioan and an 1843 graduate of West Point, found Anderson, he discovered that the North Carolinian had moved his men down the western slope of South Mountain, aligning them along the Old Sharpsburg Road with their left flank anchored on Fox's Gap. Conferring with Ripley, Anderson agreed to face his men to the right and move them farther down the slope in order to give Ripley room to move his regiments into line along the same road, forming a connection to his left. As Anderson's and Ripley's men were executing this movement, D.H. Hill came galloping down the wood road in the van of Colonel George Thomas Anderson's and General Thomas

Brigadier General Roswell Ripley. *Library of Congress.*

Drayton's brigades, both of D.R. Jones's Division. Longstreet's command had arrived.[79]

Late the night before, having received alarming reports of the rapid Federal movement and of Union troops encamped in force a few short miles east of South Mountain, Robert E. Lee had summoned General Longstreet to his headquarters in Hagerstown. There, Longstreet found Lee looking over a map. The army commander informed Longstreet of the reports and sounded out his thoughts. Longstreet urged Lee to withdraw D.H. Hill from South Mountain and to concentrate his force, along with Hill's Division, behind the Antietam Creek, immediately east of Sharpsburg and some seven miles or so west of the mountain. There, Longstreet argued, they could form a strong defensive line "and at the same time check McClellan's march towards Harpers Ferry, in case he thought to relieve the beleaguered garrison by that route, forcing him to first remove the obstacle on his flank." Having heard out his second in command, Lee demurred and instead directed Longstreet to move at daylight back toward Boonsboro.[80]

Leaving one brigade behind to guard the trains at Hagerstown, Longstreet set his columns in motion about 8:00 a.m. on the morning of September 14. "The day was hot," remembered Longstreet, "and the roads dry and beaten into impalpable powder, that rose in clouds of dust from under our feet as we marched." Due to the heat, and from sheer exhaustion, many of Longstreet's men fell by the wayside, simply unable to keep up. It was not until after noon that the head of Longstreet's column arrived at Boonsboro, having covered the ten miles from Hagerstown in four hours. The summit of South Mountain still lay more than two miles distant. Lee accompanied Longstreet's leading brigade, confined to his ambulance wagon, his hands wrapped in splints. As the ambulance creaked toward Boonsboro, Lee could hear the sounds of battle rising from the mountaintop and could see the slopes covered in smoke. He then received a frantic note from Hill; his men were being overrun, and he was in serious danger. Lee hastened Longstreet's men forward. Knowing that it would have been impossible for the wagon to deliver him to the field of battle, and knowing he was unable to do much because of his injured hands, Lee halted his driver near the foot of South Mountain. Assisted from the ambulance, Lee stood along the pike offering words of encouragement as his men shuffled past. He had no immediate direction of the battle; he was forced to rely on his subordinates and his hard-fighting, veteran troops.[81]

General David Rumph "Neighbor" Jones's Division had the lead. Lee directed Longstreet to divide this division, sending the brigades of G.T. Anderson and Drayton up the National Pike to Turner's Gap and Kemper's, Garnett's and Jenkins's Brigades south along the western foot of South Mountain in order to advance up the Old Sharpsburg Road and strike the Federal troops in Fox's Gap on their flank. Neighbor Jones led these three brigades south. Before he reached the Old Sharpsburg Road, however, Jones's orders were countermanded, and he turned his column around. Jones's men later ascended South Mountain along the National Pike to Turner's Gap, where they would be sent to the north to contend with the Federal First Corps.[82]

While Jones marched and countermarched his men at the foot of the mountain, his other two brigades, under Tige Anderson and Thomas Drayton—some eighteen hundred men total—reported to Hill at the Mountain House. By this point, a large Federal force—the First Corps under Joseph Hooker—was seen marching to the north, positioning itself to strike at Hill's left flank near Frosttown Gap, held only by Rodes's sole brigade of some twelve hundred men. But rather than reinforcing Rodes, Hill personally led G.T. Anderson's and Drayton's Brigades to the south, envisioning along the way a full-scale counterattack to drive away the Federal troops already on the mountaintop at Fox's Gap. As Hill later recorded, he "felt anxious to beat the force on my right before the Yankees made their grand attack, which I feared would be on my left."[83]

G.B. Anderson's and Ripley's men were in the process of forming into line along the Old Sharpsburg Road when Tige Anderson and Drayton arrived. Hill conferred briefly with the brigade commanders, explained his plan and placed Ripley in command of the proposed attack. Hill also directed that G.B. Anderson and Ripley move their men even farther down the mountain to make room for the new arrivals. Again, G.B. Anderson and Ripley's men faced to the right and shuffled along the Old Sharpsburg Road; Tige Anderson turned his men to the right off the wood road, forming a loose connection to Ripley's Brigade, while Drayton's men moved forward, forming to the left of Tige Anderson's Georgians and deploying in lines of battle at Fox's Gap. With these four brigades—two from D.H. Hill's Division and two from D.R. Jones's—in position, Ripley had roughly four thousand troops with which to launch the assault. Having made his orders known, Hill rode back north to the Mountain House to prepare for what he knew would be the inevitable "grand attack" against his left. He was forced to trust Ripley to lead this assault, which he hoped would drive the Federals from Fox's Gap. But things went wrong from the start, and the envisioned attack never occurred.

While the mountainous terrain, large boulders and dense laurel thickets would have made any coordination of Ripley's units nearly impossible, Anderson's Brigade on the right of the line, Ripley's in the center and G.T. Anderson's Brigade on the left had simply marched too far down the mountain slope, creating a gap of more than three hundred yards between Tige Anderson's left and the right of Drayton's Brigade, just then forming into position around Fox's Gap.

Thomas Drayton came from a prominent South Carolina family and was an 1828 graduate of West Point. Serving in the army for several years, Drayton resigned without witnessing any combat. He returned to South Carolina, where he became a wealthy plantation owner; a member of the state legislature, during which time he advocated strongly in favor of slavery and states' rights; and the president of the Charleston & Savannah Railroad.

Brigadier General Thomas F. Drayton. *The Photographic History of the Civil War.*

With the outbreak of civil war in 1861, Drayton's West Point classmate and longtime friend Jefferson Davis appointed him a brigadier general of volunteers. At South Mountain, Drayton's Brigade was composed of South Carolina and Georgia soldiers and numbered nearly thirteen hundred men. As they shuffled along the wood road that Sunday afternoon and began to form into lines of battle, they could not know that they were only minutes away from disaster.

66

That afternoon, as Ripley's, Tige Anderson's and Drayton's men were marching toward Fox's Gap, so too were additional Federal troops. Indeed, even as D.H. Hill was meeting with his subordinates and explaining his proposed assault, Federal reinforcements were nearing the front. The first to arrive was Brigadier General Orlando Bolivar Willcox's First Division, Ninth Army Corps. Willcox, an 1847 graduate of West Point, entered the conflict as colonel of the 1st Michigan Infantry. He commanded a brigade at First Bull Run, where he fell into enemy hands as a prisoner of war. Held in Richmond's notorious Libby Prison for more than a year, he was exchanged in mid-August 1862, promoted to brigadier general of volunteers and, a few weeks later, took General Isaac Stevens's place in command of the Ninth Corps's First Division, Stevens having been killed at the September 1 Battle of Chantilly.[84]

Two brigades composed Willcox's division, the First under Colonel Benjamin Christ and the Second under Colonel Thomas Welsh. In Christ's brigade marched the recently organized 17th Michigan Infantry, mustered into service just three weeks earlier. As the regiment stepped closer toward South Mountain that Sunday afternoon, Private David Lane remembered that he and his fellow Michiganders "had an inkling…that a mass meeting was to be held on that eminence to discuss the pros and cons of secession, and that we, the Seventeenth, had received a pressing invitation to be present." But the rookie soldiers could hardly have been prepared for what lay ahead. "Only two weeks from home," said Lane, "our uniforms were untarnished. Dress coats buttoned to the chin; upon our heads a high-crowned hat with a feather stuck jauntily to one side. White gloves in our pockets; a wonder we did not put them on, so little know we of the etiquette of war." They would soon learn.[85]

Willcox's two brigades left their camps a mile and a half east of Middletown about 8:00 a.m., marching west on the National Turnpike. Behind Willcox came the remaining two divisions of the Ninth Corps under Samuel Sturgis and Isaac Rodman. Willcox sent a staff officer

Brigadier General Orlando B. Willcox. *Library of Congress.*

forward to Cox asking where specifically he wanted his division to go. Cox, realizing the staffer had no clear understanding of the road network, directed that Willcox should report to Pleasonton, whom, Cox assumed, would then send Willcox's two brigades toward Fox's Gap by way of the Old Sharpsburg Road. Through a misunderstanding, however, Willcox took this to mean that he was to inquire of Pleasonton where his division should form, and when he found the cavalry chief "near his batteries" at Bolivar, Pleasonton "indicated an attack along the slope of the mountain on the right of the main pike." Instead of marching south toward Fox's Gap, Willcox's men thus began deploying in lines of battle to the right of the National Pike, as Pleasonton believed an attack up the mountain from there might sweep the Confederates from out of Turner's Gap.

Willcox began forming his lines for the advance. The 100th Pennsylvania— the famed "Roundheads"—were sent forward as skirmishers, and Willcox "was about to march Christ's brigade through the woods higher up the slope" when Burnside, knowing that Willcox should have gone south, ordered him to disengage, withdraw his division and march to Cox's support at Fox's Gap. As directed, Willcox moved his men south across the National Pike and toward Fox's Gap along the Old Sharpsburg Road. This misunderstanding cost the Federals several hours, and it was not until after 2:00 p.m. that Willcox at last reported to Cox and his men began forming next to the Kanawha Division.

Excepting the 8th Michigan and 50th Pennsylvania, which Willcox sent to the far left of Cox's line, the heavily whiskered division commander began forming his soldiers to the right of the Kanawha Division, straddling the Old Sharpsburg Road and facing west, up the mountain. But no sooner had he taken up this position than a note arrived from Reno instructing Willcox to swing back so as to overlook the National Pike, facing north. "I can hardly think the order could have been intended to effect this," Jacob Cox later wrote, "as the turnpike is deep between the hills there, and the enemy quite distant on the other side of the gorge." Still, Willcox did as directed, and while still connecting to Cox's right, his division had formed at right angles to the Kanawha Division's line along the Old Sharpsburg Road. From his position near the Mountain House at Turner's Gap, D.H. Hill noticed that the Federal line at Fox's Gap now resembled an inverted V. Confederate artillery continued to pound away while Willcox's men were being deployed. Colonel Benjamin Christ remembered that his men were "considerably annoyed by the shot and shell of the enemy." Corporal Charles Brown of Christ's 50th Pennsylvania on the far left of the line echoed this statement, writing that his regiment *crept up to the top of the mountain and over the rocks and through the brush until we got close to the Rebels. We then lay down behind a stone fence and they turned their batteries on us. Their fire knocked the limbs from the trees and the limbs fell on us. We had to help one another to get out from under them.*[86]

To contend with this annoying and damaging Confederate artillery fire, Captain Asa Cook was ordered to deploy a section of his 8th Massachusetts Battery in the Old Sharpsburg Road, in front of the angle formed by Cox's right and Willcox's left flanks. Cook brought two guns forward, which unlimbered and quickly began hurling shells toward Lane's Battery at Turner's Gap to the north. Cook's gunners were able to get off a few shots before one of the pieces became disabled. Cook ordered the gun withdrawn and sent for another to take its place. However, "while another piece was coming forward to replace it," explained Cook, "the enemy opened a very heavy fire of canister upon us from a masked battery of 12-pounders, about 150 yards off, on our flank." This "masked battery," nearly 600 yards away and not 150, belonged to Bondurant, once again in action. One of Cook's gunners fell dead and four others were wounded with the first discharge. The rest, following Cook's orders, broke to the rear in search of shelter, abandoning the guns.[87]

The renewed fire of Bondurant's guns erupted while Willcox's men were still getting into position and caused confusion, even a temporary panic among the infantry; some of the men broke to the rear. Lewis Crater of the 50th Pennsylvania recalled seeing some soldiers running down the mountain "with blanched faces, terror depicted upon their very countenances," yet the veteran officers, including Willcox, Christ and Welsh, were able to quickly restore order. Eugene Beauge of the 45th Pennsylvania was inspired by Colonel Welsh along the front line, who "by a few cool, assuring words soon allayed whatever excitement might have prevailed among the men. Order was restored," said Beauge, "and the exciting incident passed off without serious trouble."[88]

However, with his line nearly crumbling and with Bondurant's artillerists continuing to hurl shells down the length of his line, Willcox swung his division back to its original position astride the Old Sharpsburg Road, his men again facing up the mountain. Christ's brigade formed to the right, or north, of the road, with the rookie 17th Michigan on the far right and the 79th New York "Highlanders" to the left, just ahead of the 17th. These two regiments, Willcox proudly noted, "deserve credit for coolness and firmness in rallying and changing front under a heavy fire." South of the Old Sharpsburg Road went Willcox's Second Brigade under Welsh. Forming the right of Welsh's line was the 45th Pennsylvania, led by Lieutenant Colonel John I. Curtin, son of Pennsylvania's governor, Andrew Curtin. To the left of the Pennsylvanians went Lieutenant Colonel Joseph Gerhardt's 46th New York. The 50th Pennsylvania and 8th Michigan remained detached from Willcox's division, having already gone into position to the left of Cox, while the 100th Pennsylvania Roundheads was held in reserve.[89]

As they re-formed, Willcox's men were still subjected to a deadly cannon fire. "[T]he enemy's guns continued to play on us," said Willcox, "killing and wounding at all points, though few in number. We lay there silent and kept concealed." William Todd of the 79th New York remembered that Confederate shot "rattled over the tops of the stone wall, knocking the stones about." It was a tense, trying time, but it was short-lived. Soon after realigning his troops, Willcox received an order from Reno to advance and silence Bondurant's irritating—and deadly—guns on the summit. Reno also ordered Cox's men, to the left of Willcox, to move out as well.[90]

It was about 4:00 p.m., at least three and a half hours since Cox's men swept Garland's Brigade from Fox's Gap. Eugene Beauge of the 45th somewhat dramatically recalled that just prior to the advance "all had become ominously silent all along the line. Not a gun was heard. The two giants were taking breath for the final tussle. Surgeons with their knives, saws, probes and bandages had taken position nearby for their bloody work." Beauge also noted that Lieutenant Colonel Curtin was having difficulty getting his horse to move. The horse, "a spirited animal," had "either through fear or pure cussedness refused to jump a low stone wall," thus refusing to advance. Curtin was forced to dismount, let the horse go galloping back down the mountainside and then ran to catch up with his advancing troops. It was a blessing in disguise, thought Beauge, for if "the brute obeyed his master that day and carried him into that tempest of lead and iron the chances are that neither horse nor rider would have come out alive."[91]

As Willcox began his advance up South Mountain—an advance Jacob Cox later remembered was made "with the utmost enthusiasm"—on the opposite side of the mountain, Roswell Ripley was having a considerably more difficult time trying to orchestrate D.H. Hill's hoped-for assault. In forming for the attack, G.B. Anderson's, Ripley's and G.T. Anderson's men had marched too far down the Old Sharpsburg Road on the western slope of the mountain, creating a three-hundred-yard gap between the left of Tige Anderson and the right of Drayton, who was just beginning to place his regiments at Fox's Gap. The 15th South Carolina and 3rd South Carolina

Battalion formed in the Old Sharpsburg Road across from the Wise cabin, facing south. Phillips's Legion, the 51st and 50th Georgia, formed at right angles to the South Carolinians in the roadway, behind a stone wall that ran across an open field north of the Old Sharpsburg Road and some two hundred yards east, or in front of the wood road. The Georgians all faced east, down the mountain. In all, with the 550 South Carolinians in the road and with 750 Georgians behind the stone wall running north, Drayton's battle line resembled a backward *L*. When Drayton discovered the gap that had opened between his right and Tige Anderson's left, however, he sidestepped his entire brigade, sending the 15th South Carolina and 3rd South Carolina west along the Old Sharpsburg Road in an effort to close the gap and bringing Phillips's Legion into the road, which then formed to the left of the 3rd Battalion.[92]

Drayton sent Captain D.B. Miller's Company F, 3rd South Carolina Battalion, across the Wise field as skirmishers. Moments later, gunfire came echoing back up the mountain. Company F had encountered Federal skirmishers sweeping up the eastern slope; behind them, the South Carolinians could see Willcox's entire division deployed and ready to attack. Miller reported this to Drayton. Having lost contact with the rest of the Confederate line, unsure whether the proposed attack had commenced and with an enemy force now approaching his line, Drayton decided to seize the initiative and order an attack of his own, sending forward the 15th South Carolina, 3rd South Carolina Battalion and Phillips's Legion south across Wise's fields. Although he did not know it, because the brigades on his right had moved too far down the mountain, Drayton's Brigade would be forced to deal alone with Willcox's entire division.[93]

The Union skirmishers that Captain Miller's South Carolinians initially encountered belonged to Companies A and K of the 45th Pennsylvania. Nearing the crest, they caught sight of Bondurant's pieces, as well as "heavy masses of infantry, covered by trees and stone fences." The sharp crack of rifle fire soon broke out between the skirmishers, followed a short time later by Drayton's ill-fated attack. Drayton's men let out a yell as they swept forward. Jacob Cox later remembered this attack as the Confederates' "most determined effort to drive us from the summit we had gained in the morning." Colonel Welsh simply noted that the "battle became very fierce at this juncture." But Orlando Willcox was not to be outdone. He gave the command, "Forward!" and his blue line charged up the slope. "[A]fter a severe contest of several minutes," Willcox later recorded, his troops drove Drayton's men from the field. The 15th South Carolina fled while the 3rd

South Carolina Battalion fell back to the ridge road, seeking shelter behind the stone walls near the Wise cabin. Moments later, Phillips's Legion also came scurrying back across Wise's field. As they did so, they were fired into by their own men, whether from the 3rd Battalion along the ridge road or from one of the Georgia units now redeployed in the Old Sharpsburg Road. Either way, the loss was heavy.[94]

Heavy, too, were the Federal losses as they pursued the retreating Confederates up the mountain and arrived at Wise's field. On the left of Willcox's line was Welsh's brigade, with the 45th Pennsylvania on the right, anchored on the Old Sharpsburg Road, and the 46th New York advancing *en echelon* to the left of the Pennsylvanians. "Notwithstanding the terrific fire from infantry and artillery," said Welsh, a Mexican War veteran, sheriff and one-time lumber merchant from Columbia, Pennsylvania, "our troops continued to advance, utterly regardless of the slaughter in their ranks." Welsh's men had come face to face with Drayton's Georgians, well protected behind the stone walls that lined the Old Sharpsburg Road, as well as Bondurant's guns, which were belching forth shot and shell from the open fields north of the Wise cabin. Eugene Beauge remembered that the "Rebels were kneeling behind the wall nearest to our line, their own line running parallel or nearly so to ours. Only their gun barrels and the tops of their heads were visible." In front of the regiment, Beauge saw Welsh and Lieutenant Colonel Curtin encouraging the men "as cool as if on parade."

The fighting escalated as men fell one after the other. "Reports of cannon, bursting shells and musketry blended together in one continuous, deafening roar," described Beauge. "Clouds of white-blue smoke hung over the field like a thick fog, and the air was stifling with the smell of gunpowder." For their efforts that day, the 45th Pennsylvania sustained a loss of 21 men killed and 115 wounded, among the heaviest losses incurred by any Federal regiment at South Mountain.[95]

As this action unfolded south of the Old Sharpsburg Road, to the right of Welsh's brigade and north of the roadway, the rookie soldiers of the 17th Michigan Infantry, commanded by Colonel William Withington, were receiving their baptism by fire and quickly making a name for themselves. Before the order to attack, the anxious soldiers were hugging the earth, exposed to a heavy artillery fire. The order to advance thus came as a relief. Forming into line, the 17th Michigan swept gallantly forward through small woodlots and across open fields. To their front, still in position behind the stone wall that ran north from the Old Sharpsburg Road, was the 50th and 51st Georgia Infantry, veteran units, which soon opened a terrific fire into

Withington's ranks. The sharp fire of musketry reminded Captain Gabriel Campbell of the sound of a "hail storm on the roof." Michigan soldiers fell with every step, but still they pressed on. Wrote Campbell, "Although met by a terrific storm of bullets from the stone wall, we simply rushed forward giving a storm in reply." Drayton's Georgians fell back toward the wood road, and the 17th let out a cheer.[96]

Having driven back the 50th and 51st Georgia, the 17th continued to advance until coming under a terrific artillery fire from the guns positioned near the Mountain House, as well as from Bondurant's pieces. The artillery fire swept the open ground in front of the regiment, forcing Withington's men to their left, south across the Old Sharpsburg and into a tree lot where they crowded in with Curtin's 45th Pennsylvania. There, the Michiganders came under fire from Drayton's infantry along the Old Sharpsburg Road, including the 50th and 51st Georgia, which had been rallied and sent into the roadway to face south, as well as from the 3rd South Carolina Battalion behind the stone wall in front of the Wise cabin. As Captain Campbell recalled, "The batteries played upon the woods, bringing down an abundance of branches, but doing little damage. The discharge of musketry from the lane was a constant blaze." Soon, however, the Confederate artillery fire was beginning to slacken, and the Michigan men once again prepared to advance up the slope. The regiment marched northward and then advanced uphill astride the Old Sharpsburg Road, its right in the open fields to the north and heading toward the stone wall recently vacated by the 50th and 51st Georgia.[97]

Federal troops continued to converge on Drayton's line, with the Confederates desperately holding on, trying to stop this relentless blue tide. Meanwhile, more Ninth Corps troops were arriving on the field. About 3:30 p.m., Sturgis's division reached the front. Sturgis had two brigades, commanded respectively by James Nagle and Edward Ferrero, as well as two batteries—Battery D, Pennsylvania Light Artillery, under Captain George W. Durell and Battery E, 4th United States Artillery, under Captain Joseph Clark. Sturgis's men left their camps east of Middletown at 1:00 p.m. and marched west through the town. Captain Oliver Bosbyshell of the 48th Pennsylvania was struck by the sight of children attending Sunday school services: "Their gathering seemed holy and happy, as viewed through the open door of the neat little church. How great the contrast," thought the captain, "the troops marching to the field of mortal strife, they [the children] gaining strength to battle for immortality."[98]

Crossing Catoctin Creek, Sturgis's men filed to the left and advanced along the Old Sharpsburg Road. As his cannons rumbled toward Fox's Gap along this roadway, Charles Cuffel of Durell's Battery took in the situation. With Union troops advancing "in heavy columns on parallel roads towards the mountain, their bright bayonets flashing in the sunlight," it presented a "brilliant spectacle." But the men all knew there was deadly work ahead. Jesse Reno met Sturgis's columns and began deploying the troops. The 2nd Maryland and 6th New Hampshire of Nagle's brigade were detached and sent north of the National Pike. Captain Clark's Battery E, 4th U.S., was sent to the far left of the Federal line to support that end of the Kanawha Division's line. The remainder of the division moved forward in support of Willcox's attacking columns, with Ferrero's brigade in front and Nagle's remaining two regiments in the rear. Durell's Battery was deployed north of the Old Sharpsburg Road, where Asa Cook had previously unlimbered and where his guns yet remained. Durell's gunners "speedily got their guns 'in battery' between the deserted guns, and opened a vigorous fire upon the enemy."

Confederate shells soon began exploding around Durell's pieces. One Confederate shot snapped two limbs off a tree, "one quite a heavy one," which fell onto Captain George Durell, knocking him to the ground. Momentarily dazed, Durell rose to his feet, dusted himself off and refocused his efforts. It was not long before Durell's artillerists silenced Lane's guns to the north, around Turner's Gap, prompting the 17th Michigan to redeploy. Durell then turned his attention to Bondurant's indefatigable "Jeff Davis Artillery." One of Durell's first shots struck Bondurant's Napoleon, disabling it. The valiant Confederate gunners who had been raining death and destruction on the Ninth Corps since before nine o'clock that morning knew their situation was critical. With this increased Union artillery fire and with the infantry getting dangerously close, the Alabama artillerists limbered up for the final time and retreated toward the Mountain House. Their day had at last come to an end.[99]

Out in front, Drayton's men looked nervously over their shoulders as Bondurant's gunners galloped away. Their artillery support was gone, the Federal attack was relentless and they were quickly becoming surrounded. Advancing from the south, toward Drayton's right flank, was the 30th Ohio, while the 46th New York and 45th Pennsylvania of Welsh's brigade, to the right of the Ohioans, struck Drayton's line from the front. Advancing directly toward Drayton's exposed left flank in the Old Sharpsburg Road came a portion of the 17th Michigan while the balance of this regiment swept across the open fields to the north, behind Drayton's line. This was simply too much for Drayton's men to bear, and the Confederate line collapsed,

Drayton's few survivors fleeing pell-mell from the field. Holding on to the last was Lieutenant Colonel George James's 3rd South Carolina Battalion, which refused to retreat from its position near the Wise cabin. This stubborn defense cost it dearly. Of the 160 men brought into action, only 24 emerged unscathed. Among the dead was the 3rd's commander, George James.[100]

Willcox's division, along with elements of Cox's command, surged forward in the wake of the Confederate rout, sweeping what remained of Drayton's brigade from the field, pursuing them over the crest and into the woods beyond and capturing hundreds of prisoners. On the right of the Ninth Corps line, the 17th Michigan, in its first fight, emerged as conquerors of the field. Thomas Welsh declared that this regiment fought "with a bravery and constancy seldom equaled in modern warfare." Their day over, Colonel Christ relieved the 17th Michigan by advancing the 79th New York and 28th Massachusetts. To the left of the 17th Michigan and south of the Old Sharpsburg Road, the bloodied 45th Pennsylvania swept forward and over the stone fence that lined the road, gathering scores of Drayton's men who were unable to get away. Albert Allen of the 45th noted that the prisoners "said that our fire was so terrific that it was almost sure death for a man to put his head above the stone fence." Having sustained heavy losses and now nearly out of ammunition, the 45th Pennsylvania, as well as the 46th New York, was soon relieved by Sturgis's advancing troops.[101]

During the peak of the action on the summit, Sturgis, an 1846 graduate of West Point and classmate of Generals Reno and McClellan, deployed his leading brigade under Ferrero on either side of the Old Sharpsburg Road. The 51st Pennsylvania and 51st New York formed on the right, or north of the road, initially in support of Durell's gun—which, according to Captain William Bolton of the 51st Pennsylvania, was "belching forth its deadly missiles up the mountain gorge at a fearful and terrible rate"—until ordered forward. To the left of the Old Sharpsburg Road went Ferrero's remaining regiments, the 21st and 35th Massachusetts. Behind the Bay Staters went the 48th Pennsylvania and 9th New Hampshire of James Nagle's brigade. Captain Bosbyshell remembered that the 48th formed into line of battle and began pushing up the slopes "with showers of minie bullets whizzing through the air overhead, indicating the approaching conflict." Reaching a low stone fence, the soldiers unslung their knapsacks and then "Crack! Crack! Bang! Whiz! Bang! It was growing lively in front, the crowds of wounded pushing through the ranks of the Forty-eighth, on their way to the rear, showed that it was hot."[102]

Sturgis wanted to keep Nagle's men in reserve, but in front the "infantry fire had now become so warm and the ground so stubbornly disputed," that the division commander ordered Nagle's regiments forward. The veteran 48th Pennsylvania swept forward, coming up behind and relieving the 45th Pennsylvania. To their left advanced the 9th New Hampshire, a brand-new regiment that had been mustered into service only two weeks earlier and had

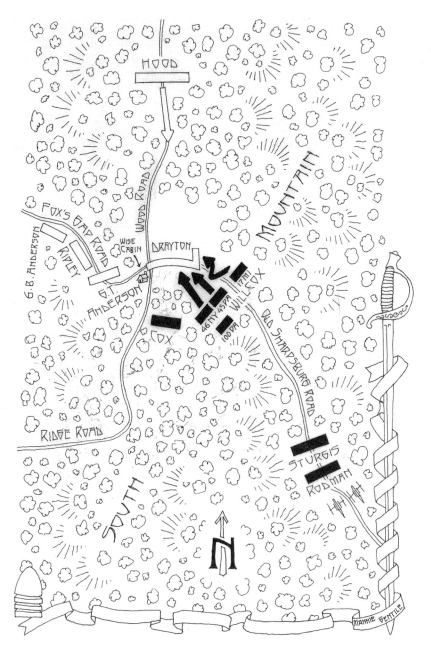

joined the brigade on the march from Washington. Thirty years later, the regimental historian provided a vivid, if somewhat dramatic, account of the 9th's entry into its first battle:

> *The cracking rattle of musketry grows nearer and nearer, the bellowing guns are louder, and just over their heads is heard the swift-sailing song of the Minie, with its devilish diminuendo...Here and there a man drops his rifle, clasps a hand to his leg, arm, or side, and falls to the rear, or sinks to the ground.*

Encouraged by Colonel Enoch Q. Fellows, the 9th continued to sweep up the mountain. As the newly minted soldiers arrived near the crest, however, they came under increased fire. With the 46th New York still to their front, the skittish soldiers of the 9th opened fire, striking some of the New Yorkers, who, Lieutenant Colonel Joseph Gerhardt later reported, "only saved themselves by throwing themselves on the ground." Order was quickly restored, and the 9th moved forward, much to the relief of Gerhardt's men.[103]

Arriving at the crest of South Mountain at Fox's Gap, Sturgis's men were greeted with the ghastly aftermath of a terrible, savage battle. In describing the Old Sharpsburg Road, Captain Bolton of the 51st Pennsylvania wrote:

> *Along its whole length the rebels laid in piles up to the very top of the stone fence. Some were found in a kneeling position in the act of firing. Death to many of them must have been instantaneous. Their arms extended and in position as in the act of firing, and in some cases the bitten cartridges in their hands.*

George Hitchcock of the 21st Massachusetts echoed Bolton, writing that the Old Sharpsburg Road was

> *literally packed with dead and dying rebels who had held so stubbornly the pass against our troops...Here the horrors of war were revealed as we see our heavy ammunition wagons go tearing up* [the road], *right over the dead and dying, mangling many in their terrible course. The shrieks of the poor fellows were heart-rendering.*[104]

Brigadier General Thomas Drayton's Brigade was destroyed at Fox's Gap. In addition to the 3rd South Carolina Battalion, which suffered an 85 percent loss, the 50th Georgia lost more than three-quarters of its men, while the 51st Georgia lost 60 percent. The Phillips's Legion sustained a 40 percent loss, some of the men shot down by their own troops, while the 15th South

Confederate dead at Fox's Gap. *Battles & Leaders of the Civil War.*

Carolina, which held the far right of Drayton's line, lost a quarter of its men. In all, 206 of Drayton's men lay dead or mortally wounded around Fox's Gap, many stacked up between the stone walls that bordered the Old Sharpsburg Road. An additional 227 lay wounded, while another 210 fell into Union hands. In all, Drayton lost half his brigade.[105]

Drayton was forced to contend alone with several divisions of the Ninth Corps at Fox's Gap. However, there was an attempt to help him. Marching down the western slope of the Old Sharpsburg Road and still attempting to get in position for an anticipated attack were the brigades of G.B. Anderson, Roswell Ripley and G.T. Anderson. As soon as the firing began at Fox's Gap, Ripley called a halt and began directing these brigades. Following Ripley's orders, Tige Anderson faced his brigade to the left and advanced through the thickets and dense trees south from the Old Sharpsburg Road. He was to support Drayton, but Anderson soon realized that the battle was raging to his left and not to his front. In an effort to establish contact with Drayton's right, Anderson faced his men to the left a second time, sent the 1st Georgia Regulars up the mountain as skirmishers and followed behind with the rest of his brigade. His skirmishers soon reported that Drayton's right had been turned and that Federal troops were pouring into the gap between his and Drayton's Brigade, threatening Anderson's own flank and rear. Hearing this, and already losing contact with Ripley, Anderson turned back around and moved northward across the Old Sharpsburg Road. Anderson's Georgians swept diagonally up the slope until they neared the wood road some distance north of Fox's Gap.[106]

G.T. Anderson's men then encountered a column of fresh Confederate troops advancing down the roadway. This was Brigadier General John Bell Hood's Division, composed of two veteran brigades under Colonels William T. Wofford and Evander Law, ably led by one of the Army of Northern Virginia's hardest-fighting generals who began the Maryland Campaign under arrest. Some two weeks earlier, Hood's men had captured several Federal ambulances. Major General Nathan Evans, who outranked John Hood, demanded that the Kentucky-born Hood turn the ambulances over to his men. "Whereas I would cheerfully have obeyed directions to deliver them to General Lee's Quartermaster for the use of the Army," explained Hood, "I did not consider it just that I should be required to yield them to another brigade of the division, which was in no manner entitled to them." Hood refused to turn over the wagons, and Evans placed him under arrest. Soon after crossing the Potomac, Longstreet directed Hood to go to Culpeper and there await a court-martial, but Lee, knowing he needed a seasoned, hard-fighting officer like Hood, intervened and ordered the general to remain with the army.[107]

As part of Longstreet's command, Hood's Division followed D.R. Jones's on the march from Hagerstown, arriving at the western base of South Mountain about 3:30 p.m. Seeing Lee standing by the roadside, Hood's men yelled out, "Give us Hood! Give us Hood!" Lee summoned Hood from the rear of the column and suspended his arrest. Restored to divisional command, Hood galloped up the National Pike to the resounding cheers of his men. At the summit, he met Longstreet, who initially ordered him north of the pike. A large body of Union troops—Hooker's First Corps—had by this time deployed and was now seen sweeping forward, at last launching the attack against the Confederate left. No sooner had Hood gotten into this position, however, than Major John Fairfax of Longstreet's staff arrived with new orders, this time sending Hood's Division in the opposite direction, toward Fox's Gap, the Confederate line there, under Drayton, having collapsed. Hood obeyed.

"The wood and undergrowth were dense," said Hood,

> and nothing but a pig path seemed to lead in the direction in which I was ordered...We marched on through the wood as rapidly as the obstacles in our passage would admit. Each step forward brought nearer and nearer to us the heavy Federal lines, as they advanced, cheering over their success and the possession of our dead and wounded.

Before encountering any Federals, Hood discovered G.T. Anderson and his panting soldiers. Hood ordered Anderson to take his brigade behind his line and form on his division's left flank.[108]

While G.T. Anderson's Brigade was marching and countermarching along the western slope of South Mountain, Roswell Ripley was still trying to coordinate his other brigades. In the confusion and nearly impossible terrain, Ripley's own brigade moved to the southwest and must have

Brigadier General John Bell Hood. *Library of Congress.*

marched obliquely across the front of G.B. Anderson's North Carolina Brigade on Ripley's right. Meanwhile, and as he had for Tige Anderson, Ripley ordered George B. Anderson to sweep south from the Old Sharpsburg Road, which he did. However, when Ripley realized that his own brigade was marching away from the fighting, he turned it around, this time marching east and again ascending the mountain. As this was going on, G.B. Anderson's men, advancing south, moved along the entire front of Ripley's Brigade. Ripley's skirmishers did not know these were Anderson's men and instead reported them to Ripley as a heavy mass of Federal troops. Ripley believed the report and, thinking he was now isolated and too far removed from any support, ordered his men to withdraw, turning around again and marching down the western slope of South Mountain. In his report, Ripley simply noted that the "natural difficulties of the ground and the condition of the troops prevented [his] movements being made with the rapidity which was desirable." D.H. Hill, however, was in no mood for excuses. His planned attack never materializing, and with his forces being driven from Fox's Gap, Hill could not hide his frustrations when in his report he noted that Ripley's men "did not draw a trigger; why, I do not know." Decades later, in an article on the Battle of South Mountain, Hill still harbored some resentment, writing that Ripley's entire brigade "did not fire a shot that day."[109]

With G.T. Anderson's men moving north and linking up with Hood's newly arrived division, and with Roswell Ripley abandoning the field, marching his men west and away from the fighting, George B. Anderson's Brigade was left alone on the eastern slope of South Mountain. George Burgwyn Anderson, an 1852 graduate of West Point destined to fall mortally wounded just three days later while defending the Bloody Lane at Antietam, led his North Carolina regiments south until reaching a point that he believed was beyond the Federal left flank on the summit. He faced his command to the left and led it up the very difficult boulder-strewn, mountainous terrain. Colonel Thomas Ruffin, whose 13th North Carolina had been attached to Anderson's Brigade since the rout of Garland's Brigade that morning, later wrote that it would be "difficult to conceive a more arduous march than this." When the summit was reached, it was clear that the North Carolinians were indeed beyond the Federal left flank. Anderson sent the 2nd and 4th North Carolina forward to reconnoiter. Advancing cautiously astride the ridge road, Captain E.A. Osborne of the 4th saw the guns of Captain Joseph Clark's Battery E, 4th U.S. Artillery, their barrels facing north, along with some infantry support.[110]

Hoping to capture these guns and create havoc on the Federal flank, Anderson organized an attack. What he and his men did not know, however, was that at the same time he was deploying for this attack, more Federal troops were just then advancing to strengthen their left. Sometime between 4:00 and 5:00 p.m., Brigadier General Isaac Rodman's Ninth Corps division neared Fox's Gap. His two brigades were divided, with Edward Harland's Connecticut and Rhode Island soldiers sent to the right of the Old Sharpsburg Road and Harrison Fairchild's New Yorkers sent to the far left to support Clark's guns. Fairchild's men were just arriving in position when Anderson commenced his attack. Matthew Graham of the 9th New York remembered that the brigade had just formed into line of battle when Anderson's men, "who were concealed in a close thicket of laurel on the west slope of the mountain, suddenly dashed from cover, and made an impetuous charge on the battery, yelling and discharging their muskets as soon as the forces were sighted." There was a momentary panic among some of Fairchild's men, but order was quickly restored, and the New Yorkers began tearing into the North Carolinians. Clark's professional gunners turned their guns toward Anderson's hard-charging men, sending double rounds of canister into their faces, "the enemy being so close that it was unnecessary to aim but simply point the guns after each discharge." Lewis Crater of the 50th Pennsylvania was nearby during this attack. "The charge was a determined one," he noted, "but the triple charges of grape and canister from these four guns and a terrific fire from the infantry at short range sent the rebel column precipitately from the field."

It was over as quickly as it began, and the results were decidedly one-sided. G.B. Anderson lost seven men killed, more than fifty wounded and nearly thirty captured. Harrison Fairchild suffered a loss of two killed and eighteen wounded. This brief flare-up marked the end of the fighting on the

Federal left, but there was still some more action unfolding on the right near Fox's Gap.[111]

After the rout of Drayton's Brigade, affairs settled down near the Wise cabin and along the Old Sharpsburg Road. The sun having already set and with twilight now descending, Sam Sturgis was busy positioning his units on the summit. To ensure that there was no immediate threat to the front, the rookie soldiers of the 35th Massachusetts, some eight hundred strong, were sent north to reconnoiter. The Bay State troops advanced across the road and into the woods north of the Wise cabin. Having detected no activity, and satisfied that there were no Confederates in the woods, the 35th fell back and resumed its place behind the 51st Pennsylvania and 51st New York on the front line of Ferrero's brigade. Meanwhile, Jesse Reno, commander of the Ninth Corps, was making his way to the front.

Born on June 20, 1823, in Wheeling, (West) Virginia, Jesse Lee Reno graduated from West Point ranked eighth in the illustrious class of 1846. He served with great distinction in the Mexican-American War, receiving two brevet promotions for gallantry at Cerro Gordo and in the storming of Chapultepec, where he had fallen wounded. Commissioned brigadier general of volunteers in November 1861, Reno turned in creditable performances during Burnside's North Carolina expedition in the spring of 1862, rising to division command. With McClellan's restructuring of the Army of the Potomac at the outset of the Maryland Campaign and Burnside's elevation to wing command, Jesse Reno advanced to command of the Ninth Corps. Augustus Woodbury, historian of the Ninth Corps, wrote:

> *In person, General Reno was of middle stature, stout, well-knit, and compact in frame. His forehead was high and broad, his face wore a genial expression, his eye beamed upon his friends with rare and quick intelligence, or, kindled in the excitement of conflict, flashed out in brave defiance of the foe. He had a magnetic kind of enthusiasm, and, when leading on his men, he seemed to inspire his followers, and make them irresistible in action.*[112]

Reno had spent most of the day with McClellan and Burnside near Bolivar, on a piece of high ground where the Federal brass could observe and direct the attacks both to the south at Fox's Gap and to the north at Frosttown Gap, the First and Ninth Corps being spread out along a nearly three-mile-wide front advancing up the mountain in execution of a double envelopment of the Confederate line. Near sunset, and with McClellan wishing a renewed attack toward Turner's Gap, Reno rode forward with his staff up the Old Sharpsburg

Road in an effort to determine why his Ninth Corps had seemingly stopped at Fox's Gap. He met briefly with Cox and Willcox, who provided summaries of the action. As he rode past his men, Reno congratulated them on their success. When he reached Fox's Gap, the 35th Massachusetts had just returned from its brief foray into the woods north of the Wise cabin. In front of Reno and near the Wise cabin, several Ninth Corps soldiers were gathering up their wounded. They were soon alerted by the sound of snapping branches and clanking accoutrements coming from the woods recently vacated by the 35th. Reporting to Reno that there was some kind of movement in the trees, the Ninth Corps commander—"his black piercing eyes flashing fire as it were"—turned to the veteran soldiers of the 51st Pennsylvania and ordered them to send forward skirmishers. Four companies moved out across the Old Sharpsburg Road, obliquing toward the tree line.

As these men swept across the road, Reno "was leaning forward peering steadily through his field glass," trying to detect if indeed there was any Confederate activity to his front. Suddenly, from the tree line a spattering of musket fire broke out—about five or six shots, recorded Captain Gabriel Campbell of the 17th Michigan, in quick succession—before a much heavier volley erupted, the flashing of the rifles illuminating the woods and revealing the Confederate position.[113]

Jesse Reno was struck down with those first scattered shots, pierced through his chest just beneath the heart. He slumped from the saddle and was helped down by his staff, who then wrapped him in a blanket and proceeded to carry him down the mountain. Captain Campbell of the 17th Michigan lent a hand and found himself helping to bear the stricken corps commander to the rear. "It was too dark to see Reno's face at all closely," Campbell recalled.

> *He seemed pale but perfectly composed. No one of us spoke. We bore our beloved commander silently, slowly, tenderly…although conscious that he was mortally wounded, I did not hear him utter a word or a groan as we were carrying him off the field.*

A stretcher was soon secured, and Campbell's services were no longer needed. Reno was borne farther down the mountain slope until the stretcher-bearers reached the base of the mountain. Sam Sturgis was there. The two had graduated together from West Point sixteen years earlier and enjoyed a good friendship. Sturgis knelt to talk with Reno, asking if the wound was serious.

"Hallo, Sam," said Reno, weakly, "I'm dead."

"No, no. Not as bad as that, I hope," replied Sturgis.

Major General Jesse Reno, commander, Ninth Corps, Army of the Potomac. *Library of Congress.*

"Yes, yes. It is all up with me. I am dead. Goodbye."

With that, the thirty-nine-year-old Jesse Reno passed away, having been struck down just yards from where Garland had received his death wound hours earlier.[114]

Reno's loss was deeply felt. Oliver Bosbyshell of the 48th Pennsylvania wrote that the "little General was well loved—his loss was a great blow to the Ninth Corps," while Thomas Parker of the 51st Pennsylvania wrote, "Thus passed away one of the army's brightest stars, as a gentleman, a friend and a soldier." General Alfred Pleasonton, commander of the Army of the Potomac's cavalry, recorded that with Reno's death, "a mastermind has passed away," while Ambrose Burnside wrote, "No more valuable [a] life than his has been lost during this contest for our country's preservation." Six days later, after the bloodshed at Antietam, Burnside circulated General Orders No. 17 through the camps of the Ninth Corps, officially announcing Reno's death:

> *By the death of this distinguished officer, the country loses one of its most devoted patriots, the army one of its most thorough soldiers. In the long list of battles in which General Reno has fought in his country's service, his name always appears with the brightest luster, and he has now bravely met a soldier's death while gallantly leading his men at the battle of South Mountain.[115]*

Confederate general Daniel Harvey Hill was not nearly as shocked or as grief-stricken with the death of Jesse Reno. In his report, Hill declared that it was a "happy shot" that killed the "renegade Virginian." Hill gave credit to the 23rd North Carolina for firing the fatal shot, but it was actually delivered by a soldier of Hood's Division. After reinforcing his line with the addition of George T. Anderson's Brigade, Hood had ordered his men to fix bayonets and creep south toward Fox's Gap. His men went into position along the wood road behind the stone fence that lined the road north of the Wise cabin only minutes after the 35th Massachusetts had departed from the woods. It was the advance of the 51st Pennsylvania's skirmishers that prompted their fire, one of the first shots striking down Reno. As Reno was being carried to the rear, the combat picked up in intensity. Many of Hood's bullets sailed over the heads of the Pennsylvanians and struck the 35th Massachusetts; one of them hit Colonel Edward Wild in the arm, which then had to be amputated. Being a new regiment, the 35th instantly opened fire directly into the skirmishers of the 51st Pennsylvania to its front, who were, said the regimental historian, "getting shot down like dogs." Commands of "Cease firing!" swept down the 35th's line, and order was soon restored. Firing continued unabated until it simply got too dark to see, and though darkness would ultimately being an end to the battle at Fox's Gap, gunfire continued until well after 10:00 p.m. when Hood received orders to withdraw his command back toward the Mountain House and Turner's Gap.[116]

Excepting the three-and-a-half-hour afternoon lull, the struggle for control of Fox's Gap raged for more than thirteen hours. The Confederates, especially those under Garland and Drayton, had put up a heroic effort but had paid a heavy price. Total Confederate casualties at Fox's Gap are difficult to determine, but they no doubt exceeded 1,100 men, with the chief loss sustained in Garland's and Drayton's shattered brigades, their respective losses totaling 40 percent and 50 percent of their total strength that morning. The Confederacy also lost a shining star with the death of Samuel Garland. Still, despite their best efforts, the Confederates were unable to hold Fox's Gap. When night fell, the Army of the Potomac's Ninth Corps held control of the crucial mountain pass, having fought valiantly for its possession. The terrain over which the Ninth Corps was forced to attack was difficult, and the Confederate position was a strong one. The Ninth Corps, too, had paid a high price for its victory: 157 killed, 691 wounded and 41 missing. Of inestimable loss was the corps commander Jesse Reno, who met his end shortly before the major fighting subsided.

As night fell across the Wise fields, and as the smoke of battle lifted over Fox's Gap, revealing more of the battle's ghoulish scenes, the exhausted soldiers of the Ninth Corps settled in for the night, victors of the field. Yet the Ninth Corps's effort that day against the right flank of the Confederate army was only half the story. As Reno's men fought for possession of Fox's Gap, to the north, General Joseph Hooker's First Corps was heavily engaged against the left of the Confederate line, north of Turner's Gap.

3

"My Men Were Fighting Like Tigers. Every Man Was a Hero"

The Fight for Frosttown and Turner's Gaps

Sergeant Evan Woodward of the 2nd Pennsylvania Reserves remembered that reveille was sounded early on the morning of September 14, about 3:00 a.m. Stirring from their camps, the bleary-eyed Pennsylvania soldiers boiled coffee and snacked on crackers until just before daybreak, when they took up their line of march. Woodward's regiment formed part of Truman Seymour's brigade in Brigadier General George Meade's Third Division, First Corps. The previous evening, the veteran First Corps troops had gone into camp along the banks of Monocacy Creek, roughly two miles from Frederick, and that Sunday morning they were now making their way through the city along the National Pike. The residents "were hardly up," noted Woodward, "yet we found many flags waving and bright eyes peering from the windows."

The morning brightened as the First Corps—Meade's division in the lead—wound its way up and over Catoctin Mountain and descended into Middletown Valley. Several miles to its front loomed South Mountain, "from whose side issued puffs of smoke from guns of the enemy, whose reports came booming over the valley," noted Woodward. By this time, Cox's Ohioans were heavily engaged with Garland's North Carolinians for possession of Fox's Gap. As they marched down the western slope of Catoctin Mountain, the First Corps soldiers saw clouds of dust kicked up by three divisions of the Ninth Corps—under Willcox, Sturgis and Rodman—ahead of them on the National Pike, tramping their way to Cox's support.[117]

About noon, the First Corps passed through Middletown, "a pretty and thriving place." The townspeople "turned out *en masse* to welcome us and cheer us on our way to battle. Never was a more cordial welcome given to troops than was given us," recorded Woodward. "Bread, cakes, milk, water, fruit and tobacco were freely given by the good people who crowded the doors and windows and lined the pavements," said the Pennsylvanian, who concluded that for the first time it felt as though they were "fighting among friends." Passing through the village and marching on "with happy hearts," the First Corps soldiers had some time to enjoy the delicacies provided by the people of Middletown when, at 12:30 p.m., they reached Catoctin Creek and were ordered to halt. Again, fires sprang up and coffee began to boil. But while the soldiers took a break from their laborious march, First Corps commander Joseph Hooker galloped to the front to see where his men would be headed and what they would confront.[118]

Forty-seven-year-old Joseph Hooker was an ambitious, aggressive officer who had earned the sobriquet "Fighting Joe" earlier that year during the Peninsula Campaign. Born in November 1814 in Hadley, Massachusetts, Hooker graduated from West Point ranked twenty-ninth in the class of 1837. As a first lieutenant, Hooker served with distinction in Mexico, earning three brevet promotions. Resigning from the army in 1853, Hooker next took up farming, meeting with varying success in California's Sonoma Valley. The outbreak of sectional hostilities in the spring of 1861 saw Hooker back in uniform. On the battlefield, he proved a capable, hard-fighting officer. He commanded a division under McClellan during the Peninsula and Seven Days' Campaigns and a division under Pope at Second Bull Run. When George McClellan inherited Pope's Army of Virginia in early September 1862, incorporating these forces into his own army, he replaced

General Joseph Hooker, commander, First Corps, Army of the Potomac. *Library of Congress.*

General Irvin McDowell as commander of what became the Army of the Potomac's First Corps with Joseph Hooker. As it was for Jesse Reno, South Mountain would also be Joe Hooker's first fight as a corps commander.[119]

Hooker galloped toward the sound of the guns, arriving at the high ground near Bolivar, where the Federal batteries continued to belch forth their shot and shell. With the cacophony of cannons raging about, Hooker sat silently on horseback, surveying the Confederate line and the mountainous terrain. The crest of the mountain "was held by the enemy in considerable force," Hooker later noted, while the slopes were "precipitous, rugged, and wooded, and difficult of ascent to an infantry force, even in absence of a foe in front." He faced a difficult task but had great confidence in his men.[120]

Hooker had three divisions in his First Corps totaling roughly twelve thousand men, plus nine artillery batteries. His command structure was in considerable flux just prior to the fight at South Mountain. Two days earlier, on September 12, at the insistence of Pennsylvania's "war governor" Andrew Curtin, who feared his state was under an imminent threat of invasion, and over the objections of both McClellan and Hooker, the popular Major General John Fulton Reynolds, commander of the First Corps's Third Division, was detached from the army and sent to Harrisburg, where he organized and took charge of the militia forces Curtin had summoned in response to the Confederate threat. Frustrated with losing Reynolds, Hooker wrote, "A scared governor ought not to be permitted to destroy the usefulness of an entire division of the army, on the eve of important operations." Still, it was permitted. Reynolds's detachment elevated Meade to command of the Third Division, composed of three brigades of Pennsylvania Reserves. "Meade was one of our most dreaded foes," Confederate general D.H. Hill admitted after the war. "He was always in deadly earnest, and eschewed all trifling."[121]

Hooker's First Division was commanded by Major General Rufus King, but on the afternoon of September 14, even as the First Corps was marching toward battle, the sickly King, suffering from bouts of epilepsy, was relieved of command and replaced by Brigadier General John Hatch. Rounding out the First Corps's division commanders was the steady and reliable Brigadier General James Ricketts, in command of the Second Division. His men were only slightly engaged that day, moving forward in support as darkness began to fall.

With the Ninth Corps marching to battle along the Old Sharpsburg Road, south of the National Pike, and striking the Confederate right flank at Fox's Gap, wing commander Burnside, orchestrating a double envelopment over very difficult terrain, desired that Hooker's First Corps now move forward, swing north and attack the Confederate left. About 1:00 p.m., unaware that Hooker was at the front conducting his survey of the Confederate line, Burnside, from his headquarters near Middletown, sent orders for the First Corps to advance. Nothing happened. Burnside sent orders once more but again came the same result. Finally, Burnside rode forward to the Catoctin and personally ordered Meade to move his division forward. Forming back into lines of march, Meade's columns once again led the First Corps toward South Mountain. Burnside rode with Meade at the head of the column. They soon encountered Hooker, just then returning from his reconnaissance. Burnside explained the plan to Hooker, and together with Meade, the three future commanders of the Army of the Potomac discussed the best way to attack the strong Confederate position. The First Corps would march west another two miles to Bolivar, it was decided, and then take a right-hand turn on Mount Tabor Road, move north and then swing west in an effort to gain the Confederate left.[122]

The First Corps stretched out nearly four miles along the National Pike. About 2:30 p.m., Meade's division reached Bolivar and turned right on Mount Tabor Road. Hooker rode along with these men while Burnside remained at Bolivar. With the First Corps preparing to deploy, Burnside scribbled off a short note to Reno, instructing him to press forward with his own attack at Fox's Gap. Moments later, Burnside heard cheering rising up from the men still

marching along the National Pike. George McClellan was just then galloping to the front on his famed mount, Dan Webster. McClellan, enthused by the reception, filed off the road and placed himself on a prominent rise, where he stood in his stirrups and pointed toward the mountain, a moving spectacle that inspired the men and hardened their resolve on their way

Major General Ambrose Burnside oversaw the First and Ninth Corps's attacks at South Mountain. *Library of Congress.*

to battle. McClellan then rode ahead to Bolivar, where he found Burnside. His wing commander explained the deployment, which, Burnside noted, McClellan "fully approved." There the two would remain for the duration of the fight.[123]

As Meade's men continued to move north along Mount Tabor Road, Hatch's division, four brigades strong, reached Bolivar. Hatch, the newly minted division commander, followed in Meade's footsteps, turning his men to the right and along the northward-running road; however, his Fourth Brigade, under the command of Brigadier General John Gibbon and the largest in the division, was detached at Bolivar and was directed to continue moving westward along the National Pike. Burnside wished to use Gibbon's regiments—three hard-fighting veteran units from Wisconsin and one from Indiana—in a demonstration against Alfred Colquitt's Georgians astride the National Pike "as soon as the movements of Generals Hooker and Reno had sufficiently progressed."[124]

Meanwhile, Hooker continued leading his main column to the north until finally arriving at Mount Tabor Church, roughly one mile north of Bolivar, where he called a halt. Captain James Cooper's Battery B, 1st Pennsylvania Light Artillery, accompanied Meade's division and unlimbered on a rise of ground northeast of the stone church. As Cooper's four three-inch rifles began shelling the Confederate line, Hooker prepared his infantry for the attack. Meade's three brigades deployed first. Facing left, Meade's men formed into lines of battle on the open ground immediately west of Mount Tabor Road. On the far right of the line—roughly one and a half miles north of the National Pike—was Brigadier General Truman Seymour's brigade.

The son of a Methodist preacher, Seymour graduated in the illustrious West Point class of 1846 and during the Civil War was one of only two Union officers to have been present at both Fort Sumter and Appomattox (the other was General Samuel W. Crawford). Following the war, and after his retirement from the army in 1876, Seymour settled in Florence, Italy, where he became a noted artist, painting Italian landscapes and Italian villas. At the Battle of South Mountain, Seymour had five regiments of Pennsylvania Reserves under his command, including the famed 13th Pennsylvania Reserves, or 1st Pennsylvania Rifles, but better known as the "Bucktails." At Hooker's behest, Seymour directed Colonel Hugh McNeil to advance his Bucktails as skirmishers. McNeil sent forward six of his companies with instructions to feel for the enemy and uncover its positions.[125]

To the left of Seymour's men, Colonel Thomas Foster Gallagher posted his four regiments, with the 9th Pennsylvania Reserves on the right, the 11th in the

Union artillery
galloping into action.
*Battles & Leaders of the
Civil War.*

center and the 12th on the left; some fifty to seventy-five paces to the rear marched the 10th Pennsylvania Reserves as support. Forty-year-old Gallagher, a native of Pleasant Unity, in western Pennsylvania, was one of the few nonprofessional soldiers in the First Corps. He was instead a merchant, but he did have extensive experience in the state militia, eventually attaining the rank of brigadier general. Gallagher was of the habit of lighting up a cigar when preparing for action, and he no doubt did so on this Sunday afternoon with his men forming up for the attack. The Pennsylvania colonel was also that day suffering from a severe case of kidney stones, which almost made it impossible for him to mount and ride a horse. Still, he was determined, and as usual, he led from the front.

Completing Meade's deployment was Colonel Albert Lewis Magilton's brigade, which formed to the left of Gallagher and held the left of Meade's line. Like Seymour and so many other Civil War notables, Magilton was an 1846 West Point graduate and Mexican War veteran who during the Civil War earned the respect and admiration of his men. Before going into position, Magilton lost the services of one of his regiments, the 3rd Pennsylvania Reserves, which had been detached and ordered about three-quarters of a mile farther north to keep an eye out for any enemy activity coming from that direction and which would not be engaged that day. Magilton then formed his remaining three regiments, with the 8th Pennsylvania Reserves on the left of his line, the 7th in the center and the 4th on the right. To the left of the 8th ran what is today known as the Dahlgren Road, on the other side of which Hatch's First Division was just then deploying.[126]

"My Men Were Fighting Like Tigers. Every Man Was a Hero"

Meade's men deployed within full view of the Confederate forces on South Mountain. Artillery fire from some of Allen Cutts's guns soon erupted from the mountaintop. Although noisy, this fire was largely ineffective. The Confederate gunners did succeed, however, in scaring away a throng of civilians that had followed Meade's march from Middletown. The veteran Pennsylvania soldiers stood by smiling while these frightened men, women and children scampered to the rear. Sergeant Woodward of the 2nd Reserves noted that the "children laid down upon the ground, the women shrieked, and the men displayed wondrous agility in leaping the fences, which caused considerable amusement among us."[127]

The levity of the moment was soon replaced by the sobering thought of what lay ahead. Looking westward, up the slopes of South Mountain, Hooker's men knew there was serious business to be done and that they faced a daunting task. The ground was ideally suited for defense. Running northward from Turner's Gap, which Hooker's men could see to their left front, South Mountain rose to a height of fifteen hundred feet. Extending from this main ridge were two projections, or spurs, both of which crawled eastward from the mountain. One ran roughly parallel for a short distance with the National Pike and was labeled the south spur. It had a fairly level plateau, which had been cleared for cultivation. On the ridge's northern side, the south spur dropped dramatically down to a deep ravine through which ran a trickle of water known as the Frosttown Branch. Across this creek the ground rose sharply once more to form the second of these two spurs, the north spur. From Hooker's position, it was seen that two roads ran up South Mountain on either side of the deep ravine between the south and north spur. A mountain trail, the Dahlgren Road, intersected with the Mount Tabor Road north of the church. It ran west for several hundred yards before turning southwesterly, running diagonally across the eastern slope of South Mountain between the south spur and the main ridge until it finally connected with the National Pike near the Mountain House behind Colquitt's position. The second road—the Frosttown Road—was farther to Hooker's right, several hundred yards north of the Dahlgren Road. This road ran west and ascended South Mountain along the southern edge of the north spur and between it and the main ridge, where it connected with another rough mountain road, the Zittlestown Road. Turning left, the Zittlestown Road ultimately connected with the National Pike on the western slope of Turner's Gap, about three-quarters of a mile west of the Mountain House.[128]

Having studied the terrain, Hooker decided on a plan of attack. Meade's division on the right would sweep up the north spur and through the ravine between it and the south spur in an effort to turn the Confederate left. While Meade's men attacked the north spur and up through the ravine, Hatch's division, to the left of Meade and south of the Dahlgren Road, would attack the south spur. Ricketts's division would be held in reserve, ready to support either Meade or Hatch.

It would be no easy task. In front of Hooker's men, the ground was broken by a series of parallel ridges with swales of varying depths between each. These ridges got increasingly steeper and more rugged as they approached the mountain. Excepting a woodlot here and there, most of the ground over which the First Corps had to advance was open until they reached the main mountain ridge. Bisecting these open fields, many of which were under cultivation, were stone walls, while several houses, barns and other outbuildings along the Dahlgren and Frosttown Roads promised to further impede Hooker's attack. Hooker's men knew that the Confederates were no doubt concealed in these buildings, behind the stone walls and behind every large boulder and tree. The regimental historian of the Pennsylvania Bucktails described the tough ground and demanding task confronted by Hooker's veteran troops:

> All up the mountain side rocks and boulders abound, and here and there, stone walls. When to these features are added the heavily wooded portions and frequent depressions in the ground itself, some idea may be gathered of the difficulty of the task laid upon the division.

To George Meade, it was simply "the most rugged country" he ever saw. Still, it had to be taken. Having completed his deployment and settled on a plan of attack, Hooker gave the order to advance. It was just minutes before 5:00 p.m.[129]

From atop the north and south spurs and spread across the gorge, a thin line of Alabamians, under the command of Brigadier General Robert Rodes, watched nervously as the First Corps moved out, advancing directly toward them. From near the Mountain House, division commander D.H. Hill watched as well, pressed heavily on both flanks. On his right, at Fox's Gap, Drayton's Brigade was just then reeling, having been driven from the field and shattered to pieces by Orlando Willcox's Ninth Corps troops. Hill could not devote his entire focus to his collapsing right, however, since, as he later recorded, "affairs were now very serious on our left." Still, despite the threat they posed, Hill could not help but marvel for a moment at the martial pageantry presented by Hooker's massed blue columns as they stepped out. The First Corps's progress was slow, Hill later wrote, but "the advance was steady and made almost with the precision of movement of a parade day." All Hill had at that time to confront the advancing First Corps was Rodes's battle-hardened Alabamians, some twelve hundred men in all, and an even smaller brigade of South Carolinians, under Colonel Peter F. Stevens, which had less than half of Rodes's numbers.[130]

Thirty-three-year-old Robert Emmett Rodes presented a striking figure. Like General Samuel Garland, Rodes was both a native of Lynchburg, Virginia, and a graduate of the Virginia Military Institute. He taught for several years at his alma mater before resigning in 1851 to pursue a career in civil engineering, ultimately settling in Alabama, where he found good and steady employment with the railroads. With the outbreak of war, Rodes entered Confederate service as colonel of the 5th Alabama Infantry. After distinguishing himself at First Manassas, he was promoted to brigadier general. Although severely wounded at Seven Pines, Rodes returned to duty before he was properly healed in order to lead his brigade throughout the Seven Days' Campaign. He was at his finest at South Mountain and several days later at Antietam.[131]

Rodes's men began the day encamped just west of Boonsboro, but as the action intensified at Fox's Gap that morning, Hill summoned both Rodes's and Ripley's Brigades to the mountaintop. Arriving at the Mountain House about noon, Ripley was sent south toward Fox's Gap while Rodes was directed north with orders to take position on the south spur, alongside and overlooking the National Pike. Rodes placed his Alabamians as directed and remained on this high ground for forty-five minutes, exposed to the fire of the massed Federal batteries near Bolivar. From the high ground, Hill and Rodes watched as Hooker's men turned right off the National Pike. With the Federals then

Brigadier General Robert Rodes. *The Photographic History of the Civil War.*

deploying on the open fields north of the pike, both Confederate officers realized that Rodes's position on the south spur could be easily turned if the Union troops got possession of the north spur, from which they could also advance up the main South Mountain ridge. Rodes was thus directed to move his entire brigade some three-quarters of a mile farther north in order to occupy this high ground.

Rodes's five Alabama regiments sidestepped to the left, marched off the south spur and crossed the deep ravine that separated it from the north spur. The young brigadier then halted his command and began positioning his five Alabama regiments. He was naturally concerned about his flanks. His movement off the south spur created a gap, some three-quarters of a mile wide, between the right of his brigade and the rest of Hill's men near the Mountain House. It also meant that Cutts's gunners now stood unsupported on the south spur. He notified Hill of this, and the division commander responded by directing Rodes to send back one of his regiments. Rodes selected Colonel Bristor B. Gayle's 12th Alabama, which turned around and headed back toward the south spur.[132]

With Gayle's men heading back, Rodes continued placing his men. On the left of his new line was Colonel John Gordon's 6th Alabama, which initially deployed along the southern slope of the north spur near the Widow Main house. To the right of the 6th went the 5th Alabama under Major Edwin Lafayette Hobson. Colonel Cullen Battle's 3rd Alabama formed to the right, or south of the 5th, near the Haupt farm, while to its right went Colonel Edward O'Neal's 26th Alabama. Including the 12th, Rodes's men were now spread out across thirty-five hundred feet of mountainous terrain, and none of his five regiments was in contact with another. Making matters worse, even in this new position Rodes saw that the Federal line still stretched at least half a mile farther north, beyond his left flank. Rodes also discovered that the Zittlestown Road ran to his left and then behind his line. Unless defended, he knew the Federals could sweep up this road, turn his position and move toward Turner's Gap simply by following this roadway. But with his line already spread thin, the only thing he could do was to send back for reinforcements and hope his men could delay the Federals from a quick sweep up the mountain. He must have taken some consolation in the fact that his men, although outnumbered, enjoyed the defensive advantage and benefited from the shelter of trees and boulders. And, unknown to Rodes, at that moment some help was on its way.[133]

Shortly after 4:00 p.m., Nathan Evans's Brigade of South Carolinians reached the Mountain House. Behind it came John Hood's two brigades under

Wofford and Law. Evans was under the impression that he wielded control over all three of these brigades—his own, plus those under Wofford and Law—not knowing that Lee had minutes earlier released Hood from arrest and restored him to command of his division. His South Carolina brigade was thus under the immediate command of Colonel Peter Stevens. When Stevens reported for orders, D.H. Hill, having just received Rodes's request for reinforcements, sent him northward with instructions to report directly to Rodes. After this, Hill sent Hood's two brigades south to strengthen his position at Fox's Gap. Evans watched as his supposed command marched off in two different directions. He sent orders for Stevens to halt, which the colonel immediately obeyed, his South Carolinians stacked up along the Dahlgren Road. No sooner had his men stopped, however, when another message arrived, this one from Rodes, who urged the South Carolinian to hurry to his support. Caught between these conflicting orders, Stevens sent back to Evans, seeking further instructions and sent a courier galloping off to Rodes to explain why he halted.

As Stevens's two staff officers raced off in different directions, the colonel looked into the valley below and saw the Federal legions advancing. There was no time to wait for an answer; his course had been chosen. Believing his position "already threatened" by the Federal advance, Stevens sent forward the Holcombe Legion as skirmishers and began deploying the rest of his brigade astride the Dahlgren Road on the eastern slope of the mountain. The 17th South Carolina deployed south of the roadway while the 18th, 22nd and 23rd South Carolina moved to the north, the left of the 23rd, Stevens later noted, "very nearly joining Rodes's right." In all, Stevens had just 550 men. Combined with Rodes's command, there were about 1,800 Confederates to contend with Meade's 4,000.[134]

By the time Stevens's men arrived and deployed on the mountainside, skirmishers from all of Rodes's regiments had already been advanced. Colonel Gayle of the 12th Alabama sent forward a skirmish force of forty men under the command of Lieutenant Robert E. Park. "I hastily deployed the men," Park later recorded, "and we moved down the mountainside. On our way down we could see the enemy, in two lines of battle, in the valley below, advancing, preceded only a few steps by their dense line of skirmishers." Park led his men to a woodlot near the base of the gorge in between the Dahlgren and Frosttown Roads. "I concealed my men behind trees, rocks and bushes," said Park, "and cautioned them to aim well before firing." Park and his small band of skirmishers waited "with beating hearts the sure and steady approach of the Pennsylvania 'Bucktails'" whom Hooker had just ordered forward.[135]

The Pennsylvania Bucktails, distinct with white deer tails pinned to their caps and armed with Sharps rifles, screened Meade's advance. A short distance behind marched the balance of the division "through open woods and over cultivating ground." Confederate gunners on the south spur re-sighted their pieces, adjusted their barrels and opened fire on the Pennsylvanians. This time the artillerists hit their mark. "The exposure was great," noted Truman Seymour, "and numbers fell under the accurate fire of the shells from these guns." Meanwhile, Lieutenant Park's anxious skirmishers drew back the hammers on their muskets, their heartbeats growing louder until, at last, the Bucktails got near enough and Park gave the order to fire. The volley staggered McNeil's skirmish line. Those who survived the initial blast, recorded Park, "rushed pell-mell to their main line, disordering it greatly." Regaining their composure, the Federal skirmishers sought shelter behind trees and rocks and soon began peppering the Confederate skirmishers with some well-aimed shots. There, boasted the regimental historian, "the Bucktails brought into play the accuracy of their marksmanship. Having in their hands Sharps rifles, they were enabled to pick off many a Confederate, who, attempting to reload his inferior weapon, was compelled to partly expose his person." Private Otis Smith of the 6th Alabama, who was on the skirmish line, remembered simply that the "pat, pat of the bullets against the rocks sounded like hail."[136]

With the gunfire erupting to his front, McNeil ordered up his four reserve companies while Seymour sent forward the 2nd Pennsylvania Reserves to bolster the right of the Bucktails' line. The strengthened Federal line advanced again and again suffered heavily; Park later claimed that "nearly every bullet did fatal work." They checked the advance a few minutes, but there were simply too many bluecoats and too few Confederates. Park could hear Union officers shouting out orders for their men: "Close up…forward!" It became clear that the Pennsylvanians would soon overwhelm the Confederate skirmishers. Park

Colonel Hugh McNeil, Pennsylvania Bucktails.
History of the Pennsylvania Bucktails.

ordered his men to fall back slowly "and to fire from everything which would screen them from observation." His own casualties up to this point had been light; indeed, Park claimed to have lost just four men wounded. However, once he gave the order to fall back, some six or eight more "became demoralized and, despite my commands, entreaties, and threats," said Park, "left me and hastily fled to the rear."

With a cheer the Pennsylvanians charged forward and chased away what remained of Park's skirmish force. The gallant lieutenant was unable to escape. Seeing one of his corporals fall wounded, Park rushed over, "raised him tenderly, [and] gave him water." Knowing there was little more he could do for the wounded man, Park was about to leave him to his fate when he looked up and saw a dozen rifles pointed right at him. He threw his arms up in surrender. Although "mortified and humiliated" at being captured, Park, while being escorted to the rear, noticed the "great execution done by my little squad as shown by the dead and wounded lying all along the route."[137]

As the skirmish fire picked up on his front, Robert Rodes knew his men would not be able to hold their position for long if the summit of the north spur remained unoccupied to his left and if the Zittlestown Road fell into Union hands. Having not heard anything from Stevens's brigade, or from any other reinforcements for that matter, Rodes ordered the 6th Alabama, on the far left of his line, to shift farther north and defend the high ground. Rodes also detached the left wing of the 5th Alabama and ordered it to sidestep to the left in an effort to fill the ground vacated by the 6th. The fire on the skirmish line was heavy as Colonel Gordon moved his regiment to the left and over the brow of the spur, which he did, Rodes noted, "in good style."[138]

Rodes was not the only one who recognized the importance of the north spur. Truman Seymour knew that if his men could gain this high ground, they would then be able to turn the entire Confederate line while at the same time sweep up the mountain toward Turner's Gap. He galloped back to Meade, who was near the center of his division's line, and reported the situation. Meade immediately ordered him to attack. Seymour raced back to his line and went "to the place where the fire was hottest." There he found McNeil and exhorted him to get his men moving. By this time, the 6th Alabama had reached the north spur and was pouring a devastating fire into Seymour's Pennsylvanians. "The task was enough to cause the boldest to hesitate," said the Bucktails historian. "The troops were expected to charge uphill, and drive from an eminently strong defensive position an equal number of opponents." Seymour and McNeil were having a difficult time getting their men to charge. Casualties mounted rapidly and the action seemed deadlocked. Seymour sent troops farther to the right in order to sweep around Gordon's left flank. At the same time, he ordered Colonel Joseph Fisher's 5th Pennsylvania Reserves to advance against Gordon's right.

With both wings now surging forward, Captain Edwin Irvin, commander of the Bucktails Company K, sought to break the deadlock in the middle. Irvin ran forward, swinging his sword and shouting, "Forward Bucktails, drive them from their position!" He soon fell, shot through the head. Yet his example inspired the men. With a cheer, and infuriated by Irvin's loss, the Bucktails charged forward. Fisher's men had meanwhile begun firing into the 6th Alabama's right. At this point, Colonel Gordon noticed the Federal force sweeping around his left and starting to move behind his line. Pressured on his flanks and now attacked in his center, Gordon knew his position was hopeless. Outnumbered and about to be overrun, he ordered a retreat, his survivors fleeing up the slopes of South Mountain. Seymour, flushed with victory, led his men to the summit and gained possession of the north spur. Rodes's left had been turned, but Seymour was not yet finished.[139]

Once his men reached high ground, Seymour noticed a line of Confederate troops behind a stone wall along the edge of a cornfield to his left. This was the left wing of the 5th Alabama, under Major Hobson, which Rodes had earlier directed to occupy the ground originally held by Gordon. Hobson's men delivered a volley that stunned Seymour's men, bringing his advance to a temporary halt. Turning to Joseph Fisher of the 5th Pennsylvania, Seymour yelled out, "Colonel, put your regiment into that corn-field and hurt somebody!"

Brigadier General Truman Seymour. *Library of Congress.*

Fisher coolly responded, "I will, general, and I'll catch one alive for you."

The confident Pennsylvania colonel turned his regiment to face left and, together with the 2nd and 6th Pennsylvania Reserves, swept forward and quickly overwhelmed Hobson's men. Eleven Confederates were sent to the rear, prisoners of war, while the rest of this small band of Alabamians retreated pell-mell up the mountain. Seymour had succeeded in turning the flank and driving away all opposition to his front. His men continued their pursuit of Rodes's retreating men, up the rugged, boulder-strewn slopes. Sergeant Woodward of the 2nd remembered:

> *All order and regularity of the lines were soon destroyed, and the battle partook of the nature of a free fight, every one going in "on his own hook," as it suited his fancy. From wall after wall, and rock after rock, the enemy were driven until our glorious banners caught the gleam of the setting sun, that he been hid from our sight by the mountain tops. Our loud cheers of victory arose from the crest, and was rolled down the mountain side.*[140]

Robert Rodes realized the dire situation that now befell his men. With his left turned and the Zittlestown Road in Federal hands, the Confederate brigadier knew that Seymour's men would surely continue to roll up his left and advance behind the remainder of his line strung out across the gorge. But all he could do was appeal again for reinforcements and prepare for what he surely knew to be the inevitable. It was not just his left that had come under attack; he was being pressured along his entire line. To the left of Seymour, the brigades of Gallagher and Magilton had also stepped forward, heading toward the gorge and directly toward the men of the 5th, 3rd, 26th and 12th Alabama.[141]

All three of Meade's brigades received the orders to advance, but because of the uneven nature of the terrain, with its rolling, undulating ridgelines, they soon lost touch with one another. Colonel Gallagher, advancing in the middle of Meade's line and to the left of Seymour, did his best to maintain contact with Seymour's men by marching his brigade at a right oblique. But he was unable to maintain a connection, and such a move only served to further the distance between his own left and the right of Magilton, advancing to his left. Ahead of these advancing Pennsylvanians was a thin line of Confederates spread out across the ravine between the north and south spurs, their fingers on the triggers, readying for the attack. All Rodes had to contest the advance of both Gallagher and Magilton was the right wing of his 5th Alabama, Colonel Battle's 3rd Alabama, the 26th Alabama under Colonel Edward O'Neil and, shouldering into position next to the 3rd, Colonel Bristor Gayle's 12th Alabama, which had just been relieved from its position near the south spur by Stevens's brigade. Most of Rodes's men were positioned directly ahead of Gallagher's brigade. Stevens's men would primarily stand in the way of Magilton.

As the Pennsylvanians neared the gorge, it erupted in a sheet of flame. The 11th Pennsylvania Reserves, in the center of Gallagher's line, suffered most heavily from a volley delivered at short range by the 3rd Alabama. Lieutenant Colonel Samuel M. Jackson, commanding the 11th, explained that he had ordered his men "to press forward rapidly to a ravine at the foot of the mountain but on reaching this we received a deadly volley from the enemy's infantry, who were strongly posted in the rocks on the mountain side and but a short distance from our lines." Jackson alleged that half of his commissioned officers fell in this single blast. The men of the 11th found whatever cover they could and soon began returning fire. Meanwhile, to the right of the 11th, the advance of Lieutenant Colonel Robert Anderson's 9th Pennsylvania Reserves also ground to a halt. Anderson's men were stalled by a small, though tenacious, band of Confederate skirmishers under Captain E.S. Ready of the 3rd Alabama, in position in the log home and outbuildings belonging to the Haupt family. The 9th formed up behind a stone wall at the base of the mountain and soon began peppering the Haupt home with bullets.[142]

As this action raged, the 12th Pennsylvania Reserves on the left of Gallagher's line did not meet with the same determined opposition, and although they also came under fire, they suffered far fewer casualties than the regiments to their right. Opposing their advance was the 26th Alabama Infantry, but it seems that soon after its commanding officer, Edward O'Neal, fell wounded, his Alabamians made haste for the rear. Rodes wrote that the 26th was "completely demoralized," and the men "mingled in utter confusion" with some of Stevens's South Carolinians, who had just taken position on the high ground behind them. Having cleared their front of Confederate troops, the 12th Pennsylvania, said Captain Andrew J. Bolar, "went on up the mountain without halting." Admittedly, the progress was slow "on account of the steepness of the hill and the rocks, logs, and brush with which the ground was covered," but still the Pennsylvanians advanced. Bolar remembered that all around them, as the day quickly turned to night, the firing was incessant and the Confederates yielded "only when routed out of their hidden positions by the balls and bayonets of our men." Casualties in the 12th Pennsylvania that day totaled six men killed and nineteen wounded.[143]

As the 12th Pennsylvania swept up the mountainside, to its right rear, at the base of the gorge, the 11th and 9th Pennsylvania were still slugging it out with Battle's 3rd Alabama and portions of the 5th and 12th Alabama. Federal casualties here were noticeably higher, and among the severely wounded was Colonel Gallagher, shot in the arm and, after collapsing from his saddle, carried from the field. The wound never properly healed, and in

December 1862, Gallagher tendered his resignation from the army. When taken to the rear, Gallagher was greeted by George McClellan. "Colonel Gallagher, this is neither the first nor the second time the Reserves have saved the army," said McClellan in effort to assuage the pained colonel. "You have reason to be proud of the wound received while leading your men to victory. God bless you and them!" Gallagher's place at the helm of Meade's Third Brigade was taken by Lieutenant Colonel Robert Anderson of the 9th Reserves.[144]

Colonel Thomas F. Gallagher. *John Boucher,* History of Westmoreland County, *Vol. 1.*

McClellan was not the only one proud of his men. Colonel Cullen Battle of the 3rd Alabama later wrote that his men were "fighting like tigers" that Sunday in the face of overwhelming numbers and that "every man was a hero." On the low ground to his left front, Battle watched Captain Ready's skirmishers on the Haupt farm duel it out with Anderson's 9th Pennsylvania Reserves. For twenty or so minutes, the 9th remained sheltered behind the stone wall before Captain Samuel Dick, who assumed command of the 9th after Anderson's elevation to brigade command, finally determined to break the stalemate by ordering a charge. With bayonets fixed, the Pennsylvanians rushed forward. "Our line moved steadily on," recorded Anderson, "not once giving way or faltering." At last, Ready's men were driven from the house, fifteen of them falling into Union hands, including a seriously wounded Captain Ready. The rest fell back toward the main Confederate line, pursued at every step by Pennsylvanians, whether individually or in small, scattered groups.

By this point, however, the soldiers of the 9th were running low on bullets and were soon relieved by Colonel Adoniram Warner's 10th Pennsylvania Reserves. Warner's regiment was initially held back, moving forward behind Gallagher's front line, but when Meade saw the advance grind to a halt and

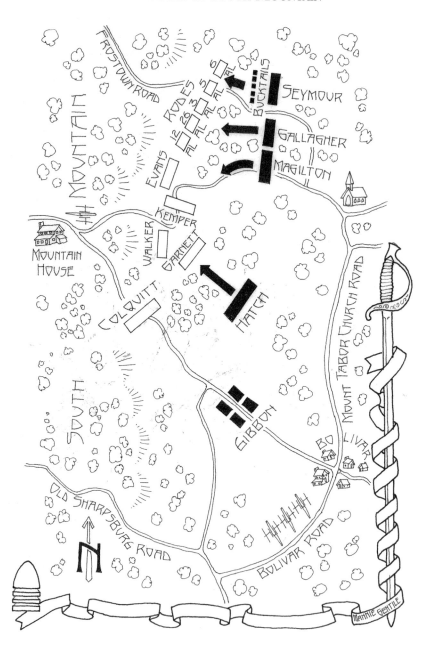

noticed the gap between Gallagher's right and Seymour's left, he sent the 10th toward this part of the line. Moving into position, the 10th came under heavy fire, causing some men to fall. Warner's horse was shot from beneath him, and he had a difficult time getting some of his men to advance. While a part of his line moved forward rapidly, firing as it went, another part was "hanging back in a way they had never done before," said Warner. "I did all in power to push them rapidly forward," wrote the colonel, and soon "confidence took the place of hesitation and all pressed rapidly forward driving the enemy from their lodgments and…fast gaining the mountainsides." Warner's men moved forward to the right of the 9th and then took their place in line.[145]

Colonel Cullen A. Battle, 3rd Alabama. *The Photographic History of the Civil War.*

Just as Captain Dick led his 9th Pennsylvania in a charge toward the Haupt house and as Warner was moving his men into position, to their left Colonel Jackson's 11th Pennsylvania, after recovering from that first, staggering blast, was again pushing forward, driving what remained of Rodes's line up the mountain. It delivered a telling fire into the 3rd Alabama, with one bullet striking Colonel Battle directly in the belt buckle. The blow knocked the colonel to the ground, and he believed he had been mortally wounded. When it was discovered that the bullet had just glanced off the plate, Battle was helped to his feet and slowly made his way to the rear, his line by this point in full retreat. A proud Colonel Jackson recorded that his men "continued to press forward with a seeming determination to win, and soon succeeded in forcing the enemy from their strong and well-selected position."[146]

Rodes's line was now gone, his men fleeing up the mountainside and being pursued at every step by the persistent Pennsylvanians of Meade's division. Alabamians were rooted out from behind nearly every tree and every boulder. D.H. Hill later wrote that it was "pitiable to see the gallant but hopeless struggle of these Alabamians against such mighty odds." Hopeless though the situation may have been, Rodes was not yet ready to abandon the fight. Having now learned that Stevens's South Carolinians had moved into position on his right, Rodes sent orders to whatever troops he could rally to fall back up the slopes and concentrate near the highest peak. There he gathered with Colonel Gordon and his "excellent regiment," the 6th Alabama. Rodes noted that Gordon, throughout the day, had handled his men "in a manner I have never heard or seen equaled during this war." Survivors of the 3rd, 5th and 12th Alabama also gathered, and Rodes fashioned a new line "under constant fire and in full view of the enemy," said the brigade commander, "now in full possession of the extreme left hill and of the gorge." Again, the fight was renewed "at close quarters" with elements of Gallagher's brigade attacking their front while Seymour's men, advancing from the left, continued to sweep around the Alabamians' flank.

The contest, though determined, was short-lived, with heavy casualties. Colonel Bristor Gayle of the 12th Alabama fell dead, and just moments later, the regiment's second in command, Lieutenant Colonel Samuel Pickens, was shot through the lungs. After delivering a few well-directed shots, the 3rd, 5th and 12th Alabama again retreated leaving just Rodes with Gordon and his indomitable 6th Alabama. The 6th "retired slowly," said Rodes, "now being under an enfilading as well as direct fire and in danger of being surrounded, but was still, fortunately for the whole command, held together by its able commander." The regiment fell back along the crest of the mountain until it reached a position about two hundred yards north of Turner's Gap, forming parallel with the National Pike and facing north.

By this time, darkness was enveloping the landscape; combined with the rugged terrain, this made further pursuit by the Federals impossible. Soon joining the 6th Alabama were handfuls of men from Rodes's other regiments. By nightfall, Rodes's Brigade had been reduced by a third; it had lost 61 men

Alfred Waud sketch of the Battle of South Mountain as seen from Boonsboro. *Library of Congress.*

killed, 157 wounded and 204 missing from the 1,200 taken into the fight. The Alabamians had put up a heroic fight in the face of Meade's entire division, and although driven from their strong position, Rodes was justly proud of his men, writing, "We did not drive the enemy back or whip him, but with 1,200 men we held his whole division at bay without assistance during four and a half hours' steady fighting, losing in that time not over half a mile of ground." D.H. Hill much more succinctly noted that Rodes's Brigade "had immortalized itself" at South Mountain.[147]

Yet Rodes's Brigade was not alone in its struggle against Meade's division, for also putting up a tough fight on the mountain and suffering heavily for it were the South Carolinians under Colonel Peter Stevens. Stevens arrived and deployed his men astride the Dahlgren Road and to the right of Rodes just moments before the Federal attack commenced. From this position, his men battled mainly with Magilton's brigade on Meade's left. Sergeant A.F. Hill of the 8th Pennsylvania Reserves, advancing on the left of Magilton's line, left a vivid account of his regiment's actions that day:

> *We toiled up the steep ascent in front of us, when we discovered that a valley lay yet between us and the main ascent of South Mountain. While passing through a corn-field upon the hill, the enemy's artillery again opened upon us with solid shot. Down the hill we went—across the small valley—up the steep ascent of the mountain.*

Several hundred yards to their front was a stone fence, said Hill, and

> *when within fifty yards of the stone-fence, a murderous fire of musketry was opened upon us by the rebels, who lay concealed behind it, and swarms of bullets whistled about our ears. With a wild shout, we dashed forward, while volley after volley was poured upon us; but we heeded it not; we rushed madly on.*

Magilton's men drove back Stevens's skirmishers of the Holcombe Legion and advanced toward his main line. One of his South Carolina colonels later wrote that he "never saw so many blue coats in my life, at one time." Stevens's men opened fire, which took effect in the ranks of Magilton's advancing troops, but they were unable to stop the blue tide from sweeping forward. "We pressed the rebels closely," wrote Sergeant Hill. "They stood awhile, loading and firing, but at last began to waver." Hill further noted that the Pennsylvanians "mowed down" the South Carolinians. "Poor fellows!" he declared. "I almost pitied

Colonel Albert Magilton. *Second Brigade, Pennsylvania Reserves at Antietam.*

Colonel Peter Fayssoux Stevens. *Courtesy of the Citadel Museum and Archives.*

them, to see them sink down by dozens at every discharge!" The 22nd and 23rd South Carolina gave way, followed soon after by the 18th and 17th South Carolina, "and from that time the fight was a retreating one," noted Stevens, "until the enemy occupied the mountain and we were driven from it."

Stevens was critical of his men during the retreat, declaring that "after once falling back I cannot commend the behavior of the men. Some two or three bravely faced the foe, but a general lack of discipline and disregard for officers prevailed around me." This may have been a bit unfair, for the South Carolinians did pay a heavy price for their short though determined stance. By the time the smoke cleared, the brigade had lost 22 men killed, 148 wounded and 45 captured or missing. This, out of the 550 they took into the fight, totaled a near 40 percent loss. Magilton's losses were fewer, with 25 killed, 64 wounded and 1 missing in action. Most of Magilton's losses occurred in the ranks of the 8th Pennsylvania.[148]

By nightfall, Meade's Pennsylvania Reserves had driven back both Rodes and Stevens's brigades, exacting a heavy toll while itself losing 95 men killed, another 296 wounded and 1 man missing in action. In the gathering darkness, Meade's division was bolstered on its right by General Abram Duryea's brigade of Ricketts's division, which had been sent forward earlier when it was feared that Seymour's flank was in danger. Moving into position, Duryea lost five men killed and an additional sixteen wounded but arrived after most of the heavy fighting. As the action drew to a close at nightfall, Meade's men began replenishing their cartridge boxes and caring for their wounded comrades. It was a hard-fought victory over challenging terrain. Hooker was naturally complimentary of Meade and his men, writing that they "moved forward with great vigor…Every step of his advance was resisted stubbornly by a numerous enemy and, besides, he had great natural obstacles to overcome, which impeded his advance but did not check it." Meade offered further praise for his Pennsylvanians, declaring that their effort that Sunday "was such to uphold its well-earned reputation for steadiness and gallantry" in battle. But Meade's men were not the only ones congratulating themselves on a hard-earned victory that night, for to their left the soldiers of General John Hatch's division were equally victorious.[149]

Major General George Gordon Meade. *Library of Congress.*

Brigadier General John Hatch. *Library of Congress.*

At 5:00 p.m., as Meade's men launched the attack against Rodes's Alabamians, Hatch's division also stepped off. Hooker's plan called for Meade and Hatch to advance simultaneously, and while Meade was instructed to carry the north spur and sweep up the ravine, Hatch was to advance straight ahead and carry the south spur. Forty-year-old John Hatch was a native of Oswego, New York, and a career military man. He graduated from West Point in 1845 and, as a lieutenant in the U.S. Mounted Rifles, served with great distinction in Mexico, being twice brevetted for his gallantry at the Battles of Contreras and Churusbusco and in the storming of Chapultepec. When civil war erupted, Hatch was a captain in the 3rd U.S. Cavalry, and throughout the first year and a half of the war he remained in the mounted arm, commanding a cavalry brigade until given an infantry command in King's division of Irvin McDowell's Third Corps under Pope. He was wounded at 2nd Bull Run but quickly returned to duty. When McDowell's Third Corps was incorporated into the Army of the Potomac, becoming the First Corps under Hooker, Hatch retained brigade command. On the afternoon of September 14, as his men marched toward South Mountain, Hatch was elevated to division command, taking the place of the sickly King.[150]

At South Mountain, Hatch had four brigades under his command, although his largest, under Gibbon, was detached at Bolivar to attack Alfred Colquitt's men astride the National Pike. Following behind Meade's men, Hatch marched his remaining three brigades north along the Mount Tabor Road until arriving in position. He then deployed for the attack, forming his brigades in three lines of battle, with Brigadier General Marsena Patrick's brigade in front followed by Hatch's own brigade, now commanded by Colonel Walter Phelps Jr., while Brigadier General Abner Doubleday's brigade brought up the rear, forming the third line. Hatch instructed Phelps to advance at a two-hundred-yard interval behind Patrick and Doubleday to advance at the same distance behind Phelps. In all, Hatch could count roughly twenty-four hundred men to make this assault.

In front, Marsena Patrick readied for the advance. A crusty old army regular, Patrick was a West Point graduate who had little respect for his peers. The day before the battle, Patrick had confided in his diary that he had "no confidence in King," was "disgusted with Hatch" and regarded Gibbon as "a despicable toady." He had that day formally requested a transfer, but Burnside, his wing commander, had more important matters to attend to. Patrick thus dutifully followed Hatch's orders. Directed to advance two of his regiments as a skirmish force for the division, he sent forward the 21st and 35th New York.[151]

"My Men Were Fighting Like Tigers. Every Man Was a Hero"

From the top of South Mountain, D.H. Hill watched in awe as Hatch's men deployed on the open fields below. The sight, declared Hill, was "grand and sublime. Hatch's general and field officers were on horseback, his colors were all flying, and the alignment of his men seemed to be perfectly preserved." There was little Hill could do at that moment but watch, for when Patrick's skirmish line stepped forward, there were just a few Confederates on the south spur to contest their advance. Indeed, only the gunners of Cutts's Battalion were then in position. They opened fire on Hatch's forming lines but did no damage, "owing," explained Hill, "to the steepness of the acclivity and the bad handling of the guns." The caustic general further noted that this "cannonade was as harmless as blank-cartridge salutes in honor of a militia general" and that Hatch's men did not even so much as duck or dodge in "honor" of these "ineffective missiles." For D.H. Hill, however, help was on its way.[152]

While Hill watched Hatch's men form for the advance, the exhausted soldiers of three Confederate brigades came panting up the National Pike on the western slopes of South Mountain. First in line were the Virginians under Brigadier General James Kemper, followed closely by Brigadier General Richard Garnett's men. Behind Garnett came the South Carolinians of Micah Jenkins's Brigade, under the command of Colonel Joseph Walker.

For these men, it had already been a long, hot day. As part of D.R. Jones's Division of Longstreet's command, they began the day at Hagerstown, some fifteen miles northwest of Turner's Gap. Captain Henry Owen of the 18th Virginia remembered that soon after sunrise that Sunday morning, "there came trembling along upon the bosom of the sultry air that low, whispering, dull, heavy sound of a distant cannon. Several minutes elapsed and then again in quivering echoes came that long, rolling sound repeated and prolonged," which told Owen of a distant battle. Orders soon arrived for the men to pack up their gear, refill their canteens and prepare to march. At last, said Owen, "the long roll was beat, the lines were rapidly formed, heading toward Boonsboro, and off we went, at a double-quick, down the long, sandy lanes with clouds of hot, suffocating dust floating around us and drifting away in heavy volumes across the fields on the roadsides." The heat, dust and "tremendous pace" forced many men to leave the ranks, collapsing by the roadside. "The perspiration welled out at every pore and ran down the neck and arms and back in little rivulets," explained Owen, while "the clouds of dust settled upon the clothes and hands and face until the hair and whiskers were so changed in color that the soldier could hardly recognize his messmate."[153]

Early that afternoon, the tired men of these three brigades limped through Boonsboro. However, while the other columns under Longstreet—including

Drayton's, Tige Anderson's and Evans's Brigades and John Bell Hood's Division—continued west up the National Pike to the Mountain House, the brigades of Kemper, Garnett and Jenkins, under the direct command of D.R. Jones, were sent south by Lee's order, with instructions to sweep up the Old Sharpsburg Road and attack the Federal force at Fox's Gap. Jones led his men at least a mile in this direction, skirting the western base of South Mountain, before orders arrived for him to halt and turn back around. This marching and countermarching added at least two additional miles to their already long day. By the time the men arrived back at the National Pike, admitted Richard Garnett, "my troops were almost exhausted," and he "consequently lost a good number of men by straggling." The brigade commander estimated that his men had covered anywhere between eighteen and twenty miles that Sunday before seeing any action. General Longstreet later wrote that because of the day's exertions, these three brigades "were thinned to skeletons" when they arrived at the front.[154]

It was nearly 5:00 p.m. and the sun was just beginning to set when Kemper's men, at the head of the column, reached the Mountain House. Also arriving on the scene was James Longstreet, who exercised the authority of his superior rank and took command of the field from Harvey Hill. Hill, who had done well in defending the mountain throughout that trying day, had a difficult time suppressing his chagrin when Longstreet took over. "I had now become familiar with the ground, and knew all the vital points," said Hill in his report of the day's action, adding with just a little hindsight, "had these troops reported to me, the result might have been different. As it was, they took wrong positions, and, in their exhausted condition after a long march, they were broken and scattered."[155]

General James Longstreet. *The Photographic History of the Civil War.*

Longstreet did not like what he saw. Almost immediately after arriving, he sent a grim note to Robert E. Lee "to prepare his mind for disappointment, and give time for arrangements for retreat." Surveying the situation—the entire Ninth

Corps was already stacked up on the Confederate right flank, secure at Fox's Gap, and now the First Corps was sweeping forward against the left—Lee's old war horse Longstreet did not believe it possible for the Confederate army to emerge victorious from this field of battle. Still, he began placing his men. From the National Pike, Kemper's men turned northeasterly along the Dahlgren Road, followed by Garnett and Jenkins.

The movement of these troops caught the attention of Captain George Durell's Ninth Corps Battery in position near the Old Sharpsburg Road, a mile or so to the south. Durell's Pennsylvania gunners took careful aim and opened a heavy fire on the advancing gray columns. John Dooley, a private in the 1st Virginia, Kemper's Brigade, remembered that the "shells of the enemy came whistling over our heads fast and furiously as we ascend the mountain. I tell you," Dooley admitted, "I was frightened." For a time, there was some confusion among the Virginians, but order was quickly restored, and the brigades began to form into lines of battle.[156]

James Kemper's brigade, just four hundred men strong, deployed first. A successful lawyer and politician, Kemper had little military experience, although he did serve in Mexico as a captain of Virginia volunteers. Still, as colonel of the 7th Virginia, he had proven himself a skilled leader on the fields of Manassas and during the Peninsula Campaign and had won promotion to brigadier general in June 1862. He formed his men near the summit of the south spur, facing northeasterly, with his five regiments in line of battle on either side of the Dahlgren Road. From their position, Kemper's men could hear but not quite see the action unfolding to their front as Magilton's Pennsylvanians battled it out with Rodes's Alabamians and Stevens's South Carolinians.[157]

Following behind Kemper was Richard Brooke Garnett, his men exposed to the same deadly fire delivered by Durell's guns. A West Point graduate, Garnett was a soldier's soldier who earned the esteem of all those who served under his command. Prior to taking command of what had been General George Pickett's Brigade just a few days before South Mountain, Garnett led the famed Stonewall Brigade until Jackson had him arrested following the Battle of Kernstown. The charges against Garnett were unfounded, and he was never convicted; still, the arrest cast a negative light on an otherwise stellar military career.

Garnett's men formed to the right of Kemper at nearly a forty-five-degree angle and stretched north–south on the summit of the south spur, with his right flank extending toward the National Pike. His men found shelter behind a stone wall that separated a woodlot from a field of standing corn, and on the far right was Colonel Eppa Hunton's 8th Virginia, followed to the left by the 18th, 19th, 28th and 56th Virginia. Forming several hundred yards to the right rear of Garnett was Walker's South Carolina brigade. In all, Garnett had roughly four hundred men. And it would be these men who would bear the brunt of Hatch's attack.[158]

As soon as his men formed into line of battle, Garnett sent forward a thin line of skirmishers. Moments later, orders arrived from D.R. Jones. During the deployment, a two-hundred-yard gap had developed between the left of Garnett and the right of Kemper, which Jones now sought to correct. He directed Garnett to detach the 56th Virginia on his far left and send it back toward Kemper's right. He then instructed him to fall back with the rest of his brigade "to a wooded ridge a little to the left and rear." Garnett complied with the first part of these instructions by sending the 56th back. However, before he could withdraw his main line, he heard scattered shots to his front followed by more severe firing. His skirmishers had made contact with Hatch's advancing troops, and the action, said Garnett, "at once became general."[159]

Marsena Patrick led Hatch's attack, his skirmishers stepping forward about 5:00 p.m. J. Harrison Mills of the 21st New York, on the right of Patrick's front line, remembered that as soon as they began their ascent, an elderly woman, "who had been frightened from her home by the threatening appearance of things," asked a passing officer where they were headed. "Only going up the hill," was the reply, to which the woman yelled out, "Don't you go

Brigadier General Richard B. Garnett. *Library of Congress.*

there! There are hundreds of 'em up there. Don't you go! Some of you will get hurt!" Her entreaties aside, the regiment continued to push on but found the going tough. The terrain hindered their progress as the men labored up the steep hill. "We cross the fence and advance," described Mills of the 21st, "slow and steady, up the mountain side, which because so broken and rocky that a halt becomes necessary every fifteen or twenty paces, to close up and dress the line." A wide gap developed in Patrick's skirmish line. The 21st New York, commanded by Colonel William Rogers, drifted too far to the right, while Colonel Newton Lord's 35[160] New York veered much too far to the left, heading toward the National Pike.[160]

General Patrick, who followed behind his skirmishers with the remainder of his brigade, noticed the gap and immediately sought to rectify it by sending his trailing regiments forward. He galloped over to Colonel Henry Hoffman of the 23rd New York, instructing him to advance his men until linking up with the right of the 35th New York. He also found Lieutenant Colonel Theodore Gates of the 80th New York and directed him to move forward until he connected with the left of the 21st. Patrick then rode forward, hoping to catch up with his skirmishers and halt their advance until the line could be restored. But Patrick galloped too far forward and somehow managed to get in between his own skirmish line and that of the Confederates. The general may have ridden right into the Confederate skirmish line had not his orderly yelled out "Gray Coats!" Patrick turned around and "plunged down the Mountain Side followed by a volley of the enemy which passed over my head." Although it was a narrow escape, Patrick had at least discovered the Confederate line.[161]

Meanwhile, Colonel Walter Phelps continued to advance with the second line of Hatch's advance, stepping off two hundred yards behind Patrick. Phelps was just a few weeks shy of his thirtieth birthday, a native of Hartford, Connecticut and a graduate of Trinity College. He enjoyed success as a lumber merchant in Glen Falls, New York, and had some experience in the New York State Militia. When John Hatch advanced to divisional command that Sunday afternoon, Phelps assumed command of his brigade, which consisted of four New York regiments and the 2nd U.S. Sharpshooters. Phelps's brigade, numerically designated as the First Brigade, First Division of the First Corps, had long referred to itself and had been known throughout the army as the Iron Brigade. But this was by no means a unique moniker. Indeed, several Federal brigades, including Phelps's and

Brigadier General Marsena R. Patrick. *Library of Congress.*

115

even Ferrero's Ninth Corps's brigade, were nicknamed the Iron Brigade. It was not until the spring of 1863, when the regiments composing Phelps's brigade were mustered out of service, that Gibbon's more famous brigade, then commanded by Solomon Meredith and consisting of the 2nd, 6th and 7th Wisconsin, 19th Indiana and 24th Michigan, inherited the title of Iron Brigade. These westerners made the name famous, but at South Mountain it was Walter Phelps's brigade, not Gibbon's, that was known as the Iron Brigade.[162]

Unaware of Patrick's difficulties up ahead, Phelps continued to lead his brigade forward until it had advanced right into the gap in the front line. Phelps's men had actually passed beyond Patrick's regiments to the right and left. Noticing that there were no skirmishers out front, Phelps halted his brigade and sent one of his orderlies back to Hatch to explain the situation. Already frustrated at the slow rate of advance, Hatch galloped forward to try and sort things out. After detaching the 2nd Sharpshooters and directing it to the far right of his division's line, Hatch, realizing that Patrick was no longer able to coordinate his advance, ordered Phelps to assume the lead by sending forward his own skirmishers and following behind them at a distance of only thirty or so yards. Phelps did as ordered, and the Federal line was once more in motion. It was a tough, exhausting climb. Minutes later, Phelps's New Yorkers encountered Garnett's skirmish line, and the battle began in earnest.[163]

Garnett's skirmishers fired a few scattered shots before falling back to their main line of battle. Phelps's men pursued, taking aim and firing at the retiring Confederates. Soon, however, they came under what was described as a murderous fire delivered by Garnett's men, well protected behind the stone wall that ran along the summit of the south spur. The fusillade staggered Phelps's line. Major George Cabell, who commanded the 120 men of the 18th Virginia Infantry, noted that the Federal advance ground to a halt with Phelps's men seeking shelter behind trees and rocks. They then opened a heavy fire, which, said Cabell, "was replied to with spirit and vigor for some time." For the next fifteen to twenty minutes, the two sides slugged it out. Phelps's men, in a more exposed position and attacking uphill, were getting the worst of it. General Hatch, who was galloping behind the troops encouraging them on, later wrote that despite the heavy fire and the Confederates' determined resistance, his men displayed "determined courage." Determined or not, Walter Phelps, whose regiments were melting away under this hot fire, realized his men would not be able to sustain this stand-up fight much longer. For Phelps, it was clear what needed to be done; he must order a charge.[164]

As Phelps's men prepared for the charge, their flanks were bolstered by Patrick's wayward regiments. Crowding in on his left were the 35th and 23rd

New York, which, said Patrick, "merged in the general line of battle that was now moving steadily toward the summit of the mountain, under a most galling fire from the enemy posted above us, posted behind the trees and among the rocks." To Phelps's right came Patrick's other two regiments, the 80th and 21st New York. In their advance on the far right of Hatch's line, these two regiments succeeded in driving back the skirmishers of Kemper's Brigade. After this, Colonel Montgomery Corse of the 17th Virginia, in command of Kemper's right wing, heard the action develop along Garnett's front. Believing his right to be endangered, and with his skirmishers falling back, Corse led the 17th, 11th and 56th Virginia to a position behind a stone wall roughly twenty yards to the rear, a position they held until after nightfall and from which they suffered not a few casualties. Of the four hundred men carried into action, Kemper lost seventy-five killed, wounded or missing, roughly 20 percent. Heavier casualties befell Garnett's men, who now faced the charging Federal line.[165]

A soldier of the 30th New York later wrote that the yell of Phelps's men as they charged toward the stone wall "could have been heard a mile away." The blue tide surged forward, up the slopes and directly into Garnett's position. Captain Henry Owen of the 8th Virginia wrote that the Confederates delivered a heavy fire, but the Federals "never paused nor faltered." Colonel Phelps later proudly noted that his men, "with a cheer, moved splendidly to the front, pouring in a deadly fire upon the enemy." The Federals soon crashed over the wall and into Garnett's line, forcing it back. Garnett noted that the 28th Virginia, on the left of his line, gave way first, those men being pressured not only by Phelps in front but also by the 21st and 80th New York of Patrick's brigade, sweeping in against their exposed left. In the center, the 18th and 19th Virginia, after a short, savage combat, were also forced back. There, the 19th Virginia lost its beloved commander, Colonel John Strange, who fell with a mortal wound.

Strange, one of the first graduates of the Virginia Military Institute, was struck down in the thickest of the fray, desperately trying to rally his men. His efforts were in vain, and when the 19th retreated, its stricken colonel was left behind. Captain Brown of the 19th remembered hearing Strange yelling out for his men to "stand firmly" even as the line crumbled around him. General Garnett paid tribute to the fallen colonel, writing that his "tried valor on other fields, and heroic conduct…will secure imperishable honor for his name and memory." Union troops buried Colonel Strange the next morning on the slopes of the mountain.[166]

The retreat of the 28th, 18th and 19th Virginia left only Colonel Eppa Hunton's 8th Virginia on the summit. But it was not long before this regiment, too, fell back. Hunton looked around and saw that the rest of the brigade had fled and that he had just thirty-four men left under his command trying desperately to hold back the advancing Union line. Captain Owen remembered that the regiment "suddenly gave way," rushing to the rear. "There was great confusion," admitted the captain, "and the broken ranks were hard to rally and reform." Long after the war, and with much hindsight, Owen suggested that had Phelps's and Patrick's men continued pursuing the retreating Confederates, they could have taken Turner's Gap "without any difficulty." But this would have been impossible. What the Virginia captain failed to consider was that Phelps's and Patrick's men were by this point thoroughly exhausted, having marched all the way from east of Frederick before attacking uphill against a strong Confederate position. Casualties in Phelps's regiments were heavy. The colonel went into battle that day with just four hundred men. Of this number, he lost ninety-five killed, wounded and missing, or almost one out of every four. Yet his Iron Brigade had turned in a heroic performance, and John Hatch had nothing but the highest

praise for the lumber merchant turned soldier, writing that he had "displayed the most distinguished courage, bringing up and handling his brigade in the most gallant manner."[167]

General John Hatch was himself listed among the casualties that Sunday. Just as his men swept over the stone wall, he fell from the saddle with a severe wound. A bullet passed through his right calf, and such was the severity of the wound that he was carried from the field and forced to relinquish command of the division to General Abner Doubleday. Hatch never truly recovered from his South Mountain wound and, at one point during his convalescence, was confined to his bed for nearly two months. He remained in the army well after the war, although he never again exercised active field command in the Civil War. In October 1893, Hatch's gallantry on September 14, 1862, was recognized with a Medal of Honor.[168]

Colonel Walter Phelps. *Massachusetts Commandery* MOLLUS; *U.S. Army Heritage & Education Center.*

"My Men Were Fighting Like Tigers. Every Man Was a Hero"

The fighting on the south spur did not end when Garnett's line caved in; it continued well into the night. With darkness descending quickly on the mountaintop, the opposing lines were distinguished only by the bright muzzle flashes. Particularly distinctive were the illuminations and thunderous salvos from Lane's guns, still in position on the high ground north of the Mountain House. Before being relieved, the 21st and 80th New York, on the right of the Federal line, took aim at the muzzle flashes and ultimately forced the gunners to withdraw. At last, Captain John Lane's pieces were silent.[169]

About this time, Abner Doubleday's brigade, nearly one thousand men strong, arrived on the summit and relieved Phelps's and Patrick's men on the front line. When Hatch's advance began, these troops formed the rear line of the division, moving out behind Phelps. Thus they had a good view of the contest as they marched forward. A.P. Smith of the 76th New York noted the strange contrast between the "beautiful, quiet, and smiling valley behind, as it lay basking in that clear September sunset, on that lovely Sabbath day," while to the front it was "the smoke and roar of battle." As he neared the front, Smith saw Phelps's men fighting their way over the stone wall "as though the fate of the country depended upon their heroic conduct." Captain George F. Noyes, also of the 76th New York, described it thus: "The air is now filled with shrieking lead, and we hear just ahead of us the cheers and yells of the opposing troops, the never ceasing rattle of musketry, and the awful din of battle." Doubleday's men would soon be drawn into that awful din.[170]

Doubleday learned of Hatch's wounding and of his own elevation to divisional command as his men approached the front. He then turned command of his brigade over to Colonel William Wainwright of the 76th New York. Moving forward, Wainwright was greeted by Phelps's adjutant, who was screaming, "Our brigade cannot sustain itself much longer, as we are nearly out of ammunition. For God's sake, to the front!" This quickened the pace, but by the time Wainwright's men reached the front, Garnett's line had fled, and the action, for the moment, had abated. Phelps's men stepped aside, replaced by Wainwright's fresh troops. With his men going into position, Wainwright detected movement to his left front. Confederates, he believed, were attempting to turn his left flank. What Wainwright saw was the advance of several regiments from Jenkins's Brigade, under Walker, sent forward to bolster the Confederate line.[171]

When Garnett's line collapsed, not all of his men fled the field. Indeed, behind a stone wall roughly two hundred yards back from their initial position, some of Garnett's men rallied, in small, scattered groups. Captain Owen of the 8th Virginia was among them. He believed that fully half of

Garnett's Brigade had disappeared, but "the survivors made a stand along the fence and endeavored to hold the enemy back until reinforcements could be brought up." They formed in squads, said Owen, "with great gaps between them and were scattered along behind the fence and bushes for half a mile, while the enemy had a strong line in front and outflanked our position on both the right and left." The Virginia captain noticed that to his right was his commander, Eppa Hunton, with a small contingent of soldiers, and then a gap, perhaps fifty yards, before he saw another group of maybe a dozen men. Major George Cabell of the 18th Virginia arrived, as did Garnett, and together they brought up another one hundred additional troops, including some from Kemper's Brigade. There, they determined to make another stand. "The sun was now behind the mountains," said Owen, "and the somber shadows of night were settling down over the smoky, bloodstained field." But there was to be yet more killing and more bloodshed.[172]

Colonel Joseph Walker initially placed his South Carolinians well to the rear of Garnett's right flank. When he saw the Virginians rally behind the stone wall to his front, Walker deemed it time to send his men forward. The 1st, 5th and 6th South Carolina soon shouldered in with the Virginians, and together the Confederates opened fire on Wainwright's men, just then arriving in position. George Noyes described "a mere pattering of musketry" as the Federal line first went into position, "then the rebel storm bursts forth afresh, and before it some of our men go down, or slowly fall back, wounded and bleeding." Some of Wainwright's uninjured men also fled from the field, unnerved. Order was restored, and the Federal troops soon began returning fire. Wainwright feared the Confederates would rush forward and strike his exposed left; he thus sought to wheel two of his regiments—the 7th Indiana and 76th New York—to the left. But the men balked, unwilling to advance into the unknown darkness. Sergeant Charlie Stamp could not believe his eyes. He rushed forward, planted the flag defiantly and yelled back to his men, "There! Come to that!" These words had hardly escaped his lips before he collapsed dead to the ground, "mustered out of the army militant," mused A.P. Smith of the 76th New York, "and mustered into the army triumphant."[173]

Stamp's example may have inspired the men, who increased the fury of their fire. "Colonel Wainwright coolly rode along the line and directed the men to fire low," explained Smith, "and never was powder and ball rammed into guns with greater energy, or discharged with greater rapidity, or more damaging effect." This seemed to do the trick, for the Confederate fire noticeably slackened. Then things grew quiet. Union troops were squinting to their front, trying to peer through the sheer darkness that had by this point entirely enshrouded the mountain. Convinced the Confederates had fled, Wainwright's men began to congratulate themselves when "suddenly out of the darkness in front" another volley tore into the blue line. Remnants of the 18th and 19th Virginia, for whatever the reason, leaped the stone fence and renewed the attack. The initial volley struck down Colonel Wainwright, shot through the arm and wounded, while his horse fell dead. Rising to his feet, a stunned Wainwright calmly tied a handkerchief around his heavily bleeding arm and then yelled for his command to open fire, himself emptying all six rounds of his revolver toward the enemy line. The Confederates were so near, said A.P. Smith, "that the blaze of our guns almost reached their faces." The fire was kept up for some time, although, as Abner Doubleday wrote, it was "too dark to see objects distinctly." Wainwright's men ran out of bullets and were replaced on the front line by Colonel William Christian's brigade of Ricketts's division, recently arrived on the field. To its right and forming a loose connection with the left of Meade's line, went Brigadier General George Hartsuff's brigade, also of Ricketts's division. "A few volleys from Ricketts ended the contest in about thirty minutes," said Doubleday, and the Confederates at last deserted the field.[174]

The shattered elements of Walker's, Garnett's and Kemper's brigades were ordered to fall back toward Turner's Gap. Near the Mountain House, they joined the fatigued survivors from Rodes's and Stevens's Brigades. These men had put up a tough, determined stand on the mountain, but they could not prevent Meade and Hatch from gaining the high ground north of the National Pike and turning the Confederate left. The price they paid for this stubborn resistance was heavy. In addition to the more than 400 casualties in Rodes's Brigade and the 210 lost in Stevens's command in their action with Meade's Pennsylvanians, Garnett suffered a near 50 percent loss, losing 196 of his 400. Kemper's and Walker's casualties were comparatively lighter, for they were not as heavily engaged. Kemper, as was noted, lost 75 men, while Walker lost just 32 men total. In Hatch's attack up the south spur, Phelps's brigade suffered the highest loss, with 95 men killed, wounded and missing. Doubleday's brigade, primarily under Wainwright's command during its heaviest fighting, lost 60 men, while Marsena Patrick counted just 25 casualties out of the 850 men he took into action. Total losses in Christian's and Hartsuff's brigades, which had arrived late on the field, were 4 men killed and 10 wounded.

Yet the Federal brigade that suffered the highest losses in the First Corps at South Mountain was neither under Meade as he attacked up the north spur nor with Hatch as he swept up the south spur. Instead, it was John Gibbon's brigade, which had been detached by Burnside at Bolivar and sent forward in an attack directly up the National Pike. And while both the right and left flanks of the Confederate army had been turned respectively by the Ninth and First Corps, its center, defended by Alfred Colquitt's Brigade directly astride the turnpike and immediately to the front of Turner's Gap, held.

Although born near Philadelphia, John Gibbon spent most of his childhood in North Carolina. An 1847 graduate of West Point, where he matriculated alongside other such Civil War notables as Ambrose Burnside and Ambrose Powell Hill, Gibbon saw some service in Mexico and in Florida battling the Seminole. An artillerist par excellence, Gibbon commanded the famed Battery B, 4th U.S. Artillery, at the outset of civil war, and while three of his brothers would don Confederate gray during the war, Gibbon maintained his loyalty to the United States. For the first year of the conflict, Gibbon served as General Irvin McDowell's chief of artillery, but in early May 1862, he received a brigadier general's commission and was placed in command of the Army of the Potomac's only all-western infantry brigade, consisting at the time of three regiments from Wisconsin and one from Indiana. Through his efforts, this brigade fast became one of the army's best-drilled, hardest-fighting, most feared units. At his insistence, his men wore their black Hardee hats instead of the regulation blue kepis, and because of this, Gibbon's brigade was soon known in both armies as the "Black Hat Brigade." In early 1863, and by then joined by the 24th Michigan, it adopted another moniker for which it is much better known today: the Iron Brigade. And although it may not have been the original or the only Iron Brigade, it certainly became the most famous one.[175]

During his days in the regular army, Gibbon befriended another adopted son of North Carolina, Daniel Harvey Hill, and had even served as a groomsman at Hill's wedding. On the evening of September 14, 1862, Gibbon would lead his westerners directly toward Hill's men defending Turner's Gap. While the rest of Hooker's First Corps deployed on the fields north of the National Pike, Gibbon's "Black Hat Brigade" halted a short distance west of Bolivar. There it waited as Meade and Hatch completed their deployments, some men boiling up coffee and some doubtlessly taking a short nap while others penned letters home. For two hours, they waited, exposed to Confederate artillery fire; one shell exploded in the ranks of the 2nd Wisconsin Infantry, killing four men and wounding three others. Finally, near 5:00 p.m., the orders went out, and Gibbon's men formed for the attack.

Gibbon formed his men on either side of the National Pike. To the right, or north of the roadway, went Captain John Callis's 7th Wisconsin. Behind the 7th, at nearly two hundred yards, was Colonel Edward Bragg's 6th

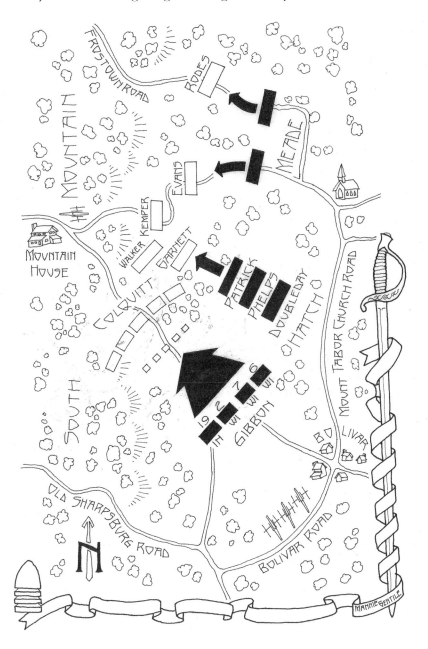

Wisconsin. South of the turnpike and to the left of the 7th Wisconsin went Colonel Solomon Meredith's 19th Indiana, while behind it, again at nearly two hundred yards, went the 2nd Wisconsin under Colonel Lucius Fairchild. In all, Gibbon went forward with roughly thirteen hundred men. Two

Brigadier General John Gibbon. *Library of Congress.*

companies of the 2nd Wisconsin, under the command of Captain Wilson Colwell, screened the advance south of the turnpike, while to the north two companies of the 6th Wisconsin went forward first as skirmishers. Two guns from Battery B, 4th U.S., under Lieutenant James Stewart, also moved ahead with Gibbon's advance. Unlimbering along the turnpike, Stewart's trained gunners began throwing shells into Colquitt's line stretched out along the road, near the summit.

Alfred Colquitt could not have asked for a better defensive position. Since very early that Sunday morning—indeed, even before the battle's opening shots at Fox's Gap—Colquitt's men had been in position astride the National Pike roughly half a mile east of the Mountain House. Two of his regiments—the 23rd and 28th Georgia, each numbering about three hundred men—formed north of the pike, their line extending up the steep and wooded slopes of the south spur, the men protected by a stone wall, which nearly ran the length of their line. South of the road, forming the right of Colquitt's line, went the 6th and 27th Georgia and the 13th Alabama, their combined numbers totaling roughly seven hundred men. These veterans stretched across a deep and heavily wooded ravine, which dropped precipitately from the National Pike. Approaching the Confederate position, the National Pike passed through a narrow defile and ascended the mountain at a steep grade, making Colquitt's defensive line an ideal one. Troops on the north side could easily command the roadway at an enfilade, and any attack would, of course, be made up a steep hill.

Not only did Colquitt have the defensive advantage, but he also had approximately the same number of men as Gibbon; thus, the odds were stacked heavily in his favor. Looking at the Confederate position from the base, Lieutenant Frank Haskell of Gibbon's staff may have said it best when he declared it was "an ugly place to attack." Colquitt had thrown out a heavy skirmish force in front of his main line. On the left, two companies each from the 23rd and 28th Georgia went forward, descending the eastern slope of the mountain, while south of the pike, four companies of skirmishers, commanded by Captain William M. Arnold, advanced about four hundred yards in front

Colonel Alfred Colquitt. *The Photographic History of the Civil War.*

of Colquitt's right, taking up sheltered positions in a thick wood lot, behind stone walls and boulders and even in the two-story house of D. Beachley. There they awaited Gibbon's advancing lines.[176]

Major Rufus Dawes of the 6th Wisconsin infantry, advancing behind the 7th Wisconsin on the right of the pike, looked off to his right soon after the orders arrived to advance and was awed by the sight of Meade's and Hatch's divisions just then sweeping forward. "Two miles away on our right, long lines and heavy columns of dark blue infantry could be seen pressing up the green slopes of the mountain, their bayonets flashing like silver in the ray of the setting sun, and their banners waving in beautiful relief against the background of green." Soon scattered musket fire to the front broke out, demanding Dawes's attention forward; the Federal skirmishers had made first contact with Colquitt's advanced troops. The gunfire soon escalated as the skirmishers of the 6th Wisconsin slowly but steadily drove back their Confederate foes. To Dawes, it was a "deadly game of 'Bo-Peep,'" the men "hiding behind logs, fences, rocks, and bushes" as they advanced. Sergeant James Sullivan of the 6th, who was on the skirmish line, remembered that "the utmost enthusiasm prevailed and our fellows were as cool and collected as if at target practice, and, in fact, on more than one occasion when gathered behind a boulder, one would ask the other to watch his shot and see where he hit." The blue line crept steadily forward in the growing twilight, "fighting," said Dawes, "for every inch of ground."

"It was now sundown," noted Sergeant Sullivan, "and being in the shadow of the mountain, it was getting dark very fast." Above the growing rattle of musket fire and between the thunderous din of Stewart's two pieces, the men could hear the familiar voice of Gibbon, on horseback and shouting, "Forward! Forward! Forward!"[177]

South of the pike, Colwell's skirmishers of the 2nd Wisconsin also came under fire, with shots ringing out from seemingly every direction by Arnold's well-placed and well-protected Confederates. Wisconsin men fell at almost every step, including Wilson Colwell, a one-time mayor of La Crosse, much admired by his men. To George Otis of the 2nd, Colwell was "an excellent adviser, a true gentleman, a thorough disciplinarian, and brave soldier." Colwell breathed his last within the hour.[178]

Seeing the skirmishers come under this heavy fire, Colonel "Long Sol" Meredith deployed his 19th Indiana into lines of battle. "We moved slowly and cautiously, but steadily forward," recorded the Indiana colonel. Noticing a large woodlot to the left of the 19th Indiana, Gibbon directed Meredith to send a few companies in that direction to flush out any Confederates that may be there. Meredith must have misunderstood, for he wheeled his entire regiment to the left. Gibbon sent forward Lieutenant Haskell, who got things sorted out. Soon, the 19th was moving in the right direction, with Meredith detaching Company B under nineteen-year-old Captain W.W. Dudley to advance on his left as flankers. But Meredith's wheeling maneuver had opened a gap between his right flank and the National Pike. To plug this gap, Colonel Fairchild was directed to move his 2nd Wisconsin forward and form on the right of the 19th Indiana. On the left, Colonel Meredith's attention was drawn to an incessant and annoying fire coming from the Beachley house. He sent his son, who served on his staff, galloping off to Lieutenant Stewart. "Father wants you to put a shot in that house; it is full of rebel sharpshooters," said the young man.

Not knowing who he was, just that he was "the youngest and tallest, as well as the thinnest" man he ever saw, Stewart barked back, "Who in thunder is your father?"

When told, the artillerist demanded a written order. The young Meredith galloped off, and minutes later Colonel Meredith himself came trotting over with the same request. Stewart now repositioned his two guns, turning their barrels toward the house, and delivered several well-aimed shots—one passing directly through the second floor—which, noted Meredith, caused a "general stampede" of the Confederates out of the building, "enabling us to go forward more rapidly and with less loss from their sharpshooters."[179]

Confederate skirmishers may have been driven out of the Beachley home, but it was not long before they began popping away once more at Meredith's advancing Hoosiers. The Indiana colonel now relied on his sheer weight of numbers, ordering his men to attack. The fire grew lively between the concealed Confederates and the more exposed Indiana soldiers. Despite some casualties, Meredith's men "gave a shout and pressed forward."

"It was a magnificent sight," wrote a proud Colonel Meredith, "to see the boys of the Nineteenth going forward, crowding the enemy, cheering all the time." The Confederate skirmishers gave way, falling back three-quarters of a mile to Captain Arnold's main skirmish line, in position behind a stout, stone wall that ran at right angles from the National Pike. Meredith's men, now joined by the 2nd Wisconsin on their right, moved forward on the heels of the retiring Confederates.[180]

Gibbon's men to the north of the National Pike were having a less difficult time advancing; however, they would pay a deadly price for having outdistanced the regiments south of the road. The two companies of skirmishers from the 6th Wisconsin continued to press forward, with the 7th following one hundred yards behind. Passing through a field of head-high corn, the Wisconsin men emerged in an open field when they came under a sudden and deadly blast from the skirmishers of the 23rd Georgia posted behind a stone wall just forty paces away. The Federal skirmishers were called in, and Callis quickly deployed his regiment for the attack. There was no protection for the 7th, yet the regiment moved forward with its left anchored on the National Pike and its right stretching toward a woodlot on the southern slopes of the south spur. No sooner had Callis's men advanced, however, than a destructive enfilading fire opened on them from a Confederate force behind a stone fence on the other side of the pike. This was Captain Arnold's skirmish force, not yet engaged on its front with Meredith's and Fairchild's men, who were at this point still moving forward. Until attacked in front, Arnold's men were able to pour a deadly, short-range fire across the pike and into the 7th's left flank. Callis's men naturally drifted in that direction and opened fire on Arnold's men. However, this left oblique exposed their right flank and rear to an equally deadly fire, which erupted from skirmishers of the 28th Georgia, well protected in a woodlot on the slope of the south spur. Callis's men, taking a heavy fire from three sides, defiantly held their ground, trading shots with their equally determined adversaries. It was at this point, said Colquitt, watching from above, that "the fight opened in earnest."[181]

Much to the relief of the 7th, Meredith's and Fairchild's regiments soon struck Arnold's skirmish line south of the pike, alleviating the flanking fire Callis's men had been taking on their left. The 19th Indiana and 2nd Wisconsin came under heavy fire but quickly returned it in intensity, showering the Confederate line with bullets. Meredith then ordered Company G on the left of his line to wheel around and strike Arnold's line in the flank and rear. Captain Clark executed the maneuver, forcing Arnold's men from the stone wall. With some satisfaction, Meredith wrote that Clark's flank attack also "gave us an opportunity of pouring upon [Arnold's men] a raking fire as they retreated." Eleven Georgians, unable to get away, fell into Union hands, while the front of the 19th Indiana and 2nd Wisconsin had been cleared.[182]

"After expending 20 rounds of ammunition," wrote Colonel Fairchild of the 2nd Wisconsin, "I discovered the enemy had entirely disappeared from our front." Looking across the National Pike, he could see Callis's men of the 7th dropping one after the other as they dealt with the 23rd Georgia's skirmishers to their front and those of the 28th on their right. He instinctively turned his regiment to the right, and the men of the 2nd soon began firing into the right flank of the 23rd Georgia across the pike. Fairchild's men kept up this fire until they exhausted their ammunition, at which point they fell back, their place taken by Meredith's 19th Indiana. Although Meredith later credited this action with causing the 23rd Georgia to abandon its position, this fire was largely ineffective in its execution. Regardless, Callis's men no doubt appreciated the support.[183]

As this action raged to the left of the 7th, across the National Pike, the 6th Wisconsin was at the same time double-quicking its way to Callis's right. The 6th had been advancing behind the 7th when Callis's men came under fire. Rufus Dawes remembered seeing the fire that erupted on the 7th's right flank, writing that from the woodlot on the slope there was "a flame of musketry which sent a shower of bullets into the backs" of Callis's men. Gibbon ordered Colonel Bragg to move his regiment to the right and flank the 28th Georgia. "The condition of the surface of the ground, and the steepness of the ascent up the mountain side, rendered this movement a difficult one," recorded Bragg, "but without hesitation the left wing moved by the flank and into the wood, firing as they went, and advancing the line." Major Dawes echoed Bragg's words, writing that the men "hurried over the rough and stony field with the utmost zeal, and while many men were struck by the bullets of the enemy, there was neither hesitation nor confusion." Bragg was able to position his regiment in a semicircular fashion around the left flank of the 28th Georgia, which continued to deliver what Bragg termed a "terrific [fire] from behind rocks and trees, and entirely under cover." At times, the lines of battle were so close that the opposing sides traded barbs with one another. Dawes remembered a Confederate shouting from behind a stone wall, "Oh, you damned Yanks! We gave you hell at Bull Run!"

"Never mind, Johnny," responded a Wisconsin soldier, "it's no McDowell after you now. 'Little Mac' and 'Johnny Gibbon' are after you now!"[184]

Gradually, the Confederate skirmish line gave way, and the sounds of battle disappeared into the night. There was, however, yet one more flare-up. On the right of Gibbon's line, Bragg's men were just beginning to settle down when they came under a brisk fire from a Confederate force that had crept close to the Federal line. Bragg's men returned the fire, which silenced their opponents' guns and drove them back. The soldiers of the 6th then gave three cheers and "sat cheerfully down to await another attack; but the enemy was no more seen." The Wisconsin men were, for the most part, entirely out of ammunition. Captain Callis of the battered 7th Wisconsin reported this to Gibbon, but the brigade commander coolly responded by telling him to "hold the ground at the point of the bayonet." Callis then ordered his men to lie down and find bullets from the cartridge boxes of the dead and wounded.[185]

In a day when Confederate forces were driven from nearly every point, Colquitt could take great pride in the fact that his men held their position against Gibbon's fierce attack. "Not an inch of ground was yielded," crowed Colquitt in his report of the day's fighting. D.H. Hill was equally prideful, writing that although the skirmishers were driven in, "the line of battle on both sides of the road was the same at 10 o'clock at night as it was at 9 o'clock in the morning." Casualties in Colquitt's Brigade totaled 110 men killed, wounded, captured or missing, less than a 10 percent loss. They inflicted a much higher loss on Gibbon's Black Hat Brigade. Thirty-seven of Gibbon's men were killed; another 251 were listed among the wounded, while 30 went down on the rolls as missing in action. Gibbon's losses totaled 318, or nearly 25 percent of his brigade's force. The 7th Wisconsin suffered the lion's share of casualties, losing 147 men in its desperate fight north of the National Pike. Not only was the number of casualties in Gibbon's brigade the highest in the First Corps, but it was also the highest of all the Army of the Potomac's brigades engaged that day at South Mountain, whether at Frostown, Fox's or Crampton's Gap.[186]

"The night was chilly, and in the woods intensely dark," wrote Rufus Dawes.

> *Our wounded were scattered over a great distance up and down the mountain, and were suffering untold agonies. Owing the difficulties of the ground and the night, no stretcher bearers had come upon the field. Several dying men were pleading piteously for water, of which there was not a drop in the regiment, nor was there any liquor.*

While the rest of Gibbon's brigade was relieved several hours later by Brigadier General Willis Gorman's brigade of John Sedgwick's Second Corps division, the 6th Wisconsin remained in its position all night in the dark woods along the southern slopes of the south spur after a thoroughly exhausting day. All around it, said Dawes, was the "dread reality of war…upon the cold, hard stones."[187]

Alfred Pleasonton was correct. Early that morning, as the Kanawha Division marched westward along the National Pike toward South Mountain, the cavalry commander told Jacob Cox that Turner's Gap was too well and too heavily defended for a direct attack. The casualties sustained by Gibbon proved this. Still, even though the Confederates technically held on to Turner's Gap, it was hard to contain the elation at Union army headquarters. McClellan relished in the reports. The Ninth Corps was able to drive the Rebels from Fox's Gap, thus turning the Confederate right flank. Add to that Joe Hooker's success in entirely routing the Confederate left and sweeping up the almost impossible terrain north of the gap. And not only had they achieved decisive tactical successes, but Reno's and Hooker's men had also exacted a heavy toll upon their foe.

That night, at 9:40 p.m., and just as his men were settling into bivouac on the damp, chilly slopes of South Mountain, George McClellan wired Henry Halleck. "After a very severe engagement the Corps of Hooker and Reno have carried the heights…The troops behaved magnificently. They never fought better," boasted the army commander. "It has been a glorious victory; I cannot yet tell whether the enemy will retreat during the night or appear in increased force in the morning," concluded McClellan, but "I am hurrying up everything from the rear to be prepared for any eventuality."[188]

When McClellan sent off this jubilant note to Halleck, he only reported on the action that had unfolded to his immediate front. As he made clear in the message, he did not yet know the results of General William Franklin's efforts at Crampton's Gap, six miles to the south. Had he known, he doubtlessly would have been even more euphoric.

4

"The Victory Was Decisive and Complete"

The Battle of Crampton's Gap

George M. Neese, a gunner in Chew's Battery of Confederate horse artillery, remembered that "the shades of night were still lingering over the landscape" early on the morning of Sunday, September 14, 1862, when he and his fellow artillerists left their camps on the western base of South Mountain and made their way to the summit. By the time the first gray light of dawn began spreading across the western Maryland sky, the gunners had arrived on the mountaintop at Crampton's Gap. Several miles to the east rose the Catoctin Mountains, which must have appeared at that early hour as dark, shadowy silhouettes, while stretched out immediately before Neese and his comrades was the "beautiful Middletown Valley…with its wooded hills, pleasant fields, hamlets, and towns reposing in the quiet calm of a peaceful Sabbath morning." Yet that quiet calm would soon be shaken. As Neese recorded:

> *Before the sun shot its first golden lance across the Catoctin range to kiss away the early dew, the booming of Yankee cannon came rolling across from the Catoctin hills, announcing in ominous thunder tones that the Yankee hosts were advancing, and that there would be but little Sunday for soldiers to-day in this part of Uncle Sam's domain.*

With the Federal advance now detected, Chew's artillerists moved halfway down the eastern slope of the mountain "and went in battery ready to work on the first bluecoats that ventured within range of our guns."[189]

The bluecoats Neese heard advancing "in ominous thunder tones" were the veteran soldiers of the Army of the Potomac's Sixth Corps. Like their adversaries across the valley, the men of the Sixth Corps were awake well before daybreak that morning, cooking their breakfasts and preparing for the day ahead. By 5:30 a.m., they were on the move. From their camps near Buckeystown, more than four miles east of Jefferson, the Sixth Corps marched west and soon began a laborious climb over Catoctin Mountain at Mountville Pass. "The ascent was long and very tedious," remembered George Bicknell of the 5th Maine, "but when upon the opposite side of the summit, the view was most magnificent." The beauty of the valley left as vivid an impression on Bicknell as it had on the Confederate gunner Neese. "A valley extending for miles, dotted here and there with snow-white villas, with little streams flowing in various directions, abounding with beautiful groves and fields, lay spread out before us," wrote the officer from Maine, concluding that it was "the loveliest landscape" he ever beheld.[190]

At the outset of the Maryland Campaign, the Sixth Corps numbered nearly thirteen thousand men and was composed of two divisions, each consisting of three brigades. Commanding the First Division was Major General Henry Warner Slocum, a solid and generally reliable officer who at age thirty-four was among the youngest generals in the Army of the Potomac. Colonels Joseph J. Bartlett and Alfred T.A. Torbert and Brigadier General John Newton commanded Slocum's three brigades, which were destined to bear the heaviest fighting and suffer the highest casualties that day at Crampton's Gap. Major General William Farrar Smith led the Sixth Corps's Second Division. Of the three brigades in Smith's division—commanded respectively by Winfield Scott Hancock, William T.H. Brooks and William Irwin—only Brooks's all-Vermont brigade would be engaged that Sunday. Excepting a handful of newly raised regiments, the Sixth Corps was made up of hard-fighting, veteran units that had witnessed much action earlier that year during the Peninsula and Seven Days' Campaigns.

Thirty-nine-year-old Major General William Buel Franklin, a career military man and gifted engineer, commanded the Sixth Corps. Although he was by most accounts an exceedingly cautious general who did not perform well in independent command, Franklin's close association with George McClellan was a large factor in his promotion to major general and his appointment to command of the Army of the Potomac's Sixth Corps. This naturally secured Franklin's unwavering support of McClellan and his highest esteem for the commanding general. Although McClellan did not necessarily return such high veneration for Franklin, the two did remain close associates.[191]

In his plans for September 14, McClellan expected much from Franklin and the soldiers of his Sixth Corps. Indeed, on their shoulders would rest the key component of carrying out his plan of cutting Lee in two and beating him in detail. While Burnside led his right wing—the First and Ninth Corps—across South Mountain at Turner's Gap and did battle with the main Confederate body under Longstreet and D.H. Hill, Franklin was to punch through the mountain at Crampton's Gap, some six miles to the south, and thus drive a wedge between Lee's divided columns while lifting the siege of Harpers Ferry by disposing of McLaws's force on Maryland Heights.

Major General William B. Franklin. *Library of Congress.*

Franklin received his orders late on the evening of September 13. McClellan left little room for doubt in his instructions. After first informing Franklin that Couch's Fourth Corps Division had been ordered to join the Sixth Corps "as rapidly as possible," but cautioning him not to await its arrival, McClellan directed Franklin to "move at daybreak in the morning by Jefferson and Burkittsville upon the road to Rohrersville," crossing South Mountain at Crampton's Gap. If Franklin found that the pass was not defended "in force," he was to "seize it as soon as practicable & debouch upon Rohrersville in order to cut off the retreat or destroy McLaws's command" on Maryland Heights. If, however, Franklin discovered "the pass held by the enemy in large force," he was to mass his columns and attack. After gaining the pass, Franklin was then instructed to first "cut off, destroy or capture McLaws's command & relieve Col. Miles" and the beleaguered garrison at Harpers Ferry. From there, Miles's liberated Federals were to link up with Franklin's Sixth Corps, and the augmented force would then move north toward Boonsboro "if the main column"—the First and Ninth Corps under Burnside—"had not succeeded in its attack." However, if Burnside's men had successfully carried Turner's Gap, Franklin was to then "take the road from Rohrersville to Sharpsburg & Williamsport in order either to cut off the retreat of Hill & Longstreet towards the Potomac, or to prevent the repassage of Jackson." McClellan further instructed Franklin to provide him with hourly updates of his movements and urged him to take strong steps to "prevent straggling and bring every available man into action." In concluding his directive, and in language that may have indicated his reservations about trusting such an important assignment to Franklin, McClellan wrote, "I believe I have sufficiently explained my intentions, I ask of you at this important moment all your intellect & the utmost activity that a general can exercise."[192]

After reading his orders and before turning in for the night, Franklin, at 10:00 p.m., sent word back to McClellan: "I have received your orders...understand them, and will do my best to carry them out. My command will commence its movement at 5 ½ A.M."[193]

True to his word, Franklin had his soldiers on the road early the following morning. Climbing the steep grade over Catoctin Mountain, the Sixth Corps set a good pace, covering more than four miles in roughly three and a half hours of tough marching and reaching Jefferson sometime after 9:00 a.m. Once in Jefferson, however, Franklin incredulously called a halt. He did so, he explained, "to afford General Couch an opportunity of coming up," despite his specific instruction from McClellan not to do so. For William Franklin, the day had gotten off to an inauspicious start. Yet his delay that morning was only a harbinger of things to come.[194]

The Sixth Corps spent nearly an hour in Jefferson, during which time the men could hear the faint though ominous sounds of battle drifting in from the northwest, where Cox's Ohioans and Garland's North Carolinians were just then slugging it out for control of Fox's Gap. Captain John Boyle of the 96th Pennsylvania later recorded that as he looked west toward South Mountain, "the smoke from the enemy's cannon planted...away off to the right, could be distinctly traced against the mountain background, and their dull, heavy thunder which 'told that battle was on again,' heard when the wind flowed from that direction."[195] Finally, and only after ascertaining that Couch's division was "still some distance in the rear," Franklin ordered his men back on the road. Six and a half miles ahead, across rolling land, lay Burkittsville, with Crampton's Gap looming beyond.[196]

Company F of Rush's Lancers, which had remained in Jefferson the previous night, screened Franklin's advance. Following closely behind the horsemen was the 96th Pennsylvania of Bartlett's brigade in the van of the entire Sixth Corps, its every step plainly visible to Confederate troops atop South Mountain. Gunner George Neese of Chew's Battery, still in position halfway up the eastern slope just below Crampton's Gap, watched "the Yankee host, about three miles away, approaching our gap cautiously and slowly. As they drew nearer, the whole country seemed to be full of bluecoats. They were so numerous," concluded the artillerist, "that it looked as if they were creeping up out of the ground."[197]

The approach of Franklin's blue columns must have been an unnerving sight even for the experienced Confederates tasked with the difficult assignment of defending the mountain passes, both at Crampton's Gap and at Brownsville Pass, a little more than one mile farther south. While Franklin could count nearly thirteen thousand men in his Sixth Corps, the entire Confederate force was skeletal at best. Making matters worse for the Confederates was the fact that they did not know which of the passes—Crampton's or Brownsville—the Federals would attempt to force their way through.

Three days earlier, when Lafayette McLaws's combined force had crossed South Mountain at Brownsville Pass and proceeded toward Maryland Heights, General Paul Semmes's mixed brigade of Georgia and Virginia soldiers was detached in Pleasant Valley with instructions to guard the rear of the column by defending the mountain passes. On September 13, McLaws sent Semmes some reinforcements in the form of Mahone's undersized brigade from R.H. Anderson's Division.

Semmes placed three of his regiments—the 53rd Georgia and 15th and 32nd Virginia—at Brownsville Pass, along with Captain Basil Manley's Battery A, 1st North Carolina Light Artillery, while keeping the 10th Georgia in Pleasant Valley to picket the Rohrersville Road.[198] Mahone's Brigade, consisting of the 6th, 12th, 16th and 41st Virginia Infantry regiments, was the smaller of the two brigades at Semmes's disposal, totaling just 520 men on the morning of September 14.[199] Since Second Manassas, where "Little Billy" Mahone had fallen wounded, the brigade was commanded by Colonel William Allen Parham, a thirty-two-year-old native of Sussex County, Virginia, who was described as a "generous, brave, high spirited gentleman."[200] Early on the morning of September 14, Semmes ordered Parham's regiments to Crampton's Gap, minus the 41st Virginia, which he sent to Solomon's Gap on Elk Ridge as per McLaws's instruction to protect the rear of General Joseph Kershaw's Brigade. Semmes also instructed Parham to call on the 10th Georgia in Pleasant Valley should it become necessary. Semmes, the highest-ranking officer in this sector, decided to remain at Brownsville Pass, convinced that the Federals would attempt passage there.[201]

When Parham's regiments reached Crampton's Gap, they joined Colonel Thomas Munford's small cavalry force, which had been forced back from

Jefferson to Burkittsville the previous day. Earlier that Sunday morning, the size of the Confederate force in the area of Crampton's Gap had been considerably larger. Wade Hampton's entire brigade of horsemen had been present. However, when Jeb Stuart reached Burkittsville early that morning after placing Thomas Rosser's 5th Virginia Cavalry at Fox's Gap, he did not detect any Federal movement east of the village and wrongly guessed that McClellan was sending the Harpers Ferry relief force farther south along the Potomac. Stuart thus ordered Hampton to move to Knoxville at the southern end of South Mountain, leaving only Munford with his 2nd and 12th Virginia Cavalry regiments—some 275 men in all—plus Chew's Battery at Crampton's Gap. Stuart then galloped out of the picture when he set off to assist McLaws in the siege of Harpers Ferry. Colonel Munford, an 1852 graduate of the Virginia Military Academy, was now left in command and saddled with the unenviable task of defending Crampton's Gap.[202]

Neither Munford at Crampton's Gap nor Semmes at Brownsville Pass needed to be reminded of the importance of holding the passes and preventing the Federals from forcing their way through. Should these gaps

fall, McLaws's command on Maryland Heights would be cut off, and Lee's entire army would be greatly imperiled. Like D.H. Hill's men some six miles north, these Confederates had to hold on at all hazards. As Franklin's blue column continued to draw closer, the anxieties of the outnumbered Confederates surely mounted.

About noon, Rush's Lancers of the 6th Pennsylvania Cavalry, riding at the head of Franklin's column, neared Burkittsville—a sleepy little village of about two hundred residents—and promptly came under fire from Munford's pickets of the 2nd Virginia Cavalry. The Federal horsemen fell back and reported the encounter to Colonel Henry

Colonel Thomas Munford. *The Photographic History of the Civil War.*

Cake of the 96th Pennsylvania, who immediately deployed Companies A and F of his regiment as skirmishers. The two companies advanced toward Burkittsville, slowly driving back Munford's men, who stubbornly resisted the Pennsylvanians' advance from behind every house and outbuilding.[203] Cake's skirmishers cleared the town and made it to within several hundred yards of the main Confederate line, in position behind a stone wall along Mountain Church Road at the base of South Mountain. As Companies A and F pushed through Burkittsville, the remaining eight companies of the 96th advanced to the eastern edge of the village and took up a position along the Knoxville road, running south of town. As the Pennsylvanians moved forward, they drew fire from the Confederate artillery pieces posted on the mountain—from Chew's Battery below Crampton's Gap and from Captain Manly's North Carolina battery at Brownsville Pass to the south. Although noisy and no doubt uncomfortable for the Pennsylvanians, this artillery fire was largely ineffective.[204]

While his skirmishers traded shots with Munford's and Parham's men behind the stone wall at the base of the mountain, Cake sought out local inhabitants in an effort to determine the size and strength of the Confederate force to his front. He interviewed an elderly resident named Otho Harley. According to Private Henry Boyer of the 96th, Harley "began at once to beg that the battle might not take place there. He declared the town to be Union almost to a man—that all the Secessionists were off in the Southern army." After assuring the frightened man that the battle would most likely occur west of town, Cake asked Harley what he knew of the Confederates in the area. "He said they intended to fight," recorded Boyer, "and did not dream of defeat." Harley greatly overestimated the Confederate force as totaling four thousand infantry, several hundred cavalry and at least two cannons. About this same time, Cake learned that his skirmishers had uncovered the main enemy body drawn up at the base of South Mountain. Cake then reported all this information, including Harley's inflated estimate, to his superiors.[205]

While Cake and his 96th Pennsylvania remained busy at the front, the rest of the Sixth Corps continued to make its way toward Burkittsville. Slocum led the balance of his division to a location roughly half a mile east of the village, while Smith's Second Division followed closely behind. Several Federal batteries were ordered into action, including Captain John Wolcott's Battery A, Maryland Light Artillery, and Captain Josiah Porter's Battery A, Massachusetts Light Artillery, which unlimbered on high ground east of town and to the south of the main road through Burkittsville, quickly exchanging rounds with Manly's guns in Brownsville Pass. Captain Romeyn Ayres's Battery F, 5th U.S. Artillery, of Smith's division also went into position, north of the road and to the rear of Wolcott's guns. Excepting these gunners and the men of the 96th Pennsylvania on the skirmish line in Burkittsville, the Sixth Corps soldiers started fires and prepared a midday meal, following the lead of their corps commander Franklin, who had just arrived on the scene.[206]

Shortly after noon, as the cannon fire began to intensify, William Franklin established his headquarters near the stately home of Martin Shafer—one mile east of Burkittsville—and then sat down to enjoy a bite to eat. He granted his footsore soldiers a reprieve, as they had covered the six miles from Jefferson in just over two hours. While his men caught their breaths, and just after he established headquarters, Franklin received an urgent note from McClellan, who was at that time overseeing Burnside's fight well to the north. "I have just been informed that the enemy have about 1500 cavalry and some artillery at Burkheadsville [sic] and that they are in considerable force in vicinity of Boonsboro," wrote the army commander. "Please lose no time in driving the rebel cavalry out of Burkheadsville [sic], and occupying the pass. Let me know first whether the enemy occupies the pass and if so the strength of their force there. Continue to bear in mind the necessity of relieving Colonel Miles if possible."[207]

At 12:30 p.m., Franklin, who by this point may have received Colonel Cake's report of at least four thousand Confederate infantry strongly posted along Mountain Church Road, sent a short response to McClellan: "I think from appearances that we may have a heavy fight to get the pass."[208] Franklin then continued with his repast. Generals Henry Slocum, Baldy Smith, Winfield Hancock, William Brooks and John Newton soon joined Franklin at headquarters, and together the officers—essentially the entire Sixth Corps brass, excepting only Colonels Bartlett, Torbert and Irwin—enjoyed a round of cigars. McClellan's urging of the previous evening for Franklin to use "the utmost activity that a general can exercise" was apparently going unheeded.

With the Sixth Corps stalled near Burkittsville, the Confederates on the mountaintop used the time to full advantage. Semmes and Munford sent urgent pleas to Lafayette McLaws for support while continuing to strengthen their positions. Semmes placed two additional guns at Brownsville Pass and sent orders to the 10th Georgia, still picketing the Rohrersville Road in Pleasant Valley, to report to Munford at Crampton's Gap. Augmenting Chew's Battery halfway up the eastern slope of South Mountain below Crampton's Gap went a section of naval howitzers from Captain Cary Grimes's Portsmouth Light Artillery. Finally, at noon and in response to the requests for support, Lafayette McLaws ordered Brigadier General Howell Cobb's Brigade, then in position at Sandy Hook, to march to Brownsville in Pleasant Valley, where it would be in position to support either Semmes or Munford. Interestingly enough, and despite the critical importance of Crampton's Gap, McLaws admitted that although he could hear cannon fire coming from the direction of the gap, he "felt no particular concern about it" since Jeb Stuart, who had by this time arrived on Maryland Heights, told McLaws "he did not believe there was more than a brigade of the enemy" advancing toward the pass. It was the second time that day that Stuart grossly underestimated the size of the Federal forces heading toward the South Mountain gaps. Still, despite Stuart's erroneous report, McLaws commanded Howell Cobb to "hold the gap even if he lost his last man doing it."[209]

Brigadier General Paul Semmes. *The Photographic History of the Civil War.*

Until Cobb's Brigade of 1,350 arrived, there were only 1,100 Confederates to defend the gaps. Semmes's force at Brownsville Pass numbered 300, which meant that Munford at Crampton's Gap had just 800 to confront Franklin's entire Sixth Corps. Munford positioned his main line of battle along Mountain Church Road, which ran parallel to South Mountain at its eastern base roughly one-third of a mile west of Burkittsville. He dismounted his horsemen and placed them on the flanks, with the 2nd Virginia Cavalry on the right of his line and the 12th Virginia Cavalry on the left, the latter up the mountain slope along what is today known as the Arnoldstown Road. Between the cavalry went the 6th, 12th and 16th Virginia Infantry regiments under Parham. (The 10th Georgia of Semmes Brigade arrived later in the afternoon and formed to the left of the 6th Virginia on the far left of the Confederate line.) As Munford oversaw the placement of Parham's three regiments, he instructed the officers "to hold the post at all hazards." So thin was Munford's line that in some places, Confederate soldiers stood eight feet apart.[210]

In total length, the Confederate line extended half a mile north along Mountain Church Road, to the right of the Jefferson–Burkittsville Pike, the main east–west roadway through Burkittsville. The 2nd Virginia Cavalry and portions of the 16th Virginia Infantry were in position south of the pike. The pike ran in northwesterly fashion from Burkittsville before its intersection with Mountain Church Road and then began a rather sharp ascent over the mountain, ultimately leveling off at Crampton's Gap, some four hundred feet above Burkittsville. Chew's Battery and the naval howitzers of the Portsmouth Artillery unlimbered next to the pike halfway up the heavily wooded mountain slope, while Confederate sharpshooters went into position in the treetops. Semmes still held on at Brownsville Pass, believing this would be the Federals' main objective. About 11:00 a.m., he sent Colonel Edgar Montague's 32nd Virginia down the eastern slope of the mountain. The Virginia colonel extended a skirmish line to the north, very loosely connecting with the right of Munford's line. However, as Montague noted, his "infantry force was not engaged, though they were ready and anxious to take part in the conflict," and he was "more of a spectator than participant in the action."[211]

The first Federals to get a good look at the Confederate defenses at Crampton's Gap were the soldiers of the 96th Pennsylvania. Captain John Boyle left a vivid description of what lay ahead of the Sixth Corps:

> *The enemy's infantry were posted behind a stout stone wall, breast high, which extended along a country road skirting the base of the mountain, which, here, was precipitous and rough...Their sharpshooters were hid and protected by the trees and boulders which cover the side of the ascent, while their artillery occupied the heights. The approach was through corn, and over stubblefields and meadows, separated from each other by stone and zig-zag fences and spotted with thickets, stone piles, rocks, gullies, and quagmires. Altogether, the rebel position was probably one of the strongest and, naturally, most defensible positions held by either party during the war, and one of the most difficult to surmount.*[212]

Also making a careful survey of the Confederate battle line at the base of Crampton's Gap was Colonel Joseph Jackson Bartlett, commander of the First Brigade, in Slocum's Sixth Corps division. The twenty-seven-year-old lawyer from Binghamton, New York, who had proven himself a skilled and brave officer, did not join his fellow Sixth Corps leaders at the Shafer House, foregoing a cigar in order to examine Munford's position. After more than an hour's worth of reconnaissance, Bartlett received a note from Slocum instructing him to report immediately to Sixth Corps headquarters.

Reaching the Shafer House, Bartlett discovered Franklin and his subordinates "resting upon the ground, in as comfortable positions as each one could assume, smoking their cigars." After some irrelevant topic of conversation between the Sixth Corps brass ended, Slocum suddenly asked Bartlett on which side of the pike they should attack. Without a moment's hesitation, Bartlett blurted out, "On the right."

At this point, Franklin piped up, "Well, gentlemen, that settles it."

Bartlett, with just a bit of impertinence, asked, "Settles what?"

"The point of attack," Franklin calmly replied.

Bartlett stood there dazed. As he later wrote, "I was naturally indignant that I should be called upon the give even an opinion upon such an important matter without previously hearing the views of such old and experienced officers upon such an important question."

Colonel Joseph J. Bartlett. *Library of Congress.*

Bartlett was, after all, the youngest officer present, the only one who did not hold the rank of general and the only one without a West Point education. In an effort to help assuage his young brigade commander, Slocum then explained the situation. While enjoying their cigars, the officers had been debating where the main attack should be made and "were equally divided in their opinions between the right and the left of the road." To break the deadlock, Franklin asked Slocum who would be leading the attack. Informed that it would be Bartlett, Franklin ordered Slocum to send for the colonel. Since Bartlett was to lead the assault, Franklin left it up to him to decide.[213]

With that, Franklin's Sixth Corps began deploying for the attack. And as though he needed some additional prodding, about this same time another message, this one more urgent, arrived at Franklin's headquarters from George McClellan. At 2:00 p.m., and in response to Franklin's 12:30 p.m. message predicting a "heavy fight to get the pass," McClellan instructed his Sixth Corps commander to "mass your troops and carry Burkittsville at any cost. We shall have strong opposition at both passes." However, if Franklin found the Confederates "in very great force at the pass," he was to inform McClellan at once and at least "amuse them as best you can so as to retain them there" while McClellan threw the weight of the army at Fox's and Turner's Gaps. Once those passes were carried, McClellan told Franklin, "it will clear the way for you, and you must then follow the enemy as rapidly as possible."[214]

About 3:00 p.m., Slocum's division began deploying for the attack. Bartlett led the deployment, attempting to do so "as secretly as possibly." His earlier reconnaissance had paid off, for as he later explained, he was able to lead the "troops under cover of the undulations of the ground through a farmyard, little ravines and a cornfield to the field I had selected to form the column in, without discovery." However, once the men reached the staging area, they emerged in full view of the Confederates on the mountain, who immediately began hurling shells in their direction. Despite this fire, as Bartlett proudly noted, the troops "formed with the coolness and precision of an exhibition drill."[215]

Slocum's three brigades formed one behind the other, with Bartlett's brigade in front. Bartlett designated the 27th New York Infantry, Lieutenant Colonel Alexander Adams commanding, as skirmishers and then formed the 5th Maine and 16th New York in a line of battle following the 27th at an interval of two hundred yards. The 96th Pennsylvania remained in Burkittsville and would stay there until the attack commenced. Bartlett's final regiment, the

121st New York, was one of the few green units in the Sixth Corps and was designated as a reserve with orders to provide battery support. Excluding this regiment, Bartlett's brigade numbered fourteen hundred men.[216]

Newton's and Torbert's brigades deployed behind Bartlett's, each brigade in two lines of battle. Composing Newton's front line was the 32nd New York on the right and the 18th New York on the left; his rear line, two hundred yards behind the first, contained the 31st New York, lining up behind the

Major General Henry W. Slocum. *Library of Congress.*

32nd on the right flank, and the Gosline's Zouaves of the 95th Pennsylvania on the left. Another two hundred yards to the rear went Torbert's New Jersey Brigade, the 1st and 2nd New Jersey composing the front line, with the 3rd and 4th New Jersey behind.

Thus deployed, Slocum's division, like a powerful battering ram, was now ready for battle. Including the skirmishers of the 27th in front, the division was stacked up six lines deep, each line separated by intervals of 150 to 200 yards. Colonel Bartlett speculated, "It must have been a grand sight from that mountain Pass to see the glistening splendor of that column as the bright September sun shone upon the arms and trappings of the moving force." And indeed it was. From his position halfway up the slope, George Neese

> *stood for a while and gazed at the magnificent splendor of the martial array that was slowly and steadily moving toward us across the plain below like a living panorama, the sheen of the glittering side-arms and thousands of bright, shiny musket barrels looking like a silver spangled sea rippling and flashing in the light of a midday sun.*[217]

Yet this martial pageantry did not last. At 4:00 p.m., Bartlett ordered Adams's skirmishers of the 27th New York forward, and the battle for Crampton's Gap commenced.

As soon as the Sixth Corps moved forward, Confederate guns stationed on the mountainside and at Brownsville Pass opened with what Slocum described as a "heavy and well-directed artillery fire." Still, wrote the division commander in typical fashion, "the troops advanced steadily, every line in the entire column preserving its alignment with as much accuracy as could have been expected at a drill or review." The skirmishers of the 27th New York pushed forward, with eyes squinted as they advanced into the sun, withstanding the worst of the Confederate artillery fire. As they reached the ever-growing shadow line cast by South Mountain over the open fields, they came under heavy musketry fire from Munford's and Parham's Confederates in position behind the stone wall along Mountain Church Road and from the well-placed sharpshooters positioned in the treetops and the numerous buildings that stood along the roadway. Having now fully developed the main Confederate line, the Union skirmishers halted their advance and commenced a steady fire.

Meanwhile, with the 27th New York moving forward, Slocum called in Colonel Cake's 96th Pennsylvania, which had been on the front lines and under fire for nearly four hours. The order to fall back was, in the words of Private Henry Boyer, "promptly and gladly obeyed." While waiting for his line to return, Cake turned to Slocum for further instruction. After first telling the Pennsylvania colonel that the regiment had done enough for the day, Slocum directed him to move to the right and "if you find something to do, do it!" With these rather vague orders, Cake led his men north, taking advantage of the same undulating ground and ravines that had previously hid Bartlett's men from view before deploying for action. But the regiment was not entirely immune from the exploding shells. As Captain Boyle of Company D remembered, "The head of the column had scarcely emerged from the cover of the ravines and thickets, which had thus far hid it from the enemy's sight, then he opened a furious fire from several of his field pieces on the mountain, hurling death through the ranks with almost every discharge." One shell exploded in front of Company B,

> kill[ing] *and wounding several of the men, while a fragment cut off the right rim of Captain* [Henry] *Royer's felt hat, close to his head, as smoothly as though it had been done with a razor. Knocked down and bewildered, that officer, after regaining his feet, with a nerve and resolution not often met with under the circumstances, pressed on at the head of his command amid appreciative cheers.*[218]

As the men of the 96th double-quicked their way behind the attacking columns, the soldiers of the 27th New York were running seriously low on ammunition. Munford's dismounted cavalrymen and Parham's foot soldiers were keeping up a relentless and well-aimed fire. To relieve the skirmishers, Bartlett ordered up his 5th Maine and 16th New York. Amid a hail of bullets, the 27th New York fell back, ordered to give way to the two advancing units. C.B. Fairchild of the 27th remembered one squad of skirmishers taking shelter "in a barn yard, behind the sheds and outbuildings, where they kept up a telling fire until the main line came up. Another squad of pickets," however, "not hearing the order to rally, found themselves between the two lines of battle, and were obliged to lie down—the bullets cutting up the ground all around them."[219]

The 5th Maine and 16th New York advanced to within three hundred yards of the Confederate line before halting and taking shelter behind a rail fence. Federal casualties mounted rapidly, the blue-clad soldiers having little protection beyond the fence. Confederate casualties were far fewer, for they benefited from the good cover provided by the stone wall. The 6th and 12th Virginia Infantry were tearing holes in Bartlett's front line, maintaining, in the words of Colonel Nathaniel Jackson of the 5th Maine, "a severe and galling fire." To the rear, Captain John Boyle of the 96th Pennsylvania wrote that "the firing had now become general along the whole line. The thunder of artillery reverberated amongst the hills, and the rattle of musketry mingled dolefully with the whiz and burst of shells and the wild execrating shouts and savage cheers of the combatants." [220] But perhaps it was George Bicknell of the 5th Maine who best summed up the action:

> *For over an hour we poured volley after volley into the enemy's ranks. Never did men work harder than the noble soldiery of those two regiments [5th Maine and 16th New York]. Almost every man seemed angry because he could not load and fire more rapidly. Hot indeed was the fire which the rebs returned; yet every one of our boys seemed determined to "send as good as received"…the fire continued brisk and hot. Death was making, in that short time, fearful havoc in the ranks of the noble soldiery. Then ammunition began to fail. Every round had been expended; and as the soldier sought in vain for another charge in his own box, he eagerly sought the cartridge boxes of the killed and the wounded, discharging their contents as rapidly as possible…It began to look alarming…Officers, as well as men began to exhibit symptoms of uneasiness…Almost every moment, some poor fellow in our lines was struck down by the fire of the rebs.[221]*

With casualties mounting rapidly and ammunition running low, Bartlett's men increasingly looked rearward, hoping to see their supports. But Newton's brigade, which was to follow closely behind Bartlett's, was lagging far behind. Indeed, Newton's front line—the 18th and 32nd New York—was still some five or six hundred yards away. The reason for this delay in movement remains unknown, but the result was that the 16th New York and 5th Maine were forced to remain at the front for well over an hour. As Bartlett wrote, "Nothing but the most undaunted courage and steadiness on the part of the two regiments forming my line maintained the fight until the arrival of the rest of the attacking column." When Newton's two leading regiments at last arrived at the front, Bartlett's bloodied regiments gladly stepped aside, retiring for what proved to be a rather short rest some twenty paces to the rear.[222]

Newton's New Yorkers, with full cartridge boxes, picked up where Bartlett had left off, trading volleys with the well-protected Confederates, still some three hundred yards away. The Federal firepower increased when Newton's second line, consisting of the 31st New York and 95th Pennsylvania, advanced, forming to the left of the 18th New York. Then, farther to the

Attack of the Sixth Corps at Crampton's Gap. *Three Years in the Sixth Corps.*

left came the four New Jersey regiments under Torbert. "We moved thus over an open country," wrote Colonel Henry Buck of the 3rd New Jersey, "intersected by high fences, the men clambering over as best they could, and quickly regaining their position in line, marching with great steadiness and precision, and so through a corn-field, still exposed to a hot fire of shell from the enemy." Once they reached the front, the 1st and 2nd New Jersey, on Torbert's advanced line, were ordered to lie down and return fire from behind a stone fence. Under a heavy fire and caught up in the moment, some New Jersey soldiers jumped on the wall, shaking their fists at the Confederates and yelling for them to come out and fight. Such senseless bravado was met with a hail of bullets.[223]

While the left of Slocum's line became nearly flooded with troops, the right flank, too, was being bolstered. Colonel Cake reported to Bartlett, who quickly rushed the colonel's indefatigable 96th Pennsylvania to form to the right of the 32nd New York on Newton's front line. Reaching its position, the 96th came under a galling fire delivered by the 175 men of the 10th Georgia Infantry, which, after spending most of the day picketing the Rohrersville Road in Pleasant Valley, had recently reported to Munford, who sent the Georgians to the north, forming to the left of the 6th Virginia.

When the 96th went into line, the whole of Slocum's division, excepting the 121st New York in reserve, had entered the fray. For more than an hour, one wave of Federal troops after the next had been sent into action, each advancing into a storm of shot and shell. Slocum's brigade commanders—Bartlett, Newton and Torbert—were relying solely on massed firepower to drive Munford's and Parham's Confederates from their position along Mountain Church Road. But despite their efforts, no headway was being made. Lieutenant Colonel George Myers of the 18th New York later reported that the Federal fire was simply "ineffectual."[224] Despite the numbers stacked against it, the Confederate line held, while the fields north of Burkittsville continued to be covered by dead and wounded Federals. Colonels Bartlett and Torbert galloped behind the lines, their faces flushed with the heat of battle, urging on their men.

With his infantry making little progress and suffering heavily, General Slocum called on his artillery. Wolcott's Battery A, 1st Maryland Light Artillery, was rushed forward. Lieutenant James Rigby later recalled that when the orders arrived, he and his battery mates began limbering up the guns and then proceeded at a gallop to the front along the Burkittsville Road. As soon as the battery turned onto the road, said Rigby,

> *the Rebels turned their guns upon us, and such a shower of shot and shell as fell around us is not easily imagined; but we went through at a gallop, and as we passed through the village, the women waved their scarves and bid us God speed, though all of them were in tears, for while they stood in front of their houses, the Rebel shells were tearing down their back fences and kitchens.*[225]

Wolcott's gunners were not the only Federal troops advancing to the front; portions of Smith's Second Division were just then moving forward as well. Hearing reports of some Confederate movement south of town, Franklin feared that Slocum's left flank might be turned. In order to prevent this, Franklin directed Smith to "throw a brigade to the left of the pass," a movement that might also enable him to turn the right flank of the Confederates along Mountain Church Road. Brigadier General William T.H. Brooks got the nod from Smith. A gruff, no-nonsense career soldier, "Bully" Brooks sent his men forward, with the 4th Vermont in the lead, followed closely by the 2nd Vermont, the men advancing through the David Arnold Farm "under a sharp fire of skirmishers."[226] Farther to the rear, Smith's remaining brigades, under Irwin and Hancock, advanced west in support of Brooks. And just like Lieutenant Rigby of Wolcott's Battery, Robert Westbrook of the 49th Pennsylvania, Hancock's Brigade, remembered that the people of Burkittsville, "regardless of the shells which were crashing through their houses, welcomed us heartily, bringing water to fill the canteens, [while] Patriotic ladies cheered the Union boys and brought them food."[227]

Despite all the efforts of the Sixth Corps—despite the waves upon waves of Federal troops being sent to the front—the Confederate line was simply not budging. The level of frustration was growing among the Federal officers, whose men were still falling rapidly while Confederate casualties remained comparatively light, for, as J. Shaw of the 95th Pennsylvania later wrote, "while clover is all right as a cow feed, when it comes to stopping bullets it don't compare with a stone wall."[228] Making no progress and unable to crack Munford's line, it soon became perfectly clear what needed to be done. As Bartlett later recorded, "It became apparent to all that nothing but a united charge would dislodge the enemy and win the battle." And the time to strike arrived soon after General Slocum galloped to the rear to bring up the artillery. Above the thunderous din of battle, Bartlett claimed to have heard cheers rising from Crampton's Gap, which could only mean that Confederate reinforcements were advancing. Bartlett sought out Torbert, who shared the New Yorker's assessment of what had to be done. On their own initiative, the two young colonels then rode down the length of the battle lines, yelling for the men to cease-fire, reload "and be ready for a charge at double-quick." It was 5:20 p.m. and daylight was fading.[229]

At that same moment, even as Bartlett and Torbert galloped behind their lines and prepared their men for the charge, General William Franklin, at his headquarters more than a mile to the rear and clearly out of touch with what was then unfolding, sent off a rather grim note to McClellan. "I report that I have been severely engaged with the enemy for the last hour," he wrote. "The force of the enemy is too great for us to take the pass tonight I am afraid."[230] Yet just ten minutes after Franklin composed this message, his veteran soldiers on the front line, with bayonets fixed, let out a cheer and charged the Confederate line.

Torbert's New Jerseymen, on the left of Slocum's line, were the first to advance, getting a slight head start on the rest of the blue column stretched out to their right. When the orders to charge arrived, the 1st and 2nd New Jersey were still on the brigade's front line, trading shots with Parham's Virginians from behind a rail fence. Torbert ordered these two units to cease-fire while his other regiments—the 3rd and 4th New Jersey—charged from their position nearly 100 yards to the rear. John Beech of the 4th New Jersey remembered that Colonel William Hatch, commanding the regiment, "with uplifted saber pointing to the enemy, his figure drawn up to its full height, and his handsome face flushed with the excitement of battle," ordered the men forward "with a voice which could be heard above the roar of battle." The 3rd and 4th New Jersey surged forward with a cheer and passed through

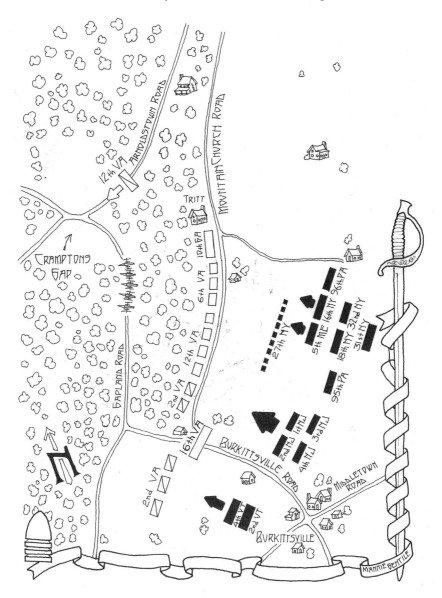

the ranks of their comrades on the front line before climbing up and over the rail fence amidst the leaden storm. When these men made it to within 150 yards of the Confederate line, Torbert ordered the 1st and 2nd New Jersey forward. [231]

James Toomer, a sergeant in Parham's 16th Virginia Infantry, remembered the sobering sight of Torbert's entire brigade now charging directly toward the thinly manned Confederate line. "They came over the field grandly, the officers all in place and cheering the men onward, the men well aligned on the colors, with the Stars and Stripes floating above them," recorded Toomer, who added that the Jerseymen roared like bulls and howled "like devils let loose from the infernal regions." Not wanting all the glory to go to the 3rd and 4th New Jersey alone, the panting soldiers of the 1st and 2nd soon caught up with their charging comrades, and together the four regiments swept up and over the stone wall lining Mountain Church Road. The Confederate line at last broke, the surviving Confederates fleeing for safety up the wooded slopes.[232]

While the New Jerseymen swept into Mountain Church Road, to their right the soldiers of Newton's and Bartlett's brigades were achieving equal success. George Bicknell of Bartlett's 5th Maine wrote that the Federal troops moved forward "like an avalanche" and that the "earth almost trembled beneath the tread of [the] mighty men."

"In an instant the enemy's cavalry were seen galloping up the hill," remembered the Maine soldier, while the "infantry looked for a moment, fired a single volley, and lo! they were scattered in all directions. Like frightened deer, they flew up the mountain, followed by the victors."[233]

Despite the comparative ease with which they carried the Confederate position along Mountain Church Road, casualties among the attacking blue columns were heavy in places. General John Newton described the charge as "short and decisive" and said that "the enemy was driven from his stronghold in a very few moments," but he was forced to admit that his "loss was severe in accomplishing this object." Colonel Bartlett echoed Newton: "The enemy was well prepared to receive us, and poured in our faces a terrible fire from behind the wall, the trees and rocks on the mountain, and a stone house on the right of the 96th Pennsylvania, which was on the right of the line." Men fell "at every step."[234]

No other Federal regiment suffered as high a loss that day as did Colonel Henry Cake's 96th Pennsylvania, and most of its casualties were sustained during this fateful charge. The 96th held the far right of the Sixth Corps line and was forced to advance across difficult ground. As Cake later described:

> *The fields through which the Ninety-Sixth charged presented many obstacles, and, in order not to meet the enemy with broken lines, I twice halted momentarily, with a stone fence for a cover…The last of the series of fields through which we had to charge was meadow and standing corn. As we emerged from the corn the enemy met us with a murderous fire.*[235]

Cake, on foot with sword in hand, presented an inspiring figure as he led the regiment forward. He was assisted by Bartlett, who galloped behind the advancing troops "waving his sword and crying at the top of his voice, 'Now, Pennsylvanians, do your duty!'"[236]

Posted directly ahead of the charging Pennsylvanians was the 10th Georgia Infantry of Semmes's Brigade, under the command of Major Willis Holt. Holt's veterans seemed to double their rate of fire, and scores of Cake's men fell, including the popular Major Lewis Martin, struck in the back of the head and mortally wounded as he turned to urge his troops forward. As Captain Boyle later wrote:

> *At every step some poor soul escaped through a bullet-hole into eternity, or some brave body fell forward, or sank to the earth, with agonizing shriek or cry of pain.* [Yet] *the excitement was now at fever heat. All fear had fled from the minds of the men, and their pale faces, begrimed with powder, and lit by frenzied, bloodshot eyes, wore the expressions of demons.*[237]

At last the 96th reached the last field over which it had to charge, with a narrow strip of standing corn. As the regiment passed through the rows of corn, an eerie silence prevailed; the Confederates held their fire until the blue line emerged. When it finally did, Holt's Georgians unleashed a murderous volley directly into the Federal faces just twenty paces to their front. "The rush and cheer and earthquake were simultaneous," wrote Private Boyer, who further admitted that "it was a dreadful shock, hardly to be withstood; and a shiver ran along the line that looked like flight." The survivors of the initial blast threw themselves flat on the ground, yet only for a moment. Still at the front, Cake cried out, "Forward into the road and then give them the bayonet! It is death for all to hesitate now!" Rising as one man, the regiment charged into another hail of bullets. Lieutenant John Dougherty of Company F was shot through the chest. As he fell, Dougherty turned his sword over to 1st Sergeant James Casey. "Here, Casey, take my sword and follow the Colonel," said the dying officer. Casey whirled the sword over his head "and called on the men who were now as fierce as bloodhounds, to move forward."[238]

Private Boyer believed that it took no longer than fifteen seconds for the men of the 96th to cover the final twenty paces from the corn and charge over the stone wall, directly into the confused ranks of the 10th Georgia. Colonel Cake simply recorded that the "road was gained in a twinkling." A brief though vicious hand-to-hand struggle ensued, during which the 96th lost two color-bearers killed and three wounded. In the fury, some of Cake's men turned to the right and charged into the stone home of the widow Susan Tritt, which stood at the immediate base of the mountain, west of Mountain Church Road and just to the north of the position held by the 10th Georgia. Some of Holt's men used the house as a sharpshooters' den, and those unable to get away were either captured or bayoneted. "The scene inside the house," said Captain Boyle, "can be better imagined than described."[239]

Despite the horrific casualties sustained during the attack—some twenty-six men killed and fifty-one wounded—the 96th Pennsylvania shattered the left of Munford's line and sent the survivors of the 10th Georgia fleeing up the mountainside. Those still in the roadway and uninjured, wrote Colonel Cake, "begged lustily for mercy." To the left of the Pennsylvanians, the 18th and 32nd New York of Newton's brigade and some additional elements of Bartlett's brigade swept into the roadway, driving what remained of the Confederate line before them. With that, the Confederate line had evaporated. Munford's and Parham's survivors now raced their way up the steep mountainside toward the summit, closely pursued by Slocum's victory-flushed Federals who had barely paused to catch their breaths and re-form after their successful charge.

While all of this was transpiring north of the Burkittsville Pike, to the south, Bully Brooks was leading his Vermonters in a similar charge toward the Confederate line. Lieutenant Colonel Charles B. Stoughton's 4th Vermont took the lead in this attack, followed closely by Major James Walbridge's 2nd Vermont. Private John Conline, in advance with the 4th, left a vivid description of the attack:

> Before we got to the wall, the rebels began to run singly, then in little squads of three or four, and finally, as we were about to reach the wall, they all broke pell-mell up the slightly inclined open plain….Many of them halted, turned and fired at us. The wall reached, we opened fire upon the rapidly vanishing Confederates for two or three minutes; and climbing over it, the line quickly advanced after the demoralized enemy, until we reached the trees at the foot of the mountain, when we were free from artillery fire. We then began to climb the steep mountain side and arrived at the crest nearly out of breath.[240]

With just his skeletal force drawn up along Mountain Church Road and on either side of the Jefferson–Burkittsville Pike, Colonel Thomas Munford had attempted to hold back the entire Sixth Corps, but by 6:00 p.m., his position had vanished. His men had put up a heroic fight, but there was little they could do once Slocum's charge began. Munford later praised Colonel William Parham, writing that "he did everything in his power to hold his position," while his small command "fought splendidly." Munford was not as praiseworthy when it came to General Paul Semmes, who was still holding on a mile to the south at Brownsville Pass. "General Semmes certainly knew the condition of things," wrote Munford, "as his artillery had been used, and he could see what was going on from his gap," the implication being that Semmes did little to support Munford at Crampton's Gap. In fact, Semmes did order something in the way of a demonstration when he sent the 32nd and 15th Virginia forward from his pass. However, it was much too late. The Virginians started forward just in time to see Brooks's Vermonters charge forward and the resulting collapse of Munford's line. Believing they could thus be of no service and fearful of being cut and surrounded if they continued forward, the Virginians aborted their endeavor and turned around.[241]

The collapse of the Confederate line along Mountain Church Road ushered in a mad scramble up the steep eastern slope of South Mountain. While General Winfield Scott Hancock, watching the battle from the rear, described this attack as "the poetry of war," Captain Boyle of the 96th Pennsylvania, on the far right of the Union line and in the midst of the heaviest fighting, did his best to describe the confusing scene, leaving a vivid account of the Confederate collapse and the struggle up the mountain:

> *Nothing human could withstand the fury of the onset, and…the enemy immediately in front, seized with a sudden panic, threw down their arms, tore off their accoutrements and fled up the steep side of the mountain like deer before the chase. Instantly their whole line gave way, and helter-skelter, pell-mell, trampling and jostling each other in their insane hurry to escape, they poured upward through the deep ravines toward the Pass. Imagine, if you can, several thousand panic-stricken, fear-haunted, powder-stained and desperate men fleeing up the steep side of a rocky mountain, dodging behind trees, crouching within the shelter of boulders, skulking with bended backs, trembling knees, and palpitating hearts among the laurel bushes and wild undergrowth, amid the gathering gloom of a September evening, pursued by as many men shouting, infuriated, battle-excited, blood-spattered, victory-flushed beings, and you have the picture as it then appeared.*[242]

Munford's and Parham's retreating soldiers were not the only Confederates with which the Sixth Corps had to contend as they advanced up the mountain, for just then arriving on the scene was Brigadier General Howell Cobb's Brigade. Born in Jefferson County, Georgia, on September 7, 1815, Howell Cobb ranked among the most prominent political figures of antebellum America. In the years prior to the outbreak of war, Cobb served as Speaker of the U.S. House of Representatives, as governor of Georgia and as secretary of the treasury under President James Buchanan. During the Maryland Campaign, Cobb's Brigade consisted of the 15th North Carolina, the 16th and 24th Georgia and Cobb's Legion, commanded by Lieutenant Colonel Jefferson Lamar.[243]

At 1:00 p.m. on that Sunday afternoon, Cobb, whose brigade was then encamped at Sandy Hook, received McLaws's order to return to Brownsville. He arrived there three hours later, at just about the same time Bartlett ordered his skirmishers of the 27th New York forward on the other side of South Mountain. Upon reaching Brownsville, Cobb was greeted by Semmes, who passed along McLaws's instruction that Cobb take command at Crampton's Gap. Semmes then headed back to Brownsville Pass, still convinced that this would be the Federal target. Cobb remained in Brownsville until shortly after 5:00 p.m., when in response to calls for help from both Munford and Parham, he led his North Carolinians and Georgians up the western slope of the mountain to Crampton's Gap. As his men reached the summit, they let out a round of high-pitched, rousing cheers. It was these same cheers that convinced Colonel Bartlett, on the fields below, to order the charge.

When Cobb reached the summit at Crampton's Gap, he was met by a fiery Thomas Munford, who immediately began directing the placement of Cobb's regiments. The 15th North Carolina was sent to the left, where it formed behind a stone wall that ran along Arnoldstown Road, which sliced diagonally across the eastern slope of the mountain. To the right of the 15th North Carolina went the 24th Georgia, forming astride Whipp's Ravine. Cobb's Legion was sent farthest to the right, racing down Gapland Road, which descended the mountain directly to Burkittsville, to roughly the same position recently occupied by the guns of Chew's Battery and those of the Portsmouth Light Artillery. With the Federal advance toward the mountain, the Confederate gunners found their fire increasingly ineffective and thus limbered up and fell back to a higher elevation on the summit. The last of Cobb's regiments, the 16th Georgia, followed behind Cobb's Legion before forming to its left. After overseeing the placement of Cobb's regiments, Munford, who had held the position all day and was thus familiar with the terrain, relinquished command of the Crampton's Gap defense to Howell Cobb, who had just arrived on the scene.[244]

In staggered lines, Cobb's Brigade went into position on the slopes of South Mountain, about halfway between the summit at Crampton's Gap and the Confederate line along Mountain Church Road. However, Cobb's men had only begun to deploy when Munford's line collapsed. Panic-stricken and routed Virginians from Munford's and Parham's commands, followed closely by the pursuing Federals, soon came crashing into Cobb's ranks, causing much confusion. Some of Cobb's men could not help but become swept up in the retreat.

Leading the Federal pursuit on the far right of the Sixth Corps line was the 96th Pennsylvania. As Private Henry Boyer recorded, the regiment "moved up the steep side of the mountain, horribly killing and wounding all we could of those who resisted or who would not stop, and mercifully sparing and capturing all who manifested a disposition to surrender." Advancing up the mountain to the left and a little to the rear of the 96th was the 32nd New York and, farther to the rear, the 18th New York, both of Newton's brigade. Following closely behind them and still a little farther to the left was the 16th New York of Bartlett's brigade. With just a bit of bravado, Lieutenant Colonel Joel Seaver, commanding the 16th New York, wrote that his soldiers "fought nobly and pressed on up the steep ascent under a perfect shower of bullets, and their example encouraged others, who faltered before the terrors of the enemy and the steepness of the hill, to follow."[245]

It was not long before the charging Sixth Corps soldiers ran headlong into Cobb's developing line halfway up the slope. There the advance came to a brief halt. Lieutenant Colonel Seaver saw a Confederate line of battle and immediately ordered his men to fall to the ground. Moments later, a volley of bullets sailed over the heads of the New Yorkers, who proceeded to return a rapid fire, which was done, said Seaver, "to good effect." Federal units to the right of Seaver's command did not fare as well. Lieutenant Colonel George Myers of the 18th New York reported, "On rising the hill to the road which ran along its side [the Arnoldstown Road], we received a terrific volley from the enemy. It was here that I met my heaviest loss, the fire of the enemy being well-directed and fatal." Myers also admitted that his men "staggered for a moment." Casualties in the 32nd New York, to the right of the 18th, were not as heavy but were nevertheless significant. Among the seriously wounded were the 32nd's commander, Colonel Roderick Matheson, and its major, Frank Lemon. Both of these men, beloved by the soldiers and highly respected by their superiors, later succumbed to their Crampton's Gap wounds.[246]

With the advance stalling, Colonel Bartlett, in command of this section of the advancing Federal line, sought to get his men once again moving up the mountainside. As he passed behind the lines, Major John McGinnis of the 18th New York told Bartlett that his men were out of ammunition. "Never mind, major," replied the red-faced brigade commander, "push on; we have got 'em on the run!" Soon, the Federal line was again in motion, Bartlett following close behind. The brigade commander struggled to make his way to the top; his horse—which he would later name Crampton—was having a difficult time negotiating his way up the steep slope. On his way up, Bartlett came across Colonel Matheson, who, although wounded, lay on the ground waving on his troops and shouting, "You've got 'em, boys! Push on!"[247]

Cobb's lines melted like wax before the flame. To Bartlett's front, all Confederate resistance dissipated, and the pursuit renewed with great intensity. Sergeant Andrew Anderson of the 96th Pennsylvania noticed the color-bearer of the 16th Georgia Infantry retreating up the mountain directly to his front. He took aim and fired, but the bullet missed its mark. The panicked Georgian instinctively dropped the burdensome flag and continued his retreat. His blood up, Anderson sidestepped the fallen colors and followed the retreating Georgian. He took another shot; this one hit its mark, and the Georgian fell to the ground.[248]

As Anderson pursued his quarry, Private James Allen of the 16th New York followed in the Pennsylvanian's footsteps. Allen, a nineteen-year-old native of

Alfred Waud sketch of the attack at Crampton's Gap. *Library of Congress.*

Ireland, along with another soldier of the 16th, became separated from his regiment during the chaotic pursuit up South Mountain. Allen's comrade fell wounded with a shot to his left leg. As Allen later related, he found "a comfortable place for the poor fellow in a crevice and gave him a drink from [his] canteen" before heading out alone, still in pursuit of the retreating Confederates. As he neared the Arnoldstown Road, Allen spotted a squad of cut-off soldiers belonging to the 16th Georgia, seemingly set adrift in the confusion. "Putting on a bold face, and waving my arms," said Allen, "I said to my imaginary company: 'Up, men, up!'" Believing they were cornered and up against greater numbers, the Georgians stacked their rifles and surrendered. As Allen approached his captives, he noticed the flag of the 16th Georgia, which was dropped earlier thanks to Sergeant Anderson of the 96th Pennsylvania. Allen gained possession of the flag and then noticed his commanding officer, Lieutenant Colonel Joel Seaver, approaching. The proud soldier turned over the captured Georgians, showed off his trophy of war and told Seaver of his wounded comrade "lying far down the mountain side." For his heroics, James Allen later received the Medal of Honor, a mark of distinction he might have shared with Anderson had the Pennsylvanian sergeant paused to collect the 16th Georgia's fallen colors.[249]

The 16th and 24th Georgia, along with the 15th North Carolina, retreated in the face of the advancing Federals. A steady stream of captured Confederates trickled down the eastern slope escorted by their Federal captors. Colonel Cake took credit for personally sending forty-two prisoners to the rear. Among the Confederate prisoners-of-war was a wounded Private Thomas Newton of the 6th Virginia Infantry, a forty-six-year-old physician from Norfolk. His cousin was Union Sixth Corps brigadier general John Newton, also a native of Norfolk, whose troops helped overrun the 6th Virginia's position along Mountain Church Road. Upon learning that his cousin was wounded and in Federal hands, General Newton had him sent to Hagerstown and directed his personal doctor to care for his stricken relative. His efforts were in vain, however, for in March 1863, Private Tom Newton succumbed to his Crampton's Gap wound.[250]

Colonel Cake's unrelenting Pennsylvanians were the first Federal troops to reach the summit of South Mountain at Crampton's Gap. The 16th, 18th and 32nd New York arrived soon after. As these panting Federals reached Crampton's Gap on the right of the Sixth Corps line, advancing along the Arnoldstown Road, to their left, Torbert's New Jerseymen approached the summit astride Gapland Road.

Although they met with less resistance and suffered fewer casualties than Bartlett's regiments, Torbert's brigade did encounter some momentary opposition in its climb up the mountainside. After punching through the

Confederate line along Mountain Church Road and forcing the retreat of Parham's Virginians, Torbert's regiments faced to the right and swept up the mountain along Gapland Road. As they advanced, the New Jerseymen raised the cry of "Kearney! Kearney!" in reverence of their first commander, General Philip Kearney, who was killed in action two weeks earlier at Chantilly. Halfway up the slope, Torbert's regiments ran into Cobb's Legion, some 250 Confederates who were just getting into position. On the left of Torbert's line, Colonel Henry Brown discovered that his 3rd New Jersey was actually behind Lamar's position; he thus ordered a right wheel, his troops now approaching Cobb's Legion from the rear. To the right of Brown's 3rd New Jersey, Colonel William B. Hatch also faced his regiment—the 4th New Jersey—to the right, while the 2nd New Jersey continued climbing straight ahead. The result of all this movement on the slope was disaster for Cobb's Legion. Lamar's regiment—outnumbered five to one—was struck on three sides: from the rear, from the flank and from the front. Torbert's Federals closed the trap, and Cobb's Legion was nearly annihilated.

Jefferson Lamar was among the first to fall, shot in the leg. He continued in command of his disintegrating regiment until, just moments after ordering a retreat, he was again shot down, this time fatally through the chest. Of the 250 men Cobb's Legion carried into action, 33 were killed or wounded, while another 156 fell into Union hands as prisoners of war—a 76 percent casualty rate. Both flags carried by Cobb's Legion were also claimed as trophies by Torbert's triumphant New Jersey soldiers.[251]

Colonel Brown of the 3rd New Jersey wrote that in the Confederates' "complete and utter rout, my men showed here what they could do when they had a fair chance, and they here well sustained the honor of New Jersey on this field." The following day, Colonel Torbert issued a Congratulatory Order to his brigade, echoing Brown's statement: "The 14th day of September, 1862, is one long to be remembered, for on that day you dashingly met and drove the enemy at every point. Your advance in line of battle under a galling artillery fire, and final bayonet charge, was a feat seldom, if ever, surpassed." Yet there was still more fighting left to do. After the destruction of Cobb's Legion, the 3rd New Jersey escorted its prisoners back down the mountain while the 2nd and 4th continued driving up the mountain.[252]

As Torbert's men finished rounding up what was left of Cobb's Legion, farther to the south, 1st Lieutenant George White Hooker of the 4th Vermont, in a daring feat similar to that of the 16th New York's James Allen, captured nearly an entire regiment single-handedly. Hooker's 4th Vermont led Brooks's brigade up the mountain, followed closely by the 2nd. The two regiments,

Colonel Alfred T.A. Torbert. *Library of Congress.*

said George Benedict, "pushed on up the rocky side of the mountain, climbing the ledges and struggling through the bushes, till they reached the crest." The 2nd Vermont continued moving forward; four companies of the 4th, however, were sent to the left, marching south along the crest. Led by Lieutenant Hooker, these Vermonters were heading toward Brownsville Pass and Manly's Battery, "whose fire from the summit," noted Benedict, "had been so annoying." Before reaching that position, Hooker stumbled across a large gathering of Confederate soldiers attempting to re-form. The young officer galloped directly into the midst of these men, told them they were being surrounded by a superior force and called upon them to surrender. Surprisingly, the Confederates laid down their weapons and threw up their arms. Lieutenant Hooker managed to capture 116 men of the 16th Virginia Infantry, including its commander, Major Francis D. Holliday, and its regimental flag. And just like Private Allen, Hooker's actions were later recognized with a Medal of Honor.[253]

Darkness was quickly descending as the heavy battle smoke enshrouded the mountain. At Crampton's Gap, a frantic Howell Cobb was desperately trying to rally what was left of his shattered command. Some men, mainly elements of the 10th, 16th and 24th Georgia, did rally, going into position behind a stone wall on the western end of a small clearing known as Padgett's Field. Most, however, continued in their retreat, running past the brigade commander and down the western slope, consumed by panic.

There was at least some help on the way. Two guns of the Georgia Troup Artillery, under the command of Lieutenant Henry Jennings, arrived at Crampton's Gap. Cobb posted the guns directly on the mountaintop, near the intersection of the Arnoldstown and Gapland Roads. One of the guns, a six-pound smoothbore nicknamed the "Sallie Craig," was positioned to fire down Gapland Road, while the barrel of the other, a twelve-pound howitzer given the sobriquet "Jennie," faced down the Arnoldstown Road. Seeing the gunners heroically unlimber in the midst of this chaos, Cobb galloped to the Georgians trying to catch their breaths behind the stone wall and shouted, "Here is the Troup Artillery, men! Rally to it!" But his efforts were in vain, and the men remained well to the rear of the guns.[254]

Jennings's gunners waited anxiously for the Federals to appear. Bartlett's and Torbert's largely disordered masses climbed up the slope and along the two roadways, converging at the crest. Finally, when the bluecoats advanced to within fifty yards, the Jennie and Sallie Craig erupted in bursts of flame, belching canister directly into the Federals' faces. The suddenness of these canister blasts staggered the Union lines, and the advance was again brought to a temporary halt. Bartlett's New Yorkers and Torbert's New Jerseymen soon started peppering the guns and their crews, inflicting some loss. Jennings's exposed Georgian gunners were able to fire off five rounds before being forced to retreat. The 4th New Jersey had moved entirely undetected to the left of the Gapland Road and approached Crampton's Gap from the south, pouring a destructive fire directly into the Confederate gunners' exposed right flank. Jennings wisely ordered his men to limber up their pieces and gallop to safety.[255]

Howell Cobb was still doing all he could to rally the men, exhorting them to hold their ground. He grabbed the flag of the 24th Georgia, carrying the banner aloft while galloping back and forth amidst his tangled troops. He was aided in his efforts by Colonels Parham and Munford and, finally, by General Semmes, who at twilight had at last arrived at Crampton's Gap after spending the day at Brownsville Pass. Semmes remembered that as he made his way to the top, he was met by Confederate soldiers "pouring down the road and through the wood, in great disorder." On the summit, he found General Cobb and his staff "at the imminent risk of their lives, using every effort to check and rally" the men. But while Semmes, like Cobb a native of Georgia, found much to praise in Cobb's heroics, Thomas Munford could only find contempt. In an effort to cast all blame for the Confederate fiasco at Crampton's Gap on the shoulders of Howell Cobb, Munford, a Virginian, wrote that Cobb's efforts were "without the least effect, and it would have been as useless to attempt to rally a flock of frightened sheep." Munford further castigated Cobb and his men by declaring, entirely unfairly, that Cobb's regiments "behaved badly."[256]

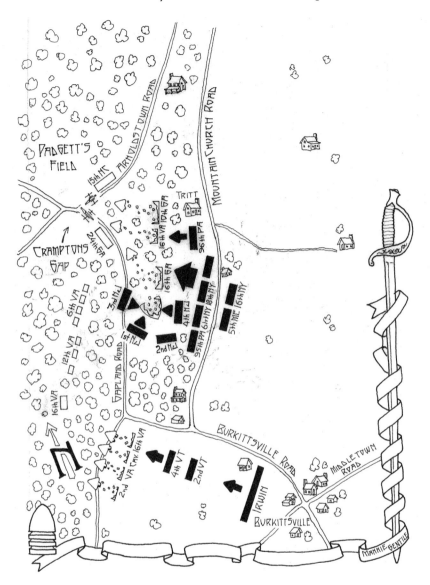

For Cobb, all was soon lost. In the same hail of gunfire that forced the retreat of Jennings's guns, Cobb's brother-in-law and volunteer aide-de-camp John Basil Lamar fell mortally wounded, shot through the chest. Seconds later, a bullet shattered the 24th Georgia's flagstaff, cutting it in two as it fell from Cobb's hands. With that, Cobb ordered a retreat. The mounted cavalcade of Confederate officers galloped down the western side of the mountain followed by the few foot soldiers who had remained on the summit.[257]

Brigadier General Howell Cobb. *Library of Congress.*

Torbert's New Jerseymen soon filled the gap, but after their long day of arduous service, they could push no further. Their place was quickly taken up by the comparatively fresh 31st New York and 95th Pennsylvania of Newton's brigade. The two regiments ventured forward and down the western slope when they were brought to a sudden and unexpected halt. In an effort to buy some time for the retreating Confederates, Lieutenant Jennings once again unlimbered his guns, and the Sallie Craig and Jennie blasted canister into the Federals' faces. Several of the Pennsylvanians fell wounded, while one was killed in the blast. However, much of the artillery fire was ineffective, passing well over the Union soldiers' heads—though tearing through the trees and showering tree limbs and branches upon them. The halt was just momentary. As the 95th's Colonel Gustavus Town recorded, "The line recoiled for a moment, and then, with shouts, charged upon it, firing as it advanced, the shots being directed by the flash of the artillery, as it was now too dark to distinguish the gunners at that distance." With the Federals charging, Jennings again ordered a retreat, but only the Sallie Craig was able to get away safely. The Jennie had suffered a broken axle and was thus abandoned on the slope. Colonel Town's Pennsylvanians swarmed around the gun but were almost immediately ordered by Bartlett to fall back to the summit. They returned sans the prize. However, later that night, pickets of the 2nd Vermont, becoming a little disoriented in the darkness, happened upon the cannon and claimed it as their own.[258]

By 6:45 p.m., the Sixth Corps held sole possession of Crampton's Gap. On the summit, Colonel Joseph Bartlett—who along with Torbert was soon afterward rewarded with a promotion to brigadier general—

began the difficult task of sorting out and disentangling the scattered regiments and forming a defensive position. Campfires began to pop up as the exhausted Federal troops brewed up some much-needed coffee and grabbed a quick bite. But not everyone rested. Search parties went out scouring the mountainside for wounded comrades. Captain Boyle of the 96th Pennsylvania explained that a detail of three men from each of the regiment's ten companies went out and "by the aid of torches and candles sought out their wounded companions and had them cared for as well as circumstances would permit."[259]

Tactically, the battle for Crampton's Gap was a victory for the Union and an utter rout for the Confederates. Esteemed historian Joseph Harsh concluded that the fight was "one of the worst routs suffered by the Army of Northern Virginia during the entire war."[260] Federal casualties totaled 533, with 113 killed in action, 418 wounded and 2 missing. Most of this loss was sustained by Slocum's division, with the 96th Pennsylvania suffering the highest casualties. Confederate casualties neared 1,000 men, or more than 40 percent of the total number of Confederates engaged. Howell Cobb's Brigade suffered the greatest loss; Cobb's Legion lost more than 70 percent of its troops, while the 16th Georgia lost more than 50 percent. Of the total Confederate casualty figure, more than 600 had fallen into Union hands as prisoners of war. Lost also to the Confederates were four flags and one disabled cannon. Colonel William Hatch of the 4th New Jersey further claimed that his men had gathered enough Confederate Springfield rifles to equip the entire regiment, replacing their outdated and "imperfect" smoothbores.[261]

In describing the aftermath, Sixth Corps soldier George Stevens wrote that the Confederate dead "strewed our path, and great care was required, as we passed along the road, to avoid treading upon the lifeless remains which lay thickly upon the ground. On every side the evidences of the fearful conflict multiplied. Trees were literally cut to pieces by shells and bullets; a continual procession of rebel wounded and prisoners lined the roadsides, while knapsacks, guns, canteens, and haversacks were scattered in great confusion." George Bicknell of the 5th Maine echoed Stevens's sentiments, writing that "it was, indeed, a sad sight to walk over the sides of that mountain, and see the strong men who had fallen in support of what we could only feel to be an unrighteous cause."[262]

General Henry Slocum was justly proud of his men:

Although greatly reduced in numbers by losses on the Peninsula, although fatigued by long marches and constant service since the opening of the spring campaign, each regiment—indeed, every man—did his whole duty, not reluctantly, but with that eagerness and enthusiasm which rendered success certain.

Colonel Bartlett recorded simply that the "victory was decisive and complete."

That night, Slocum made the final deployments, sending his division down the western slope of the mountain, where they finally went into camp. They were joined there by Irwin's brigade of Smith's division, while Brooks's Vermonters formed on their left. At Crampton's Gap, Sixth Corps commander William Franklin arrived with his staff and met up with his officers. "Congratulations were generously exchanged all around," wrote Bartlett, "and renewed confidence expressed in our brave fellows, who never had failed us when given a fair chance."[263]

All was certainly not as calm in Pleasant Valley. As the Sixth Corps began settling into bivouac and as its officers congratulated themselves on the mountaintop, all was panic and pandemonium among its Confederate adversaries. Generals Lafayette McLaws and Jeb Stuart learned of the Federal breakthrough at Crampton's Gap and immediately made their way off Maryland Heights and up Pleasant Valley toward the critical mountain pass. As they rode forward, they were met with a steady stream of retreating soldiers. Heros Von Borcke, a member of Stuart's staff, recalled the scene:

Hundreds of soldiers, many of them wounded were arriving in disorderly array from the fight, while guns and caissons, huddled together with wagons and ambulances, moving towards the rear, blocked up the road. We at once posted a strong guard along the road, with orders to arrest every man who was not too badly hurt to renew the conflict, and, taking the artillery with us, continued our ride.

Stuart and his entourage soon encountered Howell Cobb. "The poor General was in a state of the saddest excitement and disgust at the conduct of his men," wrote Von Borcke. "As soon as he recognized us in the dusk of the evening, he cried out in heartbroken accents of alarm and despair, 'Dismount, gentlemen, dismount, if your lives are dear to you! The enemy is within fifty yards of us.'" Stuart tried his best to assuage Cobb and then turned to the more serious business of assisting McLaws in patching together a last-ditch line of defense across the valley floor.[264]

Through great effort, McLaws and Stuart were able to piece together a battle line approximately one mile south of Crampton's Gap, in Pleasant

Valley, made up of elements of Cobb's, Semmes's and Mahone's Brigades. McLaws also anxiously awaited the arrival of Wilcox's Brigade of R.H. Anderson's Division, which he had summoned immediately upon hearing of the Sixth Corps's breakthrough. McLaws commented to Stuart that they were now trapped and sought out the cavalryman's advice. Stuart suggested a counterattack to reclaim Crampton's Gap, but McLaws rejected the notion and decided instead to focus on strengthening his new line of battle and preparing for any attack.

As the minutes ticked by and the Federals remained motionless, McLaws's anxieties subsided, and with darkness, the heavily bearded Georgian breathed just a little easier. "Fortunately night came on," wrote McLaws, "and allowed a new arrangement of the troops to be made to meet the changed aspect of affairs." Certain that the Federals would attack at first light, and knowing he was stuck in the valley as long as the Harpers Ferry garrison held out, McLaws withdrew Kershaw's and Barksdale's Brigades from Maryland Heights. These men, along with the Alabamians of Wilcox's Brigade, later formed alongside the remnants of Cobb's, Mahone's and Semmes's Brigades along the new Confederate line of battle and awaited what they believed would be the inevitable Union attack on the morning of September 15.[265]

Major General Lafayette McLaws. *Library of Congress.*

On September 14, 1862, General William Franklin's Sixth Corps covered more than twelve miles in just over thirteen hours of tough marching from their camps near Buckeystown and across Catoctin Mountain, through the Middletown Valley and, finally, across South Mountain, but only after achieving a decisive victory at Crampton's Gap. Franklin's halt that morning in Jefferson and his delay in attacking Munford's position once his men arrived in Burkittsville meant that he only successfully executed one aspect of his orders. Had Franklin exercised more energy by attacking earlier in the day, perhaps things might have turned out differently; maybe the Federals would have been able to achieve greater strategic goals. At the same time, it is difficult to conceive of the Sixth Corps having been able to accomplish much more that day. McClellan's instructions for Franklin to turn south after carrying Crampton's Gap in order to either cut off or destroy McLaws's command, then turn around, with Miles's liberated Harpers Ferry command in tow, to either assist Burnside in clearing Turner's Gap or cutting off Longstreet's retreat across the Potomac may have simply been asking the impossible of Franklin. Perhaps McClellan was too ambitious in his plans for September 14. No matter, for until Harpers Ferry fell, McClellan's plan for cutting the enemy in two and defeating it in detail was still possible. And both he and Robert E. Lee knew this.

5

"God Bless You and All with You. Destroy the Rebel Army If Possible"

The Road to Antietam

Late on September 14, as the dark shades of night crept over the contested passes of South Mountain, and as the thunderous roar of battle gave way to the occasional sharp crack of scattered small-arms fire and to the piteous, heart-rending cries of the wounded and dying, Robert E. Lee met with a worn-out Daniel Harvey Hill and a dispirited James Longstreet at his headquarters near Boonsboro. With his hands bandaged, Lee did not once journey to the scene of any of the day's action and was forced to rely on the reports and judgments of his subordinates. What he heard that night from both Hill and Longstreet was not encouraging.

Longstreet let Hill do much of the talking. Hill no doubt praised his men's efforts, and with good cause, for they had struggled valiantly against mighty odds. However, they were ultimately unable to prevent the Union army from gaining secure positions on both flanks. And although he still held the ground around the Mountain House, Hill explained, even this position would be untenable if they remained through the night and allowed McClellan the opportunity to renew the fighting in the morning. Longstreet agreed, believing the Union army commander "would require but little time to turn either flank," and if that happened, "our command must then be at his mercy." At this point, Lee was not yet aware of the disaster that had befallen his troops six miles to the south at Crampton's Gap, but the report from his immediate front was dire enough. It was clear to Hill and Longstreet that the Confederate army must retreat. Lee realized this as well, but for the army commander the decision meant much more than a withdrawal of his forces from the mountain. Indeed, Robert E. Lee decided that night to abandon his entire campaign—to end the bold offensive that had begun with so much promise just ten days earlier—and retreat westward through Sharpsburg and across the Potomac River at the ford at Shepherdstown.[266]

It was by no means an easy decision for Lee but one that had to be made, especially after he heard from a Union prisoner that the Federal Second Corps, the largest in the Army of the Potomac, had relieved Hooker's fought-out First Corps on the front lines and that the smaller, though still fresh Twelfth Corps had arrived near the base of the mountain. Still, even as his men silently slipped away off the mountain that night, Lee held out some hope. Sometime between 11:00 p.m. and midnight, Lee heard what proved to be an unfounded report that the Federal troops, instead of being reinforced at the front, were instead themselves falling back. He ordered Colonel Peter Stevens to send forward a small detachment to verify, if possible, this claim. Stevens entrusted this risky assignment to Lieutenant William P. DuBose of the Holcombe Legion. DuBose set out promptly into the darkness and was promptly captured, having walked right into the picket line of the 107th New York. It was clear that the Federals had not gone anywhere and were still holding their ground in strong force. The retreat would continue.[267]

Having made preparations for the withdrawal of Hill's and Longstreet's men from around Turner's and Fox's Gaps, Lee then began notifying his subordinates engaged in the siege of Harpers Ferry of his decision to retreat and arranging for the reunification of his army. "The day has gone against us," Lee wrote to Lafayette McLaws at 8:00 p.m., "and this army will go by Sharpsburg and cross the river. It is necessary for you to abandon your position to-night." Not yet knowing that the Federal Sixth Corps had punched through at Crampton's Gap and was now in Pleasant Valley, Lee directed McLaws to retire from Maryland Heights and move north with his and R.H. Anderson's commands through the valley in order to unite with Longstreet and Hill, who were just then preparing to lead their men off the mountain. After sending off this directive to McLaws, Lee sent another to Stonewall Jackson, instructing him to move north from his position west of Harpers Ferry in order to cover the Potomac River crossing at Shepherdstown. The army's trains and reserve artillery were also set in motion westward, toward Williamsport, where they were to get across the river.[268]

A somber mood prevailed among the Confederate forces as they began their retreat from the mountain. The first to withdraw, quietly in the darkness at about 10:00 p.m., were Colquitt's men, who had successfully fended off John Gibbon's assault directly up the National Pike. Reaching the Mountain House within the hour, Colquitt's soldiers continued west down the mountain, followed by Rodes's Brigade, which had battled so fiercely with Meade's Pennsylvania Reserves. As the rear of Rodes's column passed through Boonsboro, they were followed by the shattered remnants of Garland's North Carolina brigade, since early that Sunday morning commanded by Duncan McRae, who had taken the place of the lamented Garland. Behind McRae's small band came Ripley's Brigade, which D.H. Hill scornfully noted did not draw a trigger that day. Finally, there were the North Carolinians under George B. Anderson. These three brigades—McRae's, Ripley's and G.B. Anderson's—moved off South Mountain along the Old Sharpsburg Road and other trails and byroads immediately west of Fox's Gap. They were followed a short time later by the few men who remained of Drayton's Brigade, and later by Hood's Division—the brigades of Law and Wofford—now bolstered by G.T. Anderson's Brigade as they marched off the mountain. Farther north, the thoroughly exhausted survivors of Kemper's and Garnett's brigades abandoned their position just a few hundred yards from the Mountain House. They were followed by Evans's Brigade, under Stevens, which moved out about 1:00 a.m. on September 15. The last of Lee's men to slip away from South Mountain were the South Carolinians of Micah Jenkins's Brigade, under Joseph Walker. These men began their withdrawal at 4:00 a.m. and would not pass through Boonsboro until after daybreak.[269]

It was by no means an orderly retreat. The men staggered about in the darkness; many fell by the wayside, simply too worn out to continue marching, only to be gathered up the next day by the pursuing Union columns. The men were disorganized, dispirited and demoralized. That Sunday night and during the early morning hours of September 15, not one of these Confederate soldiers—not Lee, D.H. Hill or even the lowliest private—would have proclaimed the Battle of South Mountain a Confederate victory. Yet as the morning hours ticked by on September 15 and the day continued to brighten, so too did Confederate spirits, for it was only then that they began to realize what had been gained by their determined, daylong stance on the mountain. And as the fruits of the Confederates' struggle became clearer the next day, those gained by the Army of the Potomac that bloody Sunday began slipping away.

On the night of September 14, George McClellan was justifiably proud of the results of the day's actions. Just twelve days earlier he had been asked to once again assume active army command after a summer's worth of defeats, when the nation was in despair and the fortunes of war for the United States were at their nadir. He led an aggressive pursuit of Lee's invading army through Maryland, having to deal at almost every step with panicked and sometimes intrusive government officials. He had wrestled the initiative away from Lee, and that Sunday, his men forced the Confederate army from their strong, and at some places seemingly impregnable, defensive positions on South Mountain.

At 9:40 p.m., McClellan wired General in Chief Halleck, reporting that his men had carried the heights. "The troops behaved magnificently," boasted the army commander. "They have never fought better." And although McClellan, like Lee, did not yet know of the Sixth Corps's success in carrying Crampton's Gap, he proclaimed the day's action a "glorious victory." Still, McClellan knew there was much more work to be done. Of course, he did not know that Lee had already ordered a retreat, but he promised Halleck that he was "hurrying up everything from the rear to be prepared for any eventuality." And, indeed, he was.

McClellan had already ordered up Sumner's Second Corps to relieve Hooker's fought-out troops and had also advanced the Twelfth Corps to Bolivar. He further instructed his corps commanders to advance pickets at first light the following morning. Then, sometime after midnight, McClellan learned of Franklin's success. He immediately sent orders to his Sixth Corps commander to renew the offensive in the morning by marching south through Pleasant Valley and destroying McLaws's command. There was still the possibility that the siege at Harpers Ferry could be lifted and that he could inflict another blow on Lee's divided columns. After sending off these instructions to Franklin, the Union army commander turned in for a few hours' rest, hopeful that the next day his men could achieve greater victory.[270]

Early on the morning of September 15, Hartsuff's brigade of Ricketts's division, First Corps, crept forward to the Mountain House, only to discover that the Confederate army was gone. At Fox's Gap, soldiers of the Ninth Corps found that their gray-clad adversaries had also slipped away during the night. News of this filtered back to McClellan, who at once began organizing the pursuit. Brigadier General Israel B. Richardson's division of the Second Corps was to lead the advance, along with Pleasonton's cavalry, west along the National Pike. Hooker was to follow behind Richardson with his First Corps, while Sumner was to follow behind Hooker with the divisions of French and Sedgwick. The Twelfth Corps was to fall in behind Sumner. Orders then went out to Burnside to lead the Ninth Corps west from Fox's Gap along the Old Sharpsburg Road. Finally, George Sykes's division of regulars, the only Fifth Corps force immediately available, was to follow behind the Ninth Corps through Fox's Gap.

Having thus made all the necessary arrangements for a pursuit and fully expecting his subordinates to execute their orders, McClellan wired another dispatch to Halleck, informing him of Franklin's victory at Crampton's Gap and further praising his men's actions of the previous day. He also told him that Lee's men had "disappeared during the night" and that he was setting off in pursuit, "to press their retreat to the utmost." Significantly, McClellan concluded by assuring Halleck that "the morale of our own men is now restored."[271]

McClellan continued to receive encouraging reports from the front, further trumpeting the extent of the previous day's victory. Joe Hooker informed McClellan that he had heard "perfectly reliable" information that Lee's men were retreating in a "perfect panic" to the Potomac and that Lee himself admitted that the Confederate army had been "shockingly whipped." Further reports erroneously claimed that Lee was among the wounded and that the Confederate army had lost up to fifteen thousand casualties. It was clear to McClellan that Lee's army had fled "in the greatest haste and in disordered masses to the river." Having wired Washington, and before setting out for the front, McClellan took a few moments to write to his wife. The battle of September 14, declared the proud husband, resulted in a "glorious and complete victory," but he was still hoping for more. "I am pushing everything after them with the greatest rapidity & expect to gain great results…If I can believe one tenth of what is reported, God has seldom given an army a greater victory than this."[272]

While army headquarters was a flurry of activity that Monday morning, out front, any exultation McClellan's men may have felt over their victory soon gave way when they witnessed the horrid aftermath of battle. A.P. Smith of the 76th New York remembered that daylight "revealed to us the horrors of last night's work." The dead, said Smith,

lay thickly scattered, in some instances piled one upon another, over the field…Here lay a poor fellow with his head upon his arm, and his eyes closed as though in sleep; here another with gun clenched fast in his hand, and a determined look still upon his face; there, where the fire had been more deadly, lay several, the one across the other, as if the heat of battle had melted a battalion, and they had all fallen.

Such scenes forced the Union troops to become more introspective. "All animosity, at such a time, yields to the better impulses of our nature," reflected the New York soldier, "and we wonder how it is that man can lift his hand to slay his brother."[273]

The same terrible scenes dawned on the Ninth Corps troops at Fox's Gap and on Franklin's men six miles south at Crampton's Gap. "Behind us and in front of us, but especially in the angles of the stone walls, the dead bodies of the enemy lay thick," said William Todd of the 79th New York, while "near the gaps in the fences they were piled on top of each other like cordwood dumped from a cart."

"It was indeed a sad sight," echoed Allen Albert of the 45th Pennsylvania. Like A.P. Smith of the 76th New York, Albert also grew more reflective. "It was a sickening sight to see them lying there just as they had fallen and my heart went out in sympathy for them and their dear ones they had left behind. We turned away in horror," concluded the Pennsylvanian, "thankful that we had been more fortunate than they in escaping the dangers of battle." As with George McClellan, however, some of the Union troops took the time to reflect on what had been gained, realizing the victory meant much more than just a tactical battlefield win. McClellan wrote to Halleck that the men's morale had been restored, a thought shared by the regimental historian of the 35th Massachusetts. "It was our first important advantage after a series of disastrous battles," and the victory restored to the army "confidence in its prowess." Like McClellan, the men also knew there was more work to be done. Orders arrived, and the men gathered their gear and prepared to move out, more confident than they had been in quite some time.[274]

Israel Richardson got the Union pursuit off to a good start. Descending the western slopes of South Mountain along the National Pike early that morning, Richardson's veteran division, with Thomas Meagher's Irish Brigade in the lead, soon spotted a Confederate cavalry force to its front and roughly a mile and a half east of Boonsboro. A few scattered shots broke out, followed by artillery fire. Richardson halted the advance and deployed his men into lines of battle. The Confederate horsemen Richardson spotted were of General Fitzhugh Lee's Brigade, which had been entrusted with helping to cover the retreat from South Mountain. Lee had three regiments—the 3rd, 4th and 9th Virginia Cavalry—along with two guns under John Pelham. Just prior to Richardson's approach, Jenkins's South Carolina Brigade had filed past the horsemen, the last of the Confederate army to march off the mountain. After firing off a few shots, and with Richardson's division now advancing, Pelham's gunners limbered up and trotted away, followed by the cavalrymen. Richardson's men opened fire on the withdrawing troopers; moments later, thundering past the infantrymen came six companies of the

8[275] Illinois Cavalry, under Colonel John Farnsworth. Noticing the charging Federal horsemen, Fitzhugh Lee turned around his 3rd Virginia and repulsed Farnsworth's troopers, driving them back to Richardson's line. But it was only a temporary setback. The Union horsemen rallied and once more charged ahead, this time driving the 3rd Virginia back in the wildest disorder.[275]

As this unfolded east of Boonsboro, the soldiers of the 4th and 9th Virginia Cavalry, for whatever reason, were permitted to dismount in the streets of town, the men seeking some rest. They were thus caught entirely off guard when the panicked troopers of the 3rd came crashing through town, followed closely by the hard-charging 8th Illinois. It was a wild scene as Confederate horsemen attempted to remount and meet the Federal attack. Pistol and carbine fire erupted throughout sleepy Boonsboro, and many men were trampled underfoot. Fleeing town, Colonel William "Rooney" Lee, the army commander's son, was thrown violently from the saddle and seriously injured when his dead horse fell on him. He lay there, trapped, as horses thundered past, for several harrowing minutes before he was finally able to pry himself loose and crawl away, seeking a good hiding place in a field of corn. Small bands of Confederate horsemen were able to rally, stalling the Union advance and allowing the bulk of Fitzhugh Lee's shattered command to flee Boonsboro. Pleasonton brought up Captain John Tidball's artillery, which fired a few parting shots into the Confederate horsemen as they dashed away, cross-country, to the north and west. It was a sharp and bloody, though brief, encounter.

Pleasonton claimed a loss of just one man killed and fifteen wounded while Confederate casualties, he said, numbered thirty dead and fifty wounded. Two Confederate flags were also snatched up in the rout. Casualties aside, the horsemen of the 8th Illinois Cavalry chased away the Confederate screen and opened the road for Richardson's men to continue their pursuit of Robert E. Lee's retreating columns.[276]

Excepting this dust-up in the streets of Boonsboro, the retreat of the Army of Northern Virginia had been effected without much incident, although there had been much disorder and straggling. However, by the break of dawn on September 15, the situation had already drastically changed. Rather than falling all the way back to the Potomac, Lee had instead halted his retreating columns overnight. And even as McClellan was issuing orders for the pursuit that Monday morning, Lee was just then forming a new defensive line several miles to the west along the winding Antietam Creek, near Sharpsburg.

This shift in Lee's strategy was forced upon him when he learned of the Federal breakthrough at Crampton's Gap. When Lee first ordered the retreat from South Mountain about 8:00 p.m. on September 14 and sent off instructions for McLaws to abandon his position, he believed McLaws would have been able to move north unimpeded through Pleasant Valley. However, when he learned of the loss of Crampton's Gap and that a large Federal force was now in the valley and directly behind McLaws's command, he knew this was no longer possible. Further, with McLaws cut off and in a precarious position, Lee realized that if he continued with the retreat of D.H. Hill's and Longstreet's men to the Potomac, he would be abandoning McLaws—whose division, along with that of R.H. Anderson, made up a full 20 percent of his entire army—to his fate. He thus halted his men at Keedysville, a small hamlet roughly five miles west of the mountain, in order to help McLaws escape.

From this position, Longstreet and D.H. Hill would be on the flank of any Union force that moved down Pleasant Valley to attack McLaws. Yet even in this new position, Lee's concern for McLaws's command continued to grow. Throughout the night, he sent several urgent notes to the heavily bearded division commander from Georgia, informing him of his new position at Keedysville and urging him to find whatever route available and join him there. By daybreak on September 15, Lee had yet to hear anything from McLaws. He feared none of his messages had gotten through and thus sent off another: "We have fallen back to this place to enable you to more readily join us. You are desired to withdraw immediately from your position on Maryland Heights and join us here…The utmost dispatch is required." At that early hour, Lee was still fully intending on retreating but not without first seeing to the safety of McLaws's threatened command.[277]

Keedysville, however, would no longer do. Daylight revealed that there was no good defensible ground there should McClellan press his advantage and attack Longstreet and D.H. Hill. Yet just a few miles farther west, there was ideal defensive terrain on the high ground rising sharply from the Antietam Creek. And not only was there better defensive ground west of the Antietam, but also from there Lee's men would still be on the flank of any Union force moving south through Pleasant Valley. Lee issued orders for Hill and Longstreet to move their entire commands across the creek and form them into lines of battle along the dominating ridgeline.

Lee was naturally concerned about McLaws's command and was certainly aware of its dangerous position. However, he did not fully appreciate the extent of McLaws's predicament. Geography, along with Franklin's Sixth Corps, had boxed McLaws in, and there was simply no possible way that Sunday night and into the next morning for his men to escape, save for the surrender of Harpers Ferry and the hope that somehow Franklin would not attack. Throughout the evening hours of September 14 and well into the night, McLaws was desperately patching together a line of defense across the valley floor. He moved all of Kershaw's and Barksdale's brigades off Maryland Heights, except for one regiment and two cannons, and formed them in battle lines next to the shattered remnants of Semmes's, Cobb's and Parham's Brigades. He placed artillery on either flank and ordered up Wilcox's Brigade from R.H. Anderson's Division to further bolster the line. In all, McLaws had between five and six thousand men in position, bracing for the attack he was sure would come. Despite Lee's thoughts to the contrary, McLaws did receive the urgent pleas from the army commander, but he simply could not follow the orders. He tried to notify Lee of this, but his riders were unable to get through. He could not extract his command; all he could do was wait.[278]

Early on the morning of September 15, George McClellan, in addition to wanting to inflict another blow to Lee's retreating columns, still hoped to relieve the Harpers Ferry garrison, though he knew time was fast running out. The day before, as the fighting at South Mountain raged, McClellan had received a distressing report from Dixon Miles. By that point entirely surrounded and under fire from Confederate guns on all sides, Miles predicted that his men would only be able to hold out for another twenty-four hours. McClellan replied for Miles to "hold out to the last extremity" and assured him that his men were on their way. He sent this same urgent message with three different riders, each taking a different route to Harpers Ferry, but none got through. Still, that Monday morning, the chance, small though it may have been, of relieving Miles's men was still there, and it was now up to William Franklin to see it through.[279]

Franklin received his orders to move south and attack McLaws's force early that Monday morning. He could hear the cannonading to the south, which meant that Miles was still holding out. Yet Franklin advanced his men slowly down the valley and displayed no assertiveness in attempting to execute his orders. He saw McLaws's line stretched out across the valley floor and reported this to McClellan. But this was not the worst news for the Union army commander. About 8:30 a.m., the cannon fire coming from the direction of Harpers Ferry ceased; Dixon Miles had ordered the white flag of surrender raised. Any hope McClellan had of rescuing the Harpers Ferry garrison was now gone. However, Franklin still posed a great threat to McLaws's command. He promised to attack, but with other Confederate troops now freed from the siege, he was fearful that the Confederate line to his front had been bolstered and thus sought reinforcements.[280]

Meanwhile, Franklin's men continued to slowly creep their way south until they arrived within a few hundred yards of McLaws's line. All was tense and quiet between the opposing lines; a silent showdown. Then, at 10:00 a.m., the Confederates let out a resounding cheer that swept up and down their line—news of Harpers Ferry's fall had just arrived. A Union skirmisher climbed atop a stone wall and shouted, "What the hell are you fellows cheering for?"

"Because Harpers Ferry had gone up, God damn you!" came the reply.

"I thought that was it," said the Union solider before jumping off the wall.

As the hours ticked by, it became increasingly evident that there was to be no battle that day in Pleasant Valley. William Franklin saw no need for it. At 11:00 a.m., he sent off another note to McClellan. "The enemy is in large force in my front, in two lines of battle stretching across the valley, and a large column of artillery and infantry on the right of the valley looking toward Harper's Ferry," he reported. Franklin had more than fifteen thousand men available, including his own Sixth Corps, as well as General Darius Couch's wayward Fourth Corps division, which had arrived late the night before. Yet as he had the previous day at Crampton's Gap, Franklin again overestimated the Confederate force to his front. "They outnumber me two to one," declared Franklin. "It will, of course, not answer to pursue the enemy under these circumstances…I have not the force to justify an attack on the force I see in front."

McClellan took Franklin at his word and had nothing but praise for his old friend in various reports on the campaign. The army commander instead laid the blame for the loss of Harpers Ferry squarely on the shoulders of Dixon Miles, writing that the surrender of the post was both "shameful" and "premature." Miles was unable to defend himself; he was among the last casualties of the Harpers Ferry siege, falling mortally wounded in one of the final artillery salvos. However, although McClellan would not fault his Sixth Corps commander for failing to execute his instructions, the inactivity of Franklin in Pleasant Valley was just the first of several key failures that day among McClellan's subordinates to carry out his plans.[281]

With Franklin's men idle in Pleasant Valley and displaying no intention to attack, Lafayette McLaws entrusted command of his line to R.H. Anderson, instructing him to move south as soon as the bridge across the Potomac was clear. He then made his way across the river and through Harpers Ferry until he found Stonewall Jackson. He had an interesting proposal: attack the Federal force in Pleasant Valley, which would have then exposed the flank and rear of McClellan's main column as it pursued Longstreet's and

D.H. Hill's command westward from South Mountain. Jackson heard out his subordinate, probably already having considered this option, but quickly disavowed him of this notion. Jackson had received Lee's orders of the night before to make haste toward Shepherdstown to cover Lee's retiring columns, and this is what he intended to do.[282]

The surrender of Harpers Ferry altered the nature of the campaign by forcing Lee to again change his strategy. About 8:15 a.m., having already decided to fall back from Keedysville to the heights immediately west of the Antietam Creek, Lee received a message from Jackson, written the night before. This was the first report he had received from Harpers Ferry in more than twenty-four hours, and it revealed to him the imminent capture of the garrison. "Through God's Blessing," wrote Jackson, "the advance, which commenced this evening, has been successful thus far, and I look to Him for complete success to-morrow." Jackson's words reenergized Lee; perhaps, he thought, not all was lost. Perhaps he could still salvage this campaign. McClellan's advance troops were just then making their way off the mountain to the east. If he could put up a strong front along the Antietam, and if Longstreet and D.H. Hill could keep McClellan at bay long enough, then Jackson would have the time he needed to complete his operations. Jackson's force could then march north and join him there. Once again united, Lee's army could use the Hagerstown Turnpike, which ran north from Sharpsburg, to continue moving north, thereby continuing to pull McClellan after him. But if forced to fight at Antietam, the ground there did offer some defensive advantages, particularly south and east of Sharpsburg.

Lee rode across the Antietam and began overseeing the placement of Longstreet's and D.H. Hill's men into lines of battle while ordering up all his available guns. The reinvigorated army commander then cast his gaze eastward, watching as the blue Federal columns lurched westward toward his new position.[283]

The news only continued to get better for Lee. About noon he received another note from Jackson. "Through God's blessing, Harpers Ferry and its garrison are to be surrendered," announced Stonewall. Lee's hard-fighting, trusted subordinate also promised that his men would move north and join him at Sharpsburg, leaving just A.P. Hill's division behind to tend to the details of the surrender. Lee passed word of this along to his subordinates, who, in turn, passed it on to their commands, just then forming in line. The news, noted Lee, "reanimated the courage of the troops."[284]

It was only at this moment that Lee and his soldiers were able to realize what had been gained at South Mountain the previous day: time. Their determined stance held back McClellan's army long enough to give Jackson the time he needed to complete the investment of Harpers Ferry, and although a tactical defeat, it was now clear that the Battle of South Mountain was, at the same time, a successful Confederate delaying action.

While the situation continued to brighten for Robert E. Lee throughout that Monday, September 15, it only continued to worsen for George McClellan. He received word of Harpers Ferry's fall, as well as the discouraging note from Franklin claiming that a large Confederate force was in Pleasant Valley. If Franklin was to be believed—if the Confederate force to his front outnumbered him two to one—that meant more than thirty thousand Confederates in Pleasant Valley. To keep an eye on this force and to prevent their advance up the valley and toward his flank and rear, McClellan ordered Franklin to hold his position. He would remain there with his Sixth Corps until the morning of September 17. McClellan then received a report from Fitz John Porter, whose Fifth Corps troops under Sykes were supposed to follow behind Burnside westward along the Old Sharpsburg Road. The Ninth Corps, said Porter, had not so much as budged from Fox's Gap and remained in bivouac, blocking the road.

Burnside made his headquarters with McClellan's near Bolivar on the night of September 14–15 and at eight o'clock that Monday morning received orders to move out with the "utmost vigor." When Burnside arrived at Fox's Gap, however, he discovered that Jacob Cox, who had assumed command of the Ninth Corps following the death of Reno, had made no preparation for an advance. Many of the men were instead found lounging about, while others were engaged in the grim work of burying the dead. Many a letter was written home that morning, the soldiers either assuring loved ones of their survival or informing others of the deaths of their sons, brothers, husbands or fathers. Knowing the men were tired from their previous day's exertions, Burnside gave no orders to the contrary and ordered up rations.

The terrible aftermaths of battle continued to make impressions on the men of the Ninth Corps. Captain James Wren of the 48th Pennsylvania was particularly struck by a makeshift hospital established in and around a small house on the mountain's eastern slope. It was, he said, "an awful sight." In the yard were three or four large operating tables and surgeons busily going about the work of amputation. "Looking around in the yard," said Wren,

I saw a Beautiful, plump arm Laying [there], *which Drew my attention & in looking a Little* [at] *it, and seeing another of the same kind, I picked them up & Laid them together & found that they are a right* [arm] *&*

one a Left arm, which Convinced me that they were off the one man & you Could see many legs Laying in the yard with the shoes & stockings on—not taken off when amputated.

Behind the house lay a long row of dead soldiers—"side by side," said Wren, "with a Little inscription on thear breasts, giving thear Names & thear Company & Regt. and the state"—gathered for burial. Men with shovels and picks were digging a trench as a final resting place for these dead. Allen Albert of the 45th Pennsylvania was one of the men helping to bury the dead, both Union and Confederate, that morning:

In a trench a little above the old log house…wrapped in their blankets we laid them tenderly away at the front of the hill they had helped to make immortal! The enemy's dead were also left for us to bury. The poor fellows lay where they fell, singly or piled up one across the other.

Yet not all of the dead were laid "tenderly away." In one of South Mountain's more infamous stories, farmer Daniel Wise's well became the final resting place for fifty-eight Confederate soldiers, while inscribed upon a "rude board, marking the spot" were the letters CSA. "War makes brutes of human beings," rationalized Captain Oliver Bosbyshell of the 48th Pennsylvania. "These dead soldiers were men like those burying them, but no one stopped to think of that; haste to cover them out of sight was the principal thing, and the well afforded a convenient receptacle."[285]

Leaving his headquarters near Bolivar, George McClellan arrived at Fox's Gap about twelve thirty that afternoon and quickly directed the Ninth Corps to step aside, allowing Sykes's regulars to pass through, and make ready to follow. The Union army commander then took some time to view the battlefield. He stood where his friend and West Point classmate Jesse Reno had fallen. As he later recorded, "The loss of this brave and distinguished officer tempered with sadness the exultation of triumph. A gallant soldier, an able general, endeared to his troops and associates, his death is felt an irreparable misfortune." McClellan, after ensuring that the Ninth Corps would move out, then traveled north to Turner's Gap. He halted at a farmhouse near the gap that had been transformed into a field hospital. Along with his chief of staff and father-in-law, Randolph Marcy, McClellan walked among the wounded, taking them by the hand while thanking them for their service. He visited with some of the more seriously wounded inside the house before remounting, wiping away some tears and riding off to Boonsboro, once more refocused on the task at hand.[286]

As this transpired around the mountaintop, Israel Richardson's division continued to lead the Army of the Potomac's advance, marching west along the Boonsboro–Sharpsburg Turnpike. His men pushed on through Keedysville about 2:00 p.m., but as they neared the high ground east of the Antietam, they came under artillery fire. Richardson halted his columns and deployed into lines of battle while sending the 5th New Hampshire toward the creek as skirmishers. Joe Hooker, accompanying Richardson's men, galloped to the front and, together with Richardson and Alfred Pleasonton, surveyed the ground to the west. The Confederate army had halted its retreat and was now occupying a strong defensive position just across the creek. Federal guns were brought up, and a sometimes-lively artillery duel commenced; near the creek, a brisk skirmish fire broke out between the 5th New Hampshire and Confederates posted near the Middle Bridge.

McClellan's instructions were clear. As he later reported, he "had hoped to come up with the enemy during the 15th in sufficient force to beat them again and drive them into the [Potomac] river. My instructions were that if the enemy were on the march they were to be at once attacked"; if, however, "they were found in force and in position, the corps were to be placed in position for attack, but no attack was to be made until I reached the front." Now, Richardson, Hooker and Pleasonton spotted Lee's men "in force and in position." Hooker composed a note to McClellan, estimating that there were at least thirty thousand Confederates and perhaps as many as one hundred cannons lining the heights west of the Antietam. Hooker then sent an aide galloping back toward Boonsboro. Receiving Hooker's note, George McClellan made his way to the front, the rumble of artillery fire growing as he continued westward along the turnpike.[287]

Riding along the Boonsboro–Sharpsburg Turnpike, McClellan was greeted by a perfect ovation. Thousands of soldiers, the men of French's and Sedgwick's Second Corps divisions and those of Hooker's First Corps, cheered the army commander, many doffing their caps and some even throwing them high in the air. No doubt touched by this show of respect and affection, McClellan was also very likely a little troubled by the fact that these men were stacked up in the roadway—the blue column stretching for miles—instead of being brought to the front and "placed in position for attack," as his instructions had dictated. Because of this, McClellan knew these men would not be immediately available should he decide to attack. When McClellan did reach the front, sometime after 4:00 p.m., he found only Richardson's division and Sykes's Fifth Corps men formed in lines of battle.

As he neared the front, McClellan was met first by Edwin Sumner, who informed the army commander of Lee's new position, telling him that by all appearance it seemed a strong one. The two generals then rode forward to the heights immediately east of the Antietam Creek, where they were joined by Hooker. Present also in this gathering of officers was McClellan's confidant and closest subordinate, Fitz John Porter. Ambrose Burnside and Jacob Cox then galloped up to report that the Ninth Corps was making steady progress. With their staffs, this cavalcade of Union brass peered through their binoculars and field glasses, surveying the Confederate line across the creek. As McClellan later reported, Lee's new position "was one of the strongest to be found in this region of country, which is well adapted for defensive warfare," and all those present certainly shared in this assessment. McClellan's entourage caught the attention of Confederate gunners, who soon began firing shells in their direction. Coming under fire, McClellan dismissed everyone, save for Porter, instructing them to return to their commands.[288]

The sun was already in the western skies; dusk would soon settle. George McClellan wished to strike at Lee again on September 15 in order to follow up on his victory on South Mountain and deliver a more crushing blow. President Abraham Lincoln, too, clamored for action. Before setting out for the front and while still in Boonsboro, McClellan had received a telegram from the president, who, learning of the Union success on September 14, wrote, "God bless you and all with you. Destroy the Rebel army if possible." But with the lateness of the hour, with Lee's men now holding a formidable line and with only two of his divisions prepared, McClellan concluded that no attack could be made that day.[289]

Across the Antietam, and as the hours continued to tick by, Robert E. Lee breathed a little easier. That Monday morning, the Confederate army commander had been fully intending to abandon his northern campaign, but circumstances forced him to remain north of the Potomac. He could not retreat lest he leave McLaws to his fate in Pleasant Valley. He halted Longstreet and D.H. Hill on the good, defensible ground west of the Antietam, keeping a careful eye on McClellan's approaching columns. However, when he learned of the fall of Harpers Ferry, Lee's outlook brightened considerably. The retreat was called off, and he attempted to salvage something of this campaign. Even as the Union army inched its way closer to Lee's new line, Stonewall Jackson's men, including McLaws's command from Pleasant Valley, were preparing to set off from Harpers Ferry to join Lee at Sharpsburg.

After dismissing his subordinates from their exposed position, George McClellan issued a flurry of orders, calling up his artillery and identifying where he wanted his corps to be positioned. Then, with Confederate shells exploding nearby, McClellan, along with Porter, once more raised his field glass, gazing west, examining Lee's lines across the Antietam Creek.

Order of Battle

ARMY OF THE POTOMAC

MAJOR GENERAL GEORGE B. MCCLELLAN

First Corps

Major General Joseph Hooker

FIRST DIVISION
Brigadier General Rufus King[290]
Brigadier General John P. Hatch (w)*
Brigadier General Abner Doubleday

First Brigade
Colonel Walter Phelps Jr.

22nd New York
24th New York

Second Brigade
Brigadier General Abner
  Doubleday
Colonel William Wainwright (w)
Lieutenant Colonel J. William
  Hofmann

---

* (k) = killed
  (w) = wounded
  (mw) = mortally wounded

30th New York
84th New York
2nd U.S. Sharpshooters

7th Indiana
76th New York
95th New York
56th Pennsylvania

Third Brigade
Brigadier General Marsena R. Patrick
21st New York
23rd New York
35th New York
80th New York

Fourth Brigade
Brigadier General John Gibbon
19th Indiana
2nd Wisconsin
6th Wisconsin
7th Wisconsin

First Division Artillery
Captain J. Albert Monroe
New Hampshire Light, 1st Battery, Lieutenant Frederick Edgell
1st Rhode Island Light, Battery D, Captain J. Albert Monroe
1st New York Light, Battery L, Captain John A. Reynolds
4th U.S., Battery B, Captain Joseph Campbell

SECOND DIVISION
Brigadier General James Ricketts

First Brigade
Brigadier General Abram Duryee
97th New York
104th New York
105th New York
107th Pennsylvania

Second Brigade
Colonel William Christian
26th New York
94th New York
88th Pennsylvania
90th Pennsylvania

Third Brigade
Brigadier General George L. Hartsuff
12th Massachusetts
13th Massachusetts
83rd New York
11th Pennsylvania

Second Division Artillery
1st Pennsylvania Light, Battery F, Captain Ezra W. Matthews
Pennsylvania Light, Battery C, Captain James Thompson

THIRD DIVISION
Brigadier General George G. Meade

First Brigade
Brigadier General Truman Seymour
1st Pennsylvania Reserves
2nd Pennsylvania Reserves
5th Pennsylvania Reserves
6th Pennsylvania Reserves
13th Pennsylvania Reserves

Second Brigade
Colonel Albert Magilton
3rd Pennsylvania Reserves
4th Pennsylvania Reserves
7th Pennsylvania Reserves
8th Pennsylvania Reserves

Third Brigade
Colonel Thomas Gallagher (w)
Lieutenant Colonel Robert Anderson
9th Pennsylvania Reserves
10th Pennsylvania Reserves
11th Pennsylvania Reserves
12th Pennsylvania Reserves

Third Division Artillery
1st Pennsylvania Light, Battery A, Lieutenant John G. Simpson
1st Pennsylvania Light, Battery B, Captain James H. Cooper
5th U.S., Battery C, Captain Dunbar R. Ransom

Sixth Corps

Major General William B. Franklin

FIRST DIVISION
Major General Henry W. Slocum

First Brigade
Colonel Alfred T.A. Torbert
1st New Jersey
2nd New Jersey
3rd New Jersey
4th New Jersey

Second Brigade
Colonel Joseph J. Bartlett
5th Maine
16th New York
27th New York
96th Pennsylvania

Third Brigade
Brigadier General John Newton
18th New York
31st New York
32nd New York
95th Pennsylvania

First Division Artillery
Captain Emory Upton
Maryland Light, Battery A, Captain John Wolcott
Massachusetts Light, Battery A, Captain Josiah Porter
New Jersey Light, Battery A, Captain William Hexamer
2nd U.S., Battery D, Lieutenant Edward Williston

SECOND DIVISION
Major General William F. Smith

First Brigade
Brigadier General Winfield S. Hancock
6th Maine
43rd New York
49th Pennsylvania
137th Pennsylvania
5th Wisconsin

Second Brigade
Brigadier General W.T.H. Brooks
2nd Vermont
3rd Vermont
4th Vermont
5th Vermont
6th Vermont

Third Brigade
Colonel William H. Irwin
7th Maine
20th New York
33rd New York
49th New York
77th New York

Second Division Artillery
Captain Romeyn B. Ayres
Maryland Light, Battery B, Lieutenant Theodore J. Vanneman
New York Light, 1st Battery, Captain Andrew Cowan
5th U.S., Battery F, Lieutenant Leonard Martin

ORDER OF BATTLE

Ninth Corps

Major General Jesse Reno (mw)

Brigadier General Jacob Cox

FIRST DIVISION
Brigadier General Orlando B. Willcox

First Brigade
Colonel Benjamin Christ
28th Massachusetts
8th Michigan[291]
17th Michigan
79th New York
50th Pennsylvania

Second Brigade
Colonel Thomas Welsh
46th New York
45th Pennsylvania
100th Pennsylvania

First Division Artillery
Massachusetts Light, Eighth Battery, Captain Asa M. Cook
2nd U.S., Battery E, Lieutenant Samuel Benjamin

SECOND DIVISION
Brigadier General Samuel D. Sturgis

First Brigade
Colonel James Nagle
2nd Maryland
6th New Hampshire
9th New Hampshire
48th Pennsylvania

Second Brigade
Colonel Edward Ferrero
21st Massachusetts
35th Massachusetts
51st New York
51st Pennsylvania

Second Division Artillery
Pennsylvania Light, Battery D, Captain George W. Durell
4th U.S., Battery E, Captain Joseph Clark

ORDER OF BATTLE

THIRD DIVISION
Brigadier General Isaac P. Rodman

First Brigade
Colonel Harrison Fairchild
9th New York
89th New York
103rd New York

Second Brigade
Colonel Edward Harland
8th Connecticut
11th Connecticut
16th Connecticut
4th Rhode Island

Third Division Artillery
5th U.S., Battery A, Lieutenant Charles P. Muhlenberg

FOURTH (KANAWHA) DIVISION
Brigadier General Jacob Cox

First Brigade
Colonel Eliakim P. Scammon
12th Ohio
23rd Ohio
30th Ohio

Second Brigade
Colonel George Crook
11th Ohio
28th Ohio
36th Ohio

Artillery
Ohio Light Artillery, First Battery, Schambeck's Company, Chicago, Captain James McMullin Dragoons
Gilmore's Company, West Virginia Cavalry, Kentucky Light Artillery, Lieutenant James Abraham
Simmond's Battery, Harrison's Company, West Virginia Cavalry, Lieutenant Dennis Delaney

Cavalry

Brigadier General Alfred Pleasonton

First Brigade
Major Charles Whiting
5th U.S. Cavalry
6th U.S. Cavalry

Second Brigade
Colonel John Farnsworth
8th Illinois Cavalry
3rd Indiana Cavalry

1st Massachusetts Cavalry
8th Pennsylvania Cavalry

Third Brigade
Colonel Richard H. Rush
4th Pennsylvania Cavalry
6th Pennsylvania Cavalry

Fourth Brigade
Colonel Andrew T. McReynolds
1st New York Cavalry
12th Pennsylvania Cavalry

Fifth Brigade
Colonel Benjamin F. Davis
8th New York Cavalry
3rd Pennsylvania Cavalry

Artillery

2nd U.S., Battery A, Captain John Tidball
2nd U.S., Batteries B and L, Captain James M. Robertson
2nd U.S., Battery M, Lieutenant Peter Hains
3rd U.S., Batteries C and G, Captain Horatio G. Gibson

Unattached

15th Pennsylvania Cavalry

Army of Northern Virginia

General Robert E. Lee

D.H. Hill's Division

Major General Daniel Harvey Hill

RIPLEY'S BRIGADE
Brigadier General Roswell Ripley

GARLAND'S BRIGADE
Brigadier General Samuel
Garland (k)

4th Georgia
44th Georgia
1st North Carolina
3rd North Carolina

Colonel Duncan K. McRae
5th North Carolina
12th North Carolina
13th North Carolina
20th North Carolina
23rd North Carolina

RODES'S BRIGADE
Brigadier General Robert E. Rodes

3rd Alabama
5th Alabama
6th Alabama
12th Alabama
26th Alabama

ANDERSON'S BRIGADE
Brigadier General George B. Anderson
2nd North Carolina
4th North Carolina
14th North Carolina
30th North Carolina

COLQUITT'S BRIGADE
Colonel Alfred H. Colquitt
13th Alabama
6th Georgia
23rd Georgia
27th Georgia
28th Georgia

ARTILLERY
Major Pierson
Hardaway's (Alabama) Battery, Captain R.A. Hardaway
Jefferson Davis (Alabama) Artillery, Captain J.W. Bondurant
Jones's (Virginia) Battery, Captain William B. Jones
King William (Virginia) Artillery, Captain T.H. Carter

D.R. Jones's Division

Brigadier General David R. Jones

TOOMBS'S BRIGADE
Brigadier General Robert A. Toombs

DRAYTON'S BRIGADE
Brigadier General Thomas F. Drayton

2nd Georgia
15th Georgia
17th Georgia
20th Georgia

50th Georgia
51st Georgia
3rd South Carolina Battalion
15th South Carolina
Phillips (Georgia) Legion

PICKETT'S BRIGADE
Brigadier General Richard B. Garnett
8th Virginia
18th Virginia
19th Virginia
28th Virginia
56th Virginia

JENKINS'S BRIGADE
Colonel Joseph Walker
1st South Carolina (Volunteers)
2nd South Carolina Rifles
5th South Carolina
6th South Carolina
4th South Carolina Battalion
Palmetto (South Carolina)
   Sharpshooters

KEMPER'S BRIGADE
Brigadier General James L. Kemper
1st Virginia
7th Virginia
11th Virginia
17th Virginia
24th Virginia

ANDERSON'S BRIGADE
Colonel George T. Anderson
1st Georgia (Regulars)
7th Georgia
8th Georgia
9th Georgia
11th Georgia

Hood's Division

Brigadier General John B. Hood

HOOD'S BRIGADE
Colonel William T. Wofford
18th Georgia
Hampton (South Carolina) Legion
1st Texas
4th Texas
5th Texas

LAW'S BRIGADE
Colonel Evander M. Law
4th Alabama
2nd Mississippi
11th Mississippi
6th North Carolina

EVANS'S BRIGADE
Colonel Peter F. Stevens
17th South Carolina

18th South Carolina
22nd South Carolina
23rd South Carolina
Holcombe (South Carolina) Legion
Macbeth (South Carolina) Artillery

McLaws's Division

Major General Lafayette McLaws

COBB'S BRIGADE
Brigadier General Howell Cobb
16th Georgia
24th Georgia
Cobb's (Georgia) Legion
15th North Carolina

SEMMES'S BRIGADE
Brigadier General Paul J. Semmes
10th Georgia
53rd Georgia
15th Virginia
32nd Virginia

ARTILLERY
Troup (Georgia) Artillery, one section, Lieutenant Henry Jennings
1st North Carolina Artillery, Light Battery A, Captain Basil Manly
Richmond (Virginia) Fayette Artillery, Lieutenant William I. Clopton
Magruder (Virginia) Light Artillery, Captain Thomas J. Page Jr.

R.H. Anderson's Division

MAHONE'S BRIGADE
Colonel William A. Parham
6th Virginia
12th Virginia
16th Virginia
41st Virginia

ARTILLERY
Portsmouth Light Artillery, Grimes's Battery, Captain Cary F. Grimes

ORDER OF BATTLE

Cavalry

Major General James E.B. Stuart

ROBERTSON'S BRIGADE
Colonel Thomas T. Munford
2nd Virginia Cavalry
6th Virginia Cavalry
7th Virginia Cavalry
12th Virginia Cavalry
17th Virginia Cavalry

LEE'S BRIGADE
Brigadier General Fitzhugh Lee
1st Virginia Cavalry
3rd Virginia Cavalry
4th Virginia Cavalry
5th Virginia Cavalry
9th Virginia Cavalry

HORSE ARTILLERY
Captain John Pelham
Chew's (Virginia) Battery
Hart's (South Carolina) Battery
Pelham's (Virginia) Battery

HAMPTON'S BRIGADE
Brigadier General Wade Hampton
1st North Carolina Cavalry
2nd South Carolina Cavalry
10th Virginia Cavalry
Cobb's (Georgia) Legion
Jeff. Davis Legion

Notes

PREFACE

1. M. Edgar Richards to sister, September 28, 1862, Officer's Letters, February 21, 1854–March 7, 1864, Civil War Miscellaneous Collection, United States Army Heritage Education Center, Carlisle, Pennsylvania.

CHAPTER 1

2. McPherson, *Crossroads of Freedom*, 16–27.
3. Jones, *War Clerk's Diary*, 142.
4. Henry Keiser, August 31, 1862, Sergeant's Diary, September 23, 1861–July 20, 1865, Harrisburg Civil War Roundtable Collection, United States Army Heritage and Education Center, Carlisle, Pennsylvania.
5. Freeman, *Lee's Lieutenant's*, 716–21.
6. U.S. War Department, *War of the Rebellion*, series 1, vol. 51, part 2, 590–91 (hereafter cited as *OR*; citations are to series 1 unless otherwise noted).
7. For a detailed breakdown of Lee's army and his numbers at the start of the Maryland Campaign, see Harsh, *Sounding the Shallows*, 50–90, 138–39; and Harsh, *Taken at the Flood*, 33–39.
8. Von Borcke, *Memoirs*, 185.
9. Quoted in Sears, *Landscape Turned Red*, 91.

10. Lee to Davis, September 7, 1862, *OR*, vol. 51, part 1, 597; Lee to Davis, September 13, *OR*, vol. 51, part 1, 606; D.H. Hill, *OR*, vol. 19, part 1, 1026.

11. Lee to Davis, September 7, 1862, *OR*, vol. 51, part 1, 596.

12. Lee to Davis, September 12, 1862, *OR*, vol. 51, part 1, 604–05; Harsh, *Taken at the Flood*, 147–49.

13. Special Orders No. 191, *OR*, vol. 51, part 1, 603–04.

14. Harsh, *Taken at the Flood*, 147–52, 173.

15. Lee to Davis, September 8, 1862, *OR*, vol. 51, part 1, 600–01; Harsh, *Taken at the Flood*, 114–15.

16. Lee to Davis, September 12, 1862, *OR*, vol. 51, part 1, 604–05; Longstreet quoted in Sears, *Landscape Turned Red*, 96.

17. Harsh, *Taken at the Flood*, 223–26; Carman, *Maryland Campaign*, 215, 226–32.

18. George McClellan to wife, September 2, 1862, in McClellan, *Civil War Papers*, 428, 435–38.

19. Carman, *Maryland Campaign*, 122–25.

20. Rafuse, *McClellan's War*, 273–75; Hayes, *Diary and Letters*, 340–41.

21. Pope to Halleck, September 2, 1862, *OR*, vol. 12, part 3, 796–97; Bartlett "Crampton's Pass."

22. McClellan, *Civil War Papers*, 438.

23. Ibid., 445; Rafuse, *McClellan's War*, 280–81.

24. McClellan to Curtin, September 10, 1862, in McClellan, *Civil War Papers*, 446.

25. McClellan to wife, September 12, 1862, in McClellan, *Civil War Papers*, 449; Carman, *Maryland Campaign*, 186–88.

26. McClellan to wife, September 14, 1862, and Lincoln to McClellan, September 13, 1862, in McClellan, *Civil War Papers*, 452, 458.

27. Carman, *Maryland Campaign*, 192–97.

28. Harsh, *Taken at the Flood*, 232–233, 242, 257, 275.

29. McClellan quoted in Sears, *Landscape Turned Red*, 115; McClellan to Lincoln, September 13, 1862, in McClellan, *Civil War Papers*, 453; Rafuse, *McClellan's War*, 290–91.

30. Rafuse, *McClellan's War*, 291–93.

31. McClellan's Report, *OR*, vol. 19, part 1, 45–46.

32. Harsh, *Taken at the Flood*, 235–36, 246–52.

CHAPTER 2

33. Lee's Report, *OR*, vol. 19, part 1, 145; Hill, "Battle of South Mountain," 560–61; Harsh, *Taken at the Flood*, 256–57.

34. Hill, "Battle of South Mountain," 561; Harsh, *Taken at the Flood*, 257.

35. Hartwig, "My God! Be Careful," 257.

36. Hill, "Battle of South Mountain," 562; Hartwig, "My God! Be Careful," 36–37; Harsh, *Taken at the Flood*, 257.

37. Eicher and Eicher, *Civil War High Commands*, 249; Hill's Report, *OR*, vol. 19, part 1, 1026.

38. Hartwig, "My God! Be Careful," 32–33; Rafuse, *Antietam*, 178–79; Cuffel, *Durell's*, 73.

39. Hartwig, "My God! Be Careful," 37–39; Harsh, *Taken at the Flood*, 258.

40. McRae's Report, *OR*, vol. 19, part 1, 1040.

41. Harsh, *Taken at the Flood*, 260; McClellan to wife, September 14, 1862, in McClellan, *Civil War Papers*, 458.

42. Cox, *Reminiscences*, 277; Cox, "Forcing Fox's," 262.

43. Cox, *Reminiscences*, 279; Cox's Report, *OR*, vol. 19, part 1, 458; Hartwig, "My God! Be Careful," 29.

44. Hartwig, "My God! Be Careful," 30.

45. Cox, *Reminiscences*, 280.

46. Ibid.

47. Ibid., 280–81; Pleasonton's Report, *OR*, vol. 19, part 1, 210; Burnside's Report, *OR*, vol. 19, part 1, 417; Cox's Report, *OR*, vol. 19, part 1, 458; Hartwig, "My God! Be Careful," 33.

48. Cox, *Reminiscences*, 281; Rafuse, *Antietam*, 178–80.

49. Cox, *Reminiscences*, 281; Scammon's Report, *OR*, vol. 19, part 1, 461; Hayes, *Diary and Letters*, 355.

50. Cox, *Reminiscences*, 282.

51. McRae's Report, *OR*, vol. 19, part 1, 1040–41.

52. Hayes, *Diary and Letters*, 355; McRae's Report, *OR*, vol. 19, part 1, 1040; Hartwig, "My God! Be Careful," 40; Hagenboom, *Rutherford B. Hayes*, 51.

53. Hartwig, "My God! Be Careful," 40; Hayes, *Diary and Letter*, 356.

54. Hartwig, "My God! Be Careful," 40, 42; McRae's *OR*, vol. 19, part 1, 1041.

55. Hartwig, "My God! Be Careful," 42; Hayes, *Diary and Letters*, 356; Welsh, *Medical Histories*, 123.

56. Hayes, *Diary and Letters*, 356–57; Welsh, *Medical Histories*, 163; Hartwig, "My God! Be Careful," 41.

57. Cox's Report, *OR*, vol. 19, part 1, 459; Hartwig, "My God! Be Careful," 34.

58. McRae's Report, *OR*, vol. 19, part 1, 1040; Hartwig, "My God! Be Careful," 42.

59. Hartwig, "My God! Be Careful," 42–43.

60. Cox's Report, *OR*, vol. 19, part 1, 459; White's Report, *OR*, vol. 19, part 1, 464; Hartwig, "My God! Be Careful," 43.

61. Ewing's Report, *OR*, vol. 19, part 1, 462; Hartwig, "My God! Be Careful," 44.

62. Hill, "Battle of South Mountain," 563–64; Hill's Report, *OR*, vol. 19, part 1, 1020.

63. McRae's Report, *OR*, vol. 19, part 1, 1040–41; Ruffin's Report, *OR*, vol. 19, part 1, 1045–46; Ewing's Report, *OR*, vol. 19, part 1, 469.

64. Hartwig, "My God! Be Careful," 45–46; McMullin's Report, *OR*, vol. 19, part 1, 464.

65. Cox, *Reminiscences*, 283.

66. McRae's Report, *OR*, vol. 19, part 1, 1040–41; Grimes's Report, *OR*, vol. 19, part 1, 1049; Hartwig, "My God! Be Careful," 47.

67. Hartwig, "My God! Be Careful," 48; McRae's Report, *OR*, vol. 19, part 1, 1041.

68. Cox, "Forcing Fox's," 587; McRae's Report, *OR*, vol. 19, part 1, 1042; Hartwig, "My God! Be Careful," 48.

69. Horton and Teverbaugh, *Eleventh Regiment*, 72.

70. White's Report, *OR*, vol. 19, part 1, 464–65; Hartwig, "My God! Be Careful," 48; Solomon Smith quoted in Hartwig, "My God! Be Careful," 49.

71. Hill, "Battle of South Mountain," 566; Iverson quoted in Hartwig, "My God! Be Careful," 49–50; White's Report, *OR*, vol. 19, part 1, 464–65.

72. Beyer and Keydel, *Deeds of Valor*, 72–73.

73. Ruffin's Report, *OR*, vol. 19, part 1, 1046; White's Report, *OR*, vol. 19, part 1, 464–65; Hartwig, "My God! Be Careful," 52.

74. Ruffin's Report, *OR*, vol. 19, part 1, 1046–48; Hill, "Battle of South Mountain," 564; Hartwig, "My God! Be Careful," 52.

75. Hill, "Battle of South Mountain," 567; Hill's Report, *OR*, vol. 19, part 1, 1020.

76. Cox, *Reminiscences*, 287; Hartwig, "My God! Be Careful," 53.

77. Cox, *Reminiscences*, 287.

78. Hill, "Battle of South Mountain," 564.

79. Ripley's Report, *OR*, vol. 19, part 1, 1031.

80. Longstreet, *From Manassas*, 219–20.

81. Ibid., 220; Harsh, *Taken at the Flood*, 255–56.

82. Harsh, *Taken at the Flood*, 264.

83. Hill's Report, *OR*, vol. 19, part 1, 1020; Harsh, *Taken at the Flood*, 264.

84. Eicher and Eicher, *Civil War High Commands*, 564.

85. Lane, *Soldier's Diary*, 11.

86. Carman, *Maryland Campaign*, 334; Willcox's Report, *OR*, vol. 19, part 1, 428; Cox, *Reminiscences*, 288; Christ's Report, *OR*, vol. 19, part 1, 437; Brown quoted in Richards, *Company C*, 56–57.

87. Cook's Report, *OR*, vol. 19, part 1, 434; Carman, *Maryland Campaign*, 334.

88. Crater, *Fiftieth Regiment*, 32; Beauge account in Albert, *Forty-fifth Regiment*, 52.

89. Willcox's Report, *OR*, vol. 19, part 1, 428.

90. Ibid.; Todd, *The Seventy-ninth Highlanders*, 232.

91. Beauge account in Albert, *Forty-fifth Regiment*, 52.

92. Cox's Report, *OR*, vol. 19, part 1, 460; Graham, "Death of a Brigade."

93. Graham, "Death of a Brigade."

94. Welsh's Report, *OR*, vol. 19, part 1, 440; Willcox's Report, *OR*, vol. 19, part 1, 428–29; Graham, "Death of a Brigade."

95. Beauge account in Albert, *Forty-fifth Regiment*, 53–54.

96. Gabriel Campbell letter to Ezra Carman, August 23, 1899, Antietam National Battlefield Library, 17th Michigan Unit File; Carman, *Maryland Campaign*, 337.

97. Campbell Letter, August 23, 1899; Rafuse, *Antietam*, 182.

98. Lord, *Ninth Regiment*, 70; Bosbyshell, *48th in the War*, 75.

99. Cuffel, *Durell's Battery*, 73.

100. Graham, "Death of a Brigade."

101. Hill's Report, *OR*, vol. 19, part 1, 1021; Welsh's Report, *OR*, vol. 19, part 1, 440; Christ's Report, *OR*, vol. 19, part 1, 438; Albert, *Forty-fifth Regiment*, 48.

102. Bolton, *Civil War Journal*, 81; Bosbyshell, *48th in the War*, 75.

103. Sturgis's Report, *OR*, vol. 19, part 1, 443; Lord, *Ninth Regiment*, 72–73.

104. Bolton, *Civil War Journal*, 82; Hitchcock quoted in Graham, "Death of a Brigade."

105. Graham, "Death of a Brigade."

106. Carman, *Maryland Campaign*, 340.

107. Hood, *Advance and Retreat*, 39.

108. Ibid., 39–40.

109. Graham, "Death of a Brigade"; Ripley's Report, *OR*, vol. 19, part 1, 1032; Hill's Report, *OR*, vol. 19, part 1, 1021; Hill, "Battle of South Mountain," 569.

110. Carman, *Maryland Campaign*, 341–42; Ruffin's Report, *OR*, vol. 19, part 1, 1046.

111. Carman, *Maryland Campaign*, 341–42; Graham, *Ninth Regiment*, 271–72; Crater, *Fiftieth Regiment*, 34.

112. Eicher and Eicher, *Civil War High Commands*, 449; Woodbury, *Burnside and the Ninth Corps*, 131.

113. Carman, *Maryland Campaign*, 342–43; Bolton, *Civil War Journal*, 82; Campbell Letter, August 23, 1899.

114. Campbell Letter, August 23, 1899; Bosbyshell, *48th in the War*, 76; Parker, *51st Regiment*, 226.

115. Bosbyshell, *48th in the War*, 76; Parker, *51st Regiment*, 226; Pleasonton's Report, *OR*, vol. 19, part 1, 209–10; Burnside's Report, *OR*, vol. 19, part 1, 418.

116. Hill's Report, *OR*, vol. 19, part 1, 1021–22; Carman, *Maryland Campaign*, 343.

Chapter 3

117. Woodward, *Our Campaigns*, 195.

118. Ibid., 195–96.

119. Warner, *Generals in Blue*, 233–34.

120. Hooker's Report, *OR*, vol. 19, part 1, 214.

121. Hill, "Battle of South Mountain," 574; Carman, *Maryland Campaign*, 204.

122. Hartwig, "Task to Storm," 39; Rafuse, *Antietam*, 187–88.

123. Gibbs, *Bloody Eleventh*, 173; Burnside's Report, *OR*, vol. 19, part 1, 417.

124. Burnside's Report, *OR*, vol. 19, part 1, 417.

125. Meade's Report, *OR*, vol. 19, part 1, 267; Warner, *Generals in Blue*, 432; Thomson and Rauch, *Bucktails*, 204.

126. Gibbs, *Bloody Eleventh*, 26, 169; Anderson's Report, *OR*, vol. 19, part 1, 274; Hartwig, "Task to Storm," 41.

127. Woodward, *Our Campaigns*, 198.

128. Hartwig, "Task to Storm," 40.

129. Ibid.; Thomson and Rauch, *Bucktails*, 204; Meade's Report *OR*, vol. 1, part 1, 268.

130. Hill's Report, *OR*, vol. 19, part 1, 1021; Hill, "Battle of South Mountain," 573.

131. Warner, *Generals in Gray*, 263.

132. Rodes's Report, *OR*, vol. 19, part 1, 1033–34.

133. Ibid., 1034; Collins, *Robert E. Rodes*, 158–59.

134. Stevens's Report, *OR*, vol. 19, part 1, 941; Hartwig, "Task to Storm," 43.

135. Park quoted in Hill, "Battle of South Mountain," 572.

136. Seymour's Report, *OR*, vol. 19, part 1, 272; Thomson and Rauch, *Bucktails*, 204; Otis Smith quoted in Hartwig, "Task to Storm," 43.

137. Park quoted in Hill, "Battle of South Mountain," 572–73.

138. Rodes's Report, *OR*, vol. 19, part 1, 1034; Hartwig, "Task to Storm," 44.

139. Meade's Report, *OR*, vol. 19, part 1, 267; Thomson and Rauch, *Bucktails*, 204–05; Hartwig, "Task to Storm," 44–45.

140. J.R. Sypher, *Pennsylvania Reserve Corps*, 369–70; Woodward, *Our Campaigns*, 199.

141. Rodes's Report, *OR*, vol. 19, part 1, 1034.

142. Jackson's Report, *OR*, vol. 51, part 1, 153; Hartwig, "Task to Storm," 46.

143. Bolar's Report, *OR*, vol. 51, part 1, 154; Rodes's Report, *OR*, vol. 19, part 1, 1035.

144. Gibbs, *Bloody Eleventh*, 175–77.

145. Battle, *Third Alabama*, 56; Dick's Report, *OR*, vol. 51, part 1, 149; Anderson's Report, *OR*, vol. 19, part 1, 275; Hartwig, "Task to Storm," 46–47.

146. Battle, *Third Alabama*, 55; Jackson's Report, *OR*, vol. 51, part 1, 153.

147. Rodes's Report, *OR*, vol. 19, part 1, 1035–36; Hill's Report, *OR*, vol. 19, part 1, 1022.

148. Hartwig, "Task to Storm," 47–48; Hill, *Our Boys*, 395–96; Stevens's Report, *OR*, vol. 19, part 1, 941–42.

149. Hooker's Report, *OR*, vol. 19, part 1, 215; Meade's Report, *OR*, vol. 19, part 1, 268.

150. Eicher and Eicher, *Civil War High Commands*, 287.

151. Hatch's Report, *OR*, vol. 19, part 1, 220; Doubleday's Report, *OR*, vol. 19, part 1, 222; Priest, *Before Antietam*, 324–25. Hatch claimed he had 3,500 men *after* Gibbon was detached, but this is not the case. Phelps's brigade had just 520 men, while Patrick had 850 and Doubleday had roughly 1,000. Gibbon's brigade, the largest in Hatch's division, numbered 1,350; Patrick, *Inside Lincoln's Army*, 143.

152. Hill, "Battle of South Mountain," 573–74; Hill's Report, *OR*, vol. 19, part 1, 1021.

153. H.T. Owen, "South Mountain: A Confederate Record of Incidents of the Battle," *Philadelphia Weekly Times*, July 31, 1880.

154. Garnett's Report, *OR*, vol. 19, part 1, 894–95; Longstreet, *From Manassas*, 226.

155. Hill's Report, *OR*, vol. 19, part 1, 1021.

156. Longstreet, *From Manassas*, 227; Dooley, *War Journal*, 35–36.

157. Warner, *Generals in Gray*, 169; Carman, *Maryland Campaign*, 363.

158. Carman, *Maryland Campaign*, 361–62.

159. Garnett's Report, *OR*, vol. 19, part 1, 894–95.

160. Mills, *Twenty-first Regiment*, 280–81.

161. Patrick, *Inside Lincoln's Army*, 144; Patrick's Report, *OR*, vol. 19, part 1, 242.

162. Eicher and Eicher, *Civil War High Commands*, 428; Clemens, "First Fight," 59–72; Thomas Clemens, "Black Hats Off to the Original Iron Brigade," *Columbiad* (Spring 1997): 50–51.

163. Phelps's Report, *OR*, vol. 19, part 1, 231; Hatch's Report, *OR*, vol. 19, part 1, 220.

164. Cabell's Report, *OR*, vol. 19, part 1, 899; Hatch's Report, *OR*, vol. 19, part 1, 220.

165. Patrick's Report, *OR*, vol. 19, part 1, 242; Carman, *Maryland Campaign*, 362.

166. Quoted in Rafuse, *Antietam*, 191; Owens, "South Mountain," Phelps's Report, *OR*, vol. 19, part 1, 232; Cabell's Report, *OR*, vol. 19, part 1, 899; Garnett's Report, *OR*, vol. 19, part 1, 895.

167. Hunton's Report, *OR*, vol. 19, part 1, 898; Owen, "South Mountain," Phelps's Report, *OR*, vol. 19, part 1, 232; Hatch's Report, *OR*, vol. 19, part 1, 221.

168. Welsh, *Medical Histories*, 160.

169. Patrick's Report, *OR*, vol. 19, part 1, 242.

170. Smith, *Seventy-sixth Regiment*, 151–53; Noyes quoted in Mills, *Twenty-first Regiment*, 282.

171. Noyes quoted in Mills, *Twenty-first Regiment*, 282; Carman, *Maryland Campaign*, 363.

172. Owens, "South Mountain," Phelps's Report, *OR*, vol. 19, part 1.

173. Noyes, quoted in Mills, *Twenty-first Regiment*, 283; Smith, *Seventy-sixth Regiment*, 153.

174. Smith, *Seventy-sixth Regiment*, 154; Noyes quoted in Mills, *Twenty-first Regiment*, 283–84; Doubleday's Report, *OR*, vol. 19, part 1, 222.

175. Warner, *Generals in Blue*, 171.

176. Carman, *Maryland Campaign*, 363–64; Haskell quoted in Gaff, *Bloody Field*, 180; Colquitt's Report, *OR*, vol. 19, part 1, 1053.

177. Dawes, *Sixth Wisconsin*, 81; Sullivan, *Irishman*, 60–61.

178. Otis, *Second Wisconsin*, 255; Gaff, *Bloody Field*, 180–81; Fairchild's Report, *OR*, vol. 19, part 1, 253.

179. Meredith's Report, *OR*, vol. 19, part 1, 250.

180. Ibid.

181. Callis's Report, *OR*, vol. 19, part 1, 256; Carman, *Maryland Campaign*, 365–66; Colquitt's Report, *OR*, vol. 19, part 1, 1053.

182. Meredith's Report, *OR*, vol. 19, part 1, 250.

183. Fairchild's Report, *OR*, vol. 19, part 1, 252–53; Meredith's Report, *OR*, vol. 19, part 1, 250.

184. Dawes, *Sixth Wisconsin*, 81–83; Bragg's Report, *OR*, vol. 19, part 1, 254.

185. Bragg's Report, *OR*, vol. 19, part 1, 254; Callis's Report, *OR*, vol. 19, part 1, 257.

186. Colquitt's Report, *OR*, vol. 19, part 1, 1053; Hill, "Battle of South Mountain," 576–77.

187. Dawes, *Sixth Wisconsin*, 84.

188. McClellan to Halleck, September 14, 1862, in McClellan, *Civil War Papers*, 461.

Chapter 4

189. Neese, *Confederate Horse Artillery*, 119–20.

190. Bicknell, *Fifth Maine*, 133–34.

191. Snell, "William Buel Franklin," 772–73.

192. McClellan's Report, *OR*, vol. 19, part 1, 45–46.

193. Franklin to McClellan, September 13, 1862, in McClellan, *Civil War Papers*, 455.

194. Franklin's Report, *OR*, vol. 19, part 1, 374–75.

195. Boyle, "Ninety-sixth."

196. Franklin's Report, *OR*, vol. 19, part 1, 374.

197. Neese, *Confederate Horse Artillery*, 120.

198. Carman, *Maryland Campaign*, 300; Reese, *Sealed with Their Lives*, 46–48.

199. Reese, *Sealed with Their Lives*, 297.

200. Krick, *Lee's Colonels*; Allardice, *Confederate Colonels*, 298.

201. Carman, *Maryland Campaign*, 301; Reese, *Sealed with Their Lives*, 46–48; Semmes's Report, *OR*, vol. 19, part 1, 872–73.

202. Reese, *Sealed with Their Lives*, 40; Carman, *Maryland Campaign*, 300–01.

203. Reese, *Sealed with Their Lives*, 61, 57.

204. Cake's Report *OR*, vol. 19, part 1, 393.

205. Boyer, "At Crampton's Pass."

206. Carman, *Maryland Campaign*, 296–97; Reese, *Sealed with Their Lives*, 72.

207. McClellan to Franklin, September 14, 1862, in McClellan, *Civil War Papers*, 458–59.

208. Ibid., 460.

209. Reese, *Sealed with Their Lives*, 73, 126; McLaws's Report, *OR*, vol. 19, part 1, 854–55; Semmes's Report, *OR*, vol. 19, part 1, 873.

210. Reese, *Sealed with Their Lives*, 297–99, 300; Munford's Report, *OR*, vol. 19, part 1, 826.

211. Carman, *Maryland Campaign*, 299–301; Montague's Report, *OR*, vol. 19, part 1, 882.

212. Boyle, "Ninety-sixth."

213. Bartlett, "Crampton's Pass"; Reese, *Sealed with Their Lives*, 71.

214. McClellan to Franklin, September 14, 1862, in McClellan, *Civil War Papers*, 459–60.

215. Bartlett's Report, *OR*, vol. 19, part 1, 388; Bartlett, "Crampton's Pass."

216. Carman, *Maryland Campaign*, 304–05; Reese, *Sealed with Their Lives*, 69.

217. Carman, *Maryland Campaign*, 304–05; Bartlett, "Crampton's Pass"; Neese, *Confederate Horse Artillery*, 121.

218. Boyer, "At Crampton's Pass"; Boyle, "Ninety-sixth."

219. Fairchild, *27ᵗʰ Regiment*, 91.

220. Jackson's Report *OR*, vol. 19, part 1, 390; Boyle, "Ninety-sixth."

221. Bicknell, *Fifth Maine*, 137–39.

222. Bartlett's Report, *OR*, vol. 1, part 1, 389.

223. Buck's Report, *OR*, vol. 19, part 1, 384–85; Gottfried, *Kearney's Own*, 71.

224. Myers's Report, *OR*, vol. 19, part 1, 398.

225. Slocum's Report, *OR*, vol. 19, part 1, 380; Rigby account in Reese, *Sealed with Their Lives*, 105–06.

226. Smith's Report, *OR*, vol. 19, part 1, 401.

227. Westbrook, *49ᵗʰ Pennsylvania*, 124.

228. J. Shaw, *National Tribune*, October 1, 1891.

229. Bartlett's Report, *OR*, vol. 19, part 1 389; Bartlett, "Crampton's Pass."

230. Franklin to McClellan, September 14, 1862, in McClellan, *Civil War Papers*, 460.

231. Beech quoted in Reese, *Sealed with Their Lives*, 130; Torbert's Report, *OR*, vol. 19, part 1, 383; Carman, *Maryland Campaign*, 305.

232. Toomer quoted in Reese, *Sealed with Their Lives*, 130–31.

233. Bicknell, *Fifth Maine*, 140.

234. Newton's Report, *OR*, vol. 19, part 1, 396–97; Bartlett, "Crampton's Pass."

235. Cake's Report, *OR*, vol. 19, part 1, 394.

236. Boyle, "Ninety-sixth."

237. Ibid.

238. Ibid.; Boyer, "At Crampton's Pass."

239. Cake's Report, *OR*, vol. 19, part 1, 394; Boyer, "At Crampton's Pass"; Boyle, "Ninety-sixth."

240. Benedict, *Vermont in the Civil War*, 322; John Conline, "Recollections of the Battle of Antietam and the Maryland Campaign," *MOLLUS* 51: 110–19.

241. Munford's Report, *OR*, vol. 19, part 1, 827; Sears, "Fire on the Mountain," 52.

242. Hancock quoted in Bartlett, *National Tribune*; Boyle, "Ninety-sixth."

243. Eicher and Eicher, *Civil War High Commands*, 178.

244. Reese, "Cobb's Brigade," 14; Rafuse, *Antietam*, 202.

245. Boyer, "At Crampton's Pass"; Joel Seaver letter in Curtis, *From Bull Run*, 170–71.

246. Seaver's Report, *OR*, vol. 19, part 1, 391; Seaver in Curtis, *From Bull Run*, 170–71; Myers's Report, *OR*, vol. 19, part 1, 397–98.

247. Bartlett, "Crampton's Pass."

248. Boyle, "Ninety-sixth"; Reese, "Cobb's Brigade," 153–54.

249. Beyer and Keydel, *Deeds of Valor*, 73–74.

250. Reese, "Cobb's Brigade," 198.

251. Gottfried, *Kearney's Own*, 73; Rafuse, *Antietam*, 203; Reese, "Cobb's Brigade," 17–19.

252. Brown's Report, *OR*, vol. 19, part 1, 386–87; quoted in Baquet, *First Brigade*, 47.

253. Benedict, *Vermont in the Civil War*, 322; Reese, "Cobb's Brigade," 152; Brooks's Report, *OR*, vol. 19, part 1, 408.

254. Rafuse, *Antietam*, 204; Reese, "Cobb's Brigade," 47–56.

255. Rafuse, *Antietam*, 204; Bartlett, "Crampton's Pass"; Reese, *Sealed with Their Lives*; Reese, "Cobb's Brigade," 47–56.

256. Semmes's Report, *OR*, vol. 19, part 1, 872; Munford's Report, *OR*, vol. 19, part 1, 827.

257. Cobb's Report, *OR*, vol. 19, part 1, 870–71.

258. Reese, "Cobb's Brigade," 165–66; Town's Report, *OR*, vol. 19, part 1, 400–01.

259. Boyle, "Ninety-sixth."

260. Harsh, *Taken at the Flood*, 282.

261. Casualty numbers from Reese, *Sealed with Their Lives*, 297–303; Hatch's Report, *OR*, vol. 19, part 1, 388; Torbert's Report, *OR*, vol. 19, part 1, 383.

262. Stevens, *Sixth Corps*, 138; Bicknell, *Fifth Maine*, 140–41.

263 Slocum's Report, *OR*, vol. 19, part 1, 381; Bartlett's Report, *OR*, vol. 19, part 1, 389; Bartlett, "Crampton's Pass."

264. Von Borcke, *Memoirs*, 217–18.

265. McLaws's Report, *OR*, vol. 19, part 1, 856.

CHAPTER 5

266. Harsh, *Taken at the Flood*, 287–88; Longstreet, *From Manassas*, 227; Longstreet's Report, *OR*, vol. 19, part 1, 839.

267. Stevens's Report, *OR*, vol. 19, part 1, 942.

268. Carman, *Maryland Campaign*, 381–82; Lee to McLaws in *OR*, vol. 51, part 2, 618–19.

269. Harsh, *Taken at the Flood*, 294–95; Carman, *Maryland Campaign*, 387–90.

270. McClellan to Halleck, September 14, 1862, in McClellan, *Civil War Papers*, 461–62.

271. Carman, *Maryland Campaign*, 403; McClellan, *Civil War Papers*, 462.

272. McClellan to wife, in McClellan, *Civil War Papers*, 462–63; McClellan's Report, *OR*, vol. 19, part 1, 28.

273. Smith, *Seventy-sixth Regiment*, 159–60.

274. Todd, *Seventy-ninth Highlanders*, 236; Albert, *Forty-fifth Regiment*, 48; Thirty-fifth Massachusetts Infantry Regiment, *History*, 34.

275. Carman, *Maryland Campaign*, 399–401.

276. Ibid.

277. Harsh, *Taken at the Flood*, 300.

278. McLaws's Report, *OR*, vol. 19, part 1, 854–56.

279. McClellan's Report, *OR*, vol. 19, part 1, 29, 45–46.

280. Ibid., 47.

281. Rafuse, *Antietam*, 205–06; McClellan's Report, *OR*, vol. 19, part 1, 29, 47.

282. Carman, *Maryland Campaign*, 434–35.

283. Harsh, *Taken at the Flood*, 302–04.

284. Lee's Report, *OR*, vol. 19, part 1, 951.

285. Wren, *Civil Diary*, 87; Albert, *45th Regiment*, 54–55; Bosbyshell, *48th in the War*, 77.

286. McClellan's Report, *OR*, vol. 19, part 1, 27; Carman, *Maryland Campaign*, 406–08.
287. McClellan's Report, *OR*, vol. 19, part 1, 53–54.
288. Ibid., 29–30, 54; Carman, *Maryland Campaign*, 409–10.
289. Lincoln to McClellan, September 15, 1862, in McClellan, *Civil War Papers*, 463.

ORDER OF BATTLE

290. Relieved of command, September 14, 1862.
291. Transferred to Second Brigade, Colonel Welsh, September 16, 1862.

Bibliography

Primary Sources

Albert, Allen D., ed. *History of the Forty-fifth Regiment, Pennsylvania Veteran Volunteer Infantry, 1861–1865*. Williamsport, PA: Grit Publishing Company, 1912.

Baquet, Camille. *History of the First Brigade, New Jersey Volunteers, from 1861 to 1865*. Trenton, NJ: MacCrellish & Quigley, State Printers, 1910.

Bartlett, Joseph Jackson. "Crampton's Pass: The Start of the Great Maryland Campaign." *National Tribune*, December 19, 1889.

Battle, Cullen A. *Third Alabama! The Civil War Memoir of Brigadier General Cullen Andrews Battle*. Edited by Brandon H. Beck. Tuscaloosa: University of Alabama Press, 2000.

Beaudot, William J.K., and Lance J. Herdegen. *An Irishman in the Iron Brigade: The Civil War Memoirs of James P. Sullivan, Sergeant, Co. K, 6th Wisconsin Volunteers*. New York: Fordham University Press, 1993.

Beech, John P. "Crampton's Pass: And the Part Taken by the 4th New Jersey in that Engagement." *National Tribune*, May 8, 1884.

———. "The 1st New Jersey Brigade at Crampton's Pass." *Grand Army Scout and Soldiers' Mail*, October 4, 1884.

Benedict, George G. *Vermont in the Civil War*. Burlington, VT: The Free Press Association, 1886.

Beyer, Walter, and Oscar Keydel. *Deeds of Valor: How America's Civil War Heroes Won the Congressional Medal of Honor*. Stamford, CT: Longmeadow Press, 1994.

Bicknell, George W. *History of the Fifth Maine Volunteers*. Portland, ME: H.L. Davis, 1871.

Bolton, William J. *The Civil War Journal of Colonel William J. Bolton, 51st Pennsylvania, April 20, 1861–August 2, 1865*. Edited by Richard A. Sauers. Conshohocken, PA: Combined Publishing, 2000.

Bosbyshell, Oliver Christian. *The 48th in the War*. Philadelphia: Avil Printing Company, 1895.

Boyer, Henry. "At Crampton's Pass: The Ninety-sixth Pennsylvania Regiment Under Fire. Its Gallant Charge Over Rough Ground and Under Galling Fire to Achieve a Triumph of Distinction." *Evening Herald* [Shenandoah, PA], August 31, 1886; September 2, 3, 1886.

Boyle, John T. "The Ninety-sixth at Crampton's Pass, September 14, 1862." *Philadelphia Weekly Times*, September 30, 1871.

Carman, Ezra A. *The Maryland Campaign of September 1862*. Vol. 1, *South Mountain*. Edited by Thomas Clemens. New York: Savas-Beatie, 2010.

Clemens, Thomas, ed. "A Brigade Commander's First Fight: The Letters of Colonel Walter Phelps, Jr., during the Maryland Campaign." *Civil War Regiments: A Journal of the American Civil War: Antietam, The Maryland Campaign of 1862, Essays on Union and Confederate Leadership* 5, no. 3 (1997): 59–72.

Cox, Jacob Dolson. "Forcing Fox's and Turner's Gaps." In *Battles & Leaders of the Civil War*. Vol. 2. New York: The Century Company, 1887–1888.

———. *Military Reminiscences of the Civil War*. 2 vols. New York: Scribner's, 1900.

Crater, Lewis. *History of the Fiftieth Regiment, Pennsylvania Veteran Volunteers, 1861–1865*. Reading, PA: Coleman Printing House, 1884.

Cuffel, Charles A. *History of Durell's Battery in the Civil War: Independent Battery D, Pennsylvania Volunteer Artillery*. Philadelphia: Craig, Finley & Company, Printers, 1903.

Curtis, Newton. *From Bull Run to Chancellorsville: The Story of the Sixteenth New York Infantry*. New York: G.P. Putnam's Sons, 1906.

Dawes, Rufus R. *Service with the Sixth Wisconsin Volunteers*. Marietta, OH: Alderman & Sons, 1890.

Dooley, John. *John Dooley, Confederate Soldier: His War Journal*. Edited by Joseph Durkin. Washington, D.C.: Georgetown University Press, 1945.

Fairchild, Charles B. *History of the 27th Regiment, New York Volunteers*. Binghamton, NY: Carl & Mathews, Printers, 1888.

Franklin, William B. "Notes on Crampton's Gap and Antietam." In *Battles and Leaders of the Civil War*. Vol. 2. New York: The Century Company, 1887–1888.

Gates, Theodore B. *The "Ulster Guard":Twentieth New York State Militia and the War of the Rebellion.* New York: B.H. Tyrell, 1879.

Gould, Joseph. *The Story of the Forty-eighth.* Philadelphia: Alfred M. Slocum, 1908.

Graham, Matthew. *The Ninth Regiment, New York Volunteers.* New York: E.P. Coby & Co., Printers, 1900.

Hayes, Rutherford B. *Diary and Letters of Rutherford Birchard Hayes: Nineteenth President of the United States.* Vol. II, *1861–1865.* Edited by Charles Richard Williams. New York: Kraus Reprint Company, 1971.

Hill, Archibald F. *Our Boys: The Personal Experiences of a Soldier in the Army of the Potomac.* Philadelphia: John E. Potter, 1864.

Hill, Daniel Harvey. "The Battle of South Mountain, or Boonsboro." In *Battles and Leaders of the Civil War.* Vol. 2. New York: The Century Company, 1887–1888.

Hood, John Bell. *Advance and Retreat: Personal Experiences in the United States and Confederate States Armies.* New York: Da Capo Press, 1st Da Capo edition, 1993.

Horton, Joshua, and Solomon Teverbaugh. *A History of the Eleventh Regiment, Ohio Volunteer Infantry.* Dayton, OH: W.J. Shuey, Printer and Publisher, 1866.

Jackman, Lyman. *History of the Sixth New Hampshire Regiment in the War for the Union.* Concord, NH: Republican Press Association, 1891.

Johnson, Robert U., and Clarence C. Buel, eds. *Battles and Leaders of the Civil War.* 4 Vols. New York: The Century Company, 1885–1887.

Jones, John B. *A Rebel War Clerk's Diary.* Vol. 1. Philadelphia: J.B. Lippincott, 1866.

Lane, David. *A Soldier's Diary: The Story of a Volunteer, 1862–1865.* Jackson, MI, 1905.

Longstreet, James. *From Manassas to Appomattox: Memoirs of the Civil War in America.* Philadelphia: J.B. Lippincott Co., 1896.

———. "The Invasion of Maryland." In *Battles and Leaders of the Civil War.* Vol. 2. New York: The Century Company, 1887–1888.

Lord, Edward O. *History of the Ninth Regiment, New Hampshire Volunteers in the War of the Rebellion.* Concord, NH: Republican Press Association, 1895.

Marquis, Don, and Charles V. Tevis. *The History of the Fighting Fourteenth.* Brooklyn, NY: Brooklyn Eagle Press, 1911.

McClellan, George B. *The Civil War Papers of George B. McClellan: Selected Correspondence, 1860–1865.* Edited by Stephen W. Sears. New York: Ticknor & Fields, 1989.

McDonald, William N. *A History of the Laurel Brigade: Originally the Ashby Cavalry of the Army of Northern Virginia and Chew's Battery*. Baltimore: Published by Mrs. Kate McDonald, 1907.

Meade, George Gordon. *The Life and Letters of George Gordon Meade*. 2 vols. Edited by George Gordon Meade Jr. New York: Charles Scribner's Sons, 1913.

Mills, John Harrison. *Chronicles of the Twenty-first Regiment, New York State Volunteers*. Buffalo, NY: J.M. Lawton, 1867.

Morgan, William H. *Personal Reminiscences of the War of 1861–5*. Lynchburg, VA: J.P. Bell Company, Inc., 1911.

Neese, George M. *Three Years in the Confederate Horse Artillery*. New York: Neale Publishing Company, 1911.

Otis, George. *The Second Wisconsin Infantry*. Edited by Alan D. Gaff. Dayton, OH: Press of Morningside Bookshop, 1984.

Park, Robert Emory. *Sketch of the Twelfth Alabama Infantry of Battle's Brigade, Rodes' Division, Early's Corps, of the Army of Northern Virginia*. Richmond, VA: W.E. Jones, Book and Job Printer, 1906.

Parker, Francis Marion. *To Drive the Enemy from Southern Soil: The Letters of Col. Francis Marion Parker and the History of the 30ᵗʰ Regiment North Carolina Troops*. Edited by Michael W. Taylor. Dayton, OH: Morningside, 1998.

Parker, Thomas H. *History of the 51ˢᵗ Regiment of Pennsylvania Volunteers*. Philadelphia: King & Baird Printers, 1869.

Patrick, Marsena. *Inside Lincoln's Army: The Diary of Marsena Rudolph Patrick, Provost Marshal General, Army of the Potomac*. Edited by David S. Sparks. New York: Yoseloff, 1964.

Pinto, Francis E. *History of the 32ⁿᵈ Regiment, New York Volunteers, in the Civil War, 1861–1863*. Brooklyn, NY, 1895.

Smith, Abram P. *History of the Seventy-sixth Regiment New York Volunteers*. Cortland, NY: Truair, Smith and Miles, 1867.

Smith, William Alexander. *The Anson Guards: Company C, Fourteenth North Carolina Volunteers, 1861–1865*. Charlotte, NC: Stone Publishing Company, 1914.

Stevens, George T. *Three Years in the Sixth Corps*. Albany, NY: S.R. Gray, Publisher, 1866.

Stevenson, James H. *"Boots and Saddles": A History of the First Volunteer Cavalry of the War, Known as the First New York (Lincoln) Cavalry*. Harrisburg, PA: Patriot Publishing Company, 1879.

Sullivan, John. *An Irishman in the Iron Brigade: The Civil War Memoirs of Sergeant John P. Sullivan*. Edited by William Beaudout and Lance Herdegen. New York: Fordham University Press, 1993.

Sypher, J.R. *History of the Pennsylvania Reserve Corps.* Lancaster, PA: Elias Barr, 1865.

Thirty-fifth Massachusetts Infantry Regiment. *History of the Thirty-fifth Regiment Massachusetts Volunteers, 1862–1865.* Boston: Mills, Knight & Company, 1884.

Thomson, O.R. Howard, and William H. Rauch. *History of the "Bucktails": Kane Rifle Regiment of the Pennsylvania Reserve Corps.* Philadelphia: Electric Printing Company, 1906.

Thomson, Orville. *Narrative of the Service of the Seventh Indiana Infantry in the War for the Union.* Baltimore: Butternut and Blue, 1993.

Todd, William. *The Seventy-ninth Highlanders, New York Volunteers in the War of the Rebellion, 1861–1865.* Albany, NY: Press of Brandow, Barton & Co., 1886.

U.S. War Department. *The War of the Rebellion: A Compilation of the Official Records of the Union and Confederate Armies.* 128 vols. Washington, D.C.: Government Printing Office, 1880–1901.

Von Borcke, Heros. *Memoirs of the Confederate War for Independence.* Vol. 1. Philadelphia: J.B. Lippincott, 1867.

Walcott, Charles F. *History of the Twenty-first Regiment, Massachusetts Volunteers in the War for the Preservation of the Union.* Boston: Houghton, Mifflin & Company, 1882.

Ward, James E.D. *Twelfth Ohio Volunteer Infantry.* Ripley, OH, 1864.

Westbrook, Robert S. *History of the 49th Pennsylvania Volunteers.* Altoona, PA: Altoona Times Print, 1898.

Willcox, Orlando B. *Forgotten Valor: The Memoirs, Journals and Civil War Letters of Orlando B. Willcox.* Edited by Robert G. Scott. Kent, OH: Kent State University Press, 1999.

Wingate, George W. *History of the Twenty-second Regiment of the National Guard of the State of New York, from Its Organization to 1895.* New York: E.W. Dayton, 1895.

Woodbury, Augustus. *Major General Ambrose Burnside and the Ninth Army Corps.* Providence, RI: S.S. Rider & Brother, 1867.

Woodward, E.M. *Our Campaigns, or The Marches, Bivouacs, Battles, Incidents of Camp Life and History of Our Regiment during Its Three Year' Term of Service.* Philadelphia: J.E. Potter, 1865.

Wren, James. *Captain James Wren's Civil Diary, From New Bern to Fredericksburg.* Edited by John Michael Priest. Shippensburg, PA: White Mane, 1991.

SECONDARY SOURCES

Allardice, Bruce S. *Confederate Colonels: A Biographical Roster.* Columbia: University of Missouri Press, 2008.

Bailey, Ronald H. *The Bloodiest Day: The Battle of Antietam.* Alexandria, VA: Time Life Books, 1984.

Collins, Darrell L. *Major General Robert E. Rodes of the Army of Northern Virginia: A Biography.* New York: Savas Beatie, 2008.

Eberly, Robert E. *Bouquets from the Cannon's Mouth: Soldiering with the Eighth Regiment of the Pennsylvania Reserves.* Shippensburg, PA: White Mane Books, 2005.

Eicher, John H., and David J. Eicher. *Civil War High Commands.* Stanford, CA: Stanford University Press, 2001.

Ernst, Kathleen. *Too Afraid to Cry: Maryland Civilians in the Antietam Campaign.* Mechanicsburg, PA: Stackpole Books, 1999.

Freeman, Douglas Southall. *Lee's Lieutenant's: A Study in Command.* Vol. 2. New York: Charles Scribner's Sons, 1943.

Gaff, Alan D. *On Many a Bloody Field: Four Years in the Iron Brigade.* Bloomington: Indiana University Press, 1996.

Gibbs, Joseph. *Three Years in the Bloody Eleventh: The Campaigns of a Pennsylvania Reserves Regiment.* University Park: Pennsylvania State University Press, 2002.

Gottfried, Bradley M. *Kearney's Own: The History of the First New Jersey Brigade in the Civil War.* New Brunswick, NJ: Rutgers University Press, 2005.

Graham, Kurt. "Death of a Brigade: Drayton's Brigade at Fox's Gap, September 14, 1862." *N.C. South Mountain Monument News* (Fall 2000). [Available at Antietam Park Library, T.F. Drayton File.]

Hagenboom, Ari. *Rutherford B. Hayes: "One of the Good Colonels."* Abilene, TX: McWhiney Foundation Press, 1999.

Harsh, Joseph L. *Sounding the Shallows: A Confederate Companion for the Maryland Campaign of 1862.* Kent, OH: Kent State University Press, 2000.

———. *Taken at the Flood: Robert E. Lee and Confederate Strategy in the Maryland Campaign 1862.* Kent, OH: Kent State University Press, 1999.

Hartwig, D. Scott. "It Looked Like a Task to Storm: The Pennsylvania Reserves Assault South Mountain, September 14, 1862." *North & South* 5 (October 2002): 36–49.

———. "'My God! Be Careful': Morning Battle at Fox's Gap, September 14, 1862." *Civil War Regiments* 5, no. 3 (1997): 27–58.

Herdegen, Lance J. *The Men Stood Like Iron: How the Iron Brigade Won Its Name.* Bloomington: Indiana University Press, 1997.

Hoptak, John David. *Our Boys Did Nobly: Schuylkill County, Pennsylvania, Soldiers at the Battles of South Mountain and Antietam*. N.p., 2009.

Johnston, Terry A., Jr. "From Fox's Gap to the Sherrick Farm: The 79th New York Highlanders in the Maryland Campaign." *Civil War Regiments* 6, no. 2 (1997).

Krick, Robert K. *Lee's Colonels: A Biographical Register of the Field Officers of the Army of Northern Virginia*. 3rd ed. Dayton, OH: Morningside, 1991.

Marvel, William. *Burnside*. Chapel Hill: University of North Carolina Press, 1991.

———. *Race of the Soil: The Ninth New Hampshire Regiment in the Civil War*. Wilmington, NC: Broadfoot Publishing Company, 1988.

McPherson, James. *Crossroads of Freedom: Antietam, The Battle that Changed the Course of the Civil War*. New York: Oxford University Press, 2002.

Murfin, James V. *The Gleam of Bayonets: The Battle of Antietam and the Maryland Campaign of 1862*. New York: T. Yoseloff, 1965.

Nicholas, Alexander F. *Second Brigade of Pennsylvania Reserves at Antietam*. Harrisburg: Harrisburg Publishing Company, 1908.

Nolan, Alan T. *The Iron Brigade: A Military History*. New York: MacMillan, 1961.

Priest, John M. *Before Antietam: The Battle of South Mountain*. Shippensburg, PA: White Mane Publishing Company, 1992.

Rafuse, Ethan S. *Antietam, South Mountain, & Harpers Ferry: A Battlefield Guide*. Lincoln: University of Nebraska Press, 2008.

———. *McClellan's War: The Failure of Modernization in the Struggle for the Union*. Bloomington: Indiana University Press, 2005.

Reese, Timothy J. *High Water Mark: The 1862 Maryland Campaign in Strategic Perspective*. Baltimore: Butternut and Blue, 2004.

———. "Howell Cobb's Brigade at Crampton's Gap." *Blue & Gray* 15 (1998): 6–21, 47–56.

———. *Sealed with Their Lives: The Battle for Crampton's Gap*. Baltimore: Butternut and Blue, 1998.

Richards, J. Stuart. *A History of Company C, 50th Pennsylvania Veteran Volunteer Infantry Regiment: From the Camp, the Battlefield and the Prison Pen, 1861–1865*. Charleston, SC: The History Press, 2006.

Sears, Stephen W. *George B. McClellan: The Young Napoleon*. New York: Ticknor & Fields, 1988.

———. "Fire on the Mountain: The Battle of South Mountain, September 14, 1862." *Blue & Gray* (December–January 1986–1987).

———. *Landscape Turned Red: The Battle of Antietam*. New Haven, CT: Ticknor & Fields, 1983.

Snell, Mark. *From First to Last: The Life of Major General William B. Franklin.* New York: Fordham University Press, 2002.

———. "William Buel Franklin." In *Encyclopedia of the American Civil War.* Edited by David S. and Jeanne T. Heidler. New York: W.W. Norton, 2000.

Stotlemyer, Steven R. *Bivouacs of the Dead: The Story of Those Who Died at Antietam and South Mountain.* Baltimore: Toomey Press, 1992.

Time-Life Books. *Antietam: Voices of the Civil War.* Alexandria, VA: Time-Life Books, 1996.

Warner, Ezra. *Generals in Blue: The Lives of the Union Commanders.* Baton Rouge: Louisiana State University Press, 1964.

———. *Generals in Gray: The Lives of the Confederate Commanders.* Baton Rouge: Louisiana State University Press, 1959.

Welsh, Jack. *Medical Histories of Union Generals.* Kent, OH: Kent State University Press, 1996.

Index

A

Anderson
  General George B. 55, 60, 61, 63,
    65, 70, 78, 80, 81, 169
  General George T. 65, 66, 67, 70,
    71, 78, 80, 84, 112
  General Richard H. 18, 22, 135,
    165, 168, 174, 175, 176
Antietam Creek 64, 81, 84, 95, 167,
    173, 174, 177, 180, 181, 182
Army of Northern Virginia
  Cobb's Legion (Georgia) 154, 158
  Phillips Legion (Georgia) 71, 72, 77
  2nd Virginia Cavalry 136, 139
  3rd Alabama 96, 101, 102, 103, 105
  3rd South Carolina Battalion 70,
    71, 72, 73, 75, 77
  5th Alabama 95, 96, 99, 100, 101
  5th North Carolina 41, 42, 47,
    50, 56
  5th Virginia Cavalry 33, 40, 46,
    48, 56, 136
  6th Alabama 96, 98, 99, 100, 106

6th Virginia 139, 146, 157
8th Virginia 113, 117, 119
9th Virginia Cavalry 172, 173
10th Georgia 135, 138, 139, 146,
    151, 152
12th Alabama 96, 97, 101, 102, 106
12th North Carolina 42, 48, 52
12th Virginia 31, 136, 139, 144
12th Virginia Cavalry 31, 136, 139
13th North Carolina 48, 51, 52,
    55, 59, 60, 81
15th North Carolina 154, 157
15th South Carolina 70, 71, 78
16th Georgia 154, 156, 157, 163
16th Virginia 139, 140, 149, 159
20th North Carolina 42, 51, 55,
    57, 58, 59
23rd North Carolina 42, 48, 51,
    53, 56, 58, 84
24th Georgia 154, 157, 159, 160, 161
26th Alabama 96, 101, 102
41st Virginia 135
50th Georgia 71, 77
51st Georgia 72, 73, 77

Army of the Potomac
2nd Vermont 147, 152, 159, 162
2nd Wisconsin 122, 123, 124, 126, 127, 128
3rd New Jersey 146, 158
4th New Jersey 158
4th Vermont 147, 152, 158
5th Maine 132, 142, 144, 145, 150, 163
5th Pennsylvania Reserves 100
6th Wisconsin 123, 124, 125, 127, 128, 130
7th Wisconsin 116, 122, 123, 125, 129
8th Illinois Cavalry 173
8th Pennsylvania Reserves 92, 107
9th New Hampshire 75, 76
9th New York 81
9th Pennsylvania Reserves 91, 102, 103
10th Pennsylvania Reserves 92, 103
11th Ohio 54
11th Pennsylvania Reserves 102
12th Ohio 46, 49, 51, 53, 54, 56, 58, 59, 60
12th Pennsylvania Reserves 102
13th Pennsylvania Reserves (Bucktails) 91, 94, 97, 98, 99, 100
17th Michigan 67, 69, 72, 74, 75, 83, 199
19th Indiana 116, 123, 126, 128
21st New York 114, 117
23rd Ohio 27, 42, 46, 48, 49, 51, 53, 54, 56, 58, 61
27th New York 142, 143, 144, 154
28th Ohio 54
30th Ohio 52, 54, 55, 60
35th Massachusetts 75, 82, 83, 85, 172
36th Ohio 45, 54, 56, 58, 59

45th Pennsylvania 69, 70, 71, 72, 73, 74, 75, 76, 172, 179
46th New York 70
48th Pennsylvania 73, 75, 76, 84, 178, 179
51st Pennsylvania 75, 77, 82, 83, 85
76th New York 119, 120, 172
79th New York 172
96th Pennsylvania 15, 134, 137, 138, 140, 142, 143, 145, 146, 150, 152, 153, 155, 156, 157, 163

B

Bartlett, Colonel Joseph J. 27, 132, 134, 138, 140, 141, 142, 143, 144, 145, 146, 147, 148, 150, 151, 152, 154, 155, 156, 157, 160, 162, 164
Bondurant, Captain James 37, 40, 42, 45, 46, 49, 50, 52, 53, 59, 62, 69, 70, 71, 72, 73, 74
Boonsboro, Maryland 22, 23, 24, 33, 35, 36, 37, 39, 43, 55, 62, 64, 95, 111, 133, 138, 167, 169, 172, 173, 179, 180, 181
Brooks, General William T.H. 132, 138, 147, 152, 153, 158, 164
Burkittsville, Maryland 32, 33, 35, 36, 133, 134, 136, 137, 138, 139, 140, 141, 142, 147, 152, 154, 166
Burnside, General Ambrose E. 13, 15, 27, 28, 30, 35, 42, 43, 68, 82, 84, 89, 90, 91, 110, 122, 133, 138, 166, 170, 178, 181

C

Catoctin Mountain 16, 20, 23, 31, 32, 33, 35, 41, 43, 44, 73, 87, 88, 90, 131, 132, 134, 166

Christ, Colonel Benjamin 67, 68, 69, 75

Christie, Colonel Daniel 42, 48, 51, 56, 58

Cobb, General Howell 138, 139, 154, 155, 159, 163, 164

Colquitt, General Alfred 33, 35, 37, 39, 40, 43, 61, 91, 93, 110, 122, 124, 125, 128, 129, 168, 169

Cox, General Jacob 30, 42, 43, 44, 45, 46, 50, 51, 53, 56, 60, 61, 62, 68, 69, 70, 71, 75, 83, 87, 130, 134, 178, 181, 197

Crook, Colonel George 44, 45, 54, 61, 188

D

Doubleday, General Abner 110, 118, 119, 121

Drayton, General Thomas 64, 65, 66, 67, 70, 71, 72, 73, 74, 75, 77, 78, 79, 82, 85, 94, 112, 169

F

Fairchild, Colonel Harrison 33, 81

Franklin, General William B. 28, 31, 35, 42, 130, 132, 133, 134, 135, 136, 138, 139, 140, 141, 142, 147, 148, 164, 166, 170, 171, 172, 174, 175, 176, 178

Frederick, Maryland 16, 19, 20, 21, 22, 23, 25, 28, 29, 30, 31, 33, 34, 35, 36, 42, 44, 45, 87, 118

G

Gallagher, Colonel Thomas 91, 92, 101, 102, 103, 104, 106

Garland, General Samuel 35, 37, 39, 40, 41, 42, 43, 47, 48, 50, 51, 52, 58, 60, 61, 70, 81, 84, 85, 87, 95, 134, 169

Garnett, General Richard B. 65, 111, 112, 113, 114, 116, 117, 119, 120, 121, 169

Gibbon, General John 34, 91, 110, 116, 121, 122, 123, 124, 125, 126, 127, 128, 129, 130, 169

Gordon, Colonel John B. 96, 99, 100, 106

H

Hagan's Gap 31, 32, 34

Hagerstown, Maryland 20, 21, 22, 24, 30, 35, 43, 64, 79, 111, 157, 177

Halleck, General Henry W. 26, 27, 28, 29, 30, 130, 170, 171, 172

Hampton, General Wade 18, 30, 31, 32, 44, 136

Harpers Ferry 21, 22, 24, 30, 33, 34, 35, 36, 37, 39, 42, 63, 64, 133, 136, 165, 166, 168, 170, 175, 176, 177, 178, 181

Hatch, General John 89, 91, 92, 94, 109, 110, 111, 114, 115, 116, 117, 118, 119, 121, 122, 125, 148, 158, 163

Hayes, Lieutenant Colonel Rutherford B. 27, 46, 47, 48, 49, 51

Hill, General Daniel H. 18, 20, 22, 31, 33, 35, 36, 37, 40, 43, 52, 55, 56, 58, 60, 61, 63, 64, 66, 67, 68, 70, 80, 84, 89, 94, 97, 105, 107, 111, 122, 129, 133, 136, 167, 169, 174, 177, 181

Hood, General John B. 18, 78, 79, 80, 84, 85, 96, 97, 112, 169

Hooker, General Joseph 28, 31, 35, 65, 79, 85, 88, 89, 90, 91, 93, 94, 95, 97, 109, 110, 122, 130, 158, 159, 168, 170, 171, 180, 181

J

Jones, General David R. 18, 64, 66, 79, 111, 112, 114

K

Kemper, General James 65, 111, 112, 113, 114, 117, 120, 121, 169

L

Lee, General Robert E. 13, 14, 15, 16, 17, 18, 19, 20, 21, 22, 23, 24, 25, 26, 27, 28, 29, 30, 31, 33, 34, 35, 36, 37, 40, 42, 63, 64, 65, 79, 82, 97, 112, 113, 133, 136, 166, 167, 168, 169, 170, 171, 172, 173, 174, 175, 177, 178, 180, 181, 182

Longstreet, General James 18, 21, 22, 24, 35, 36, 43, 61, 64, 65, 79, 111, 112, 113, 133, 134, 166, 167, 168, 174, 176, 177, 181

M

Magilton, Colonel Albert L. 92, 101, 107, 108, 113

Martinsburg, (West) Virginia 21, 24

McClellan, General George B. 14, 15, 17, 25, 26, 27, 28, 29, 30, 31, 33, 34, 35, 36, 42, 43, 62, 63, 64, 75, 82, 88, 89, 90, 91, 103, 130, 132, 133, 134, 136, 138, 141, 142, 148, 166, 167, 169, 170, 171, 172, 173, 174, 175, 176, 177, 178, 179, 180, 181, 182

McLaws, General Lafayette 18, 22, 24, 35, 36, 133, 135, 136, 138, 139, 154, 164, 165, 166, 168, 170, 174, 175, 176, 181

McRae, Colonel Duncan 41, 42, 47, 48, 50, 51, 52, 53, 55, 56, 58, 169

Meade, General George 87, 89, 90, 91, 92, 93, 94, 97, 98, 99, 101, 103, 105, 107, 108, 109, 110, 121, 122, 125, 169

Middletown, Maryland 22, 32, 33, 34, 35, 42, 43, 44, 49, 61, 67, 73, 87, 88, 90, 93, 131, 166

Miles, Colonel Dixon 21, 24, 30, 42, 138, 175, 176

Moor, Colonel Augustus 30, 44

Munford, Colonel Thomas 31, 32, 33, 135, 136, 137, 138, 139, 140, 143, 144, 146, 148, 152, 153, 154, 155, 160, 166

O

Orr's Gap 39

P

Parham, Colonel William A. 135, 137, 139, 143, 144, 146, 148, 149, 152, 153, 154, 155, 158, 160, 175

Patrick, General Marsena 110, 111, 114, 115, 116, 117, 118, 119, 121

Pelham, Captain John 40, 42, 46, 48, 56, 62, 172

Phelps, Colonel Walter 110, 115, 116, 117, 118, 119, 121

Pleasonton, General Alfred 28, 30, 31, 34, 43, 44, 45, 68, 84, 130, 170, 173, 180

Pope, General John 15, 17, 26, 27, 28, 88, 110

Q

Quebec Schoolhouse 32

R

Reno, General Jesse 28, 35, 44, 46, 68, 70, 74, 75, 82, 83, 84, 85, 89, 90, 91, 130, 178, 179

Ripley, General Roswell 39, 62, 63, 65, 66, 67, 70, 78, 79, 80, 95, 169

Rodes, General Robert 39, 62, 65, 94, 95, 96, 97, 99, 100, 101, 102, 105, 106, 107, 108, 110, 113, 121, 169

Rosser, Colonel Thomas 33, 40, 42, 46, 48, 53, 56, 136

Ruffin, Colonel Thomas 51, 52, 53, 55, 59, 60, 81

S

Scammon, General Eliakim P. 43, 44, 45, 46, 49, 51, 53, 54, 59, 61

Semmes, General Paul 135, 136, 138, 139, 140, 151, 153, 154, 160, 165, 175

Seymour, General Truman 87, 91, 92, 98, 99, 100, 101, 104, 106, 109

Sharpsburg, Maryland 21, 23, 36, 40, 41, 42, 45, 51, 54, 55, 59, 62, 63, 64, 65, 68, 69, 70, 71, 72, 73, 74, 75, 77, 78, 80, 81, 82, 83, 89, 112, 113, 133, 168, 169, 170, 173, 177, 178, 180, 181

Slocum, General Henry W. 132, 137, 138, 140, 141, 142, 143, 144, 146, 147, 148, 152, 153, 163, 164

Special Orders No. 191 22, 23, 24, 33, 34, 37, 43

Stevens, Colonel Peter 97, 107, 168

Stuart, General James E.B. 18, 22, 23, 25, 31, 32, 33, 35, 37, 38, 40, 43, 63, 136, 139, 164, 165

Sturgis, General Samuel S. 67, 73, 74, 75, 77, 82, 83, 87

T

Torbert, Colonel Alfred T.A. 132, 138, 142, 143, 146, 147, 148, 149, 157, 158, 160, 162

W

Welsh, Colonel Thomas 67, 69, 70, 71, 72, 74, 75

Willcox, General Orlando B. 67, 68, 69, 70, 71, 72, 74, 75, 83, 87, 94

Wise Farm, Fox's Gap 41, 42, 50, 55, 59, 60, 71, 72, 73, 75, 82, 83, 85, 179

About the Author

John David Hoptak was born on the 116th anniversary of the Battle of South Mountain, on September 14, 1978, in Schuylkill County, Pennsylvania. A lifelong student of the American Civil War, Hoptak holds a bachelor's degree in history from Kutztown University and a master's degree in history from Lehigh University. Hoptak serves as an interpretative park ranger at the Antietam National Battlefield and teaches courses in American history, Civil War history

Photograph by Mannie Gentile.

and Mexican-American War history as an adjunct instructor at American Military University. He is the author of several other books, including *First in Defense of the Union: The Civil War History of the First Defenders*, *Antietam: September 17, 1862* and *Our Boys Did Nobly: Schuylkill County, Pennsylvania, Soldiers at the Battles of South Mountain and Antietam*. Hoptak has also written articles for *America's Civil War*, *Civil War Times* and *Pennsylvania Heritage* and maintains a Civil War–themed blog at www.48thpennsylvania.blogspot.com. John and his wife, Laura, currently reside near Gettysburg, Pennsylvania, with their cats.

Visit us at
www.historypress.net